Martin Booth is internationally known as a writer and biographer. An acclaimed novelist, his *The Industry of Souls* was shortlisted for the Booker Prize in 1998. When he was diagnosed with a brain tumour in 2002 he was inspired to delve into his Hong Kong childhood and write *Gweilo*. He died in February 2004, shortly after completing the manuscript.

Acclaim for Martin Booth's *Gweilo*:

'A more than worthy legacy to his prolific literary life, but also stands as one of the most original and engaging memoirs of recent years, all the more telling because it is so personal, witty and true' *The Times*

'Wonderful . . . it has such pace and power. The theme of good fortune may be ironic in the light of his death, but his memoir is, above all, a celebration of an enviable start in life . . . The portrait of his parents is particularly fine. There are some great comic moments too' *Sunday Telegraph*

'Highly evocative . . . As a sharp-eyed, sensitive child of a vanished Hong Kong, Booth earns his nostalgia. Booth has a grimmer excuse for recalling the past, writing these memoirs for his children before his death from cancer this February. His family are not the only ones who will enjoy the book' *Daily Telegraph*

'The best autobiographies are written by observers rather than participants, evoking memories and emotions familiar to us all . . . *Gweilo* is admirably evocative of the noise and bustle of Hong Kong half a century ago, but none of the characters Booth meets on his wanderings is anything like as interesting as his increasingly embattled parents . . . One longs to learn what happened next; but, alas, we never will' *Sunday Times*

'His finest work. Full of local colour and packed with incident' *Evening Standard* 'Books of the Year'

'Booth must rank as a giant of modern English letters . . . it is alive with delight in the new . . . Sadly there will be no sequel. So this sunny, luminous account of a very special time and place will have to serve as an epitaph . . . ensuring that he will remain forever young' *Time* magazine

'Full of colour and anecdote, wit and originality, his tale of the young "gweilo" (pale fellow) loose in an exotic motley of rickshaw coolies, street magicians, Triads, drunken expats and others is crafted with deftness and aplomb. My type of leisure reading – off-beat and polished' *Good Book Guide*

www.**books**attranswo P9-EMH-724

Also by Martin Booth

NON-FICTION
CARPET SAHIB: A Life of Jim Corbett

THE TRIADS

RHINO ROAD: The Natural History and Conservation of the African Rhino

THE DRAGON AND THE PEARL: A HONG KONG NOTEBOOK

OPIUM: A HISTORY

THE DOCTOR, THE DETECTIVE AND ARTHUR CONAN DOYLE:
A Biography of Sir Arthur Conan Doyle

THE DRAGON SYNDICATES

A MAGICK LIFE: A Biography of Aleister Crowley

CANNABIS: A HISTORY

FICTION
HIROSHIMA JOE

THE JADE PAVILION

BLACK CHAMELEON

DREAMING OF SAMARKAND

A VERY PRIVATE GENTLEMAN

THE HUMBLE DISCIPLE

THE IRON TREE

TOYS OF GLASS

ADRIFT IN THE OCEANS OF MERCY

THE INDUSTRY OF SOULS

ISLANDS OF SILENCE

CHILDREN'S FICTION
WAR DOG

MUSIC ON THE BAMBOO RADIO

PANTHER

PoW

DR ILLUMINATUS

SOUL STEALER

GWEILO

Memories of a Hong Kong Childhood

MARTIN BOOTH

BANTAM BOOKS

LONDON · TORONTO · SYDNEY · AUCKLAND · JOHANNESBURG

GWEILO
A BANTAM BOOK : 9780553816723

Originally published in Great Britain by Doubleday,
a division of Transworld Publishers

PRINTING HISTORY
Doubleday edition published 2004
Bantam edition published 2005

20

Copyright © Martin Booth 2004

The right of Martin Booth to be identified as the author of this work
has been asserted in accordance with sections 77 and 78 of the
Copyright, Designs and Patents Act 1988.

Condition of Sale
This book is sold subject to the condition that is shall not,
by way of trade or otherwise, be lent, re-sold, hired out or otherwise
circulated in any form of binding or cover other than that in which it is
published and without a similar condition including this condition
being imposed on the subsequent purchaser.

Typeset in 12/13½pt Granjon by
Kestrel Data, Exeter, Devon.

Bantam Books are published by Transworld Publishers,
61–63 Uxbridge Road, London W5 5SA,
a division of The Random House Group Ltd,

Addresses for companies within The Random House Group Limited
can be found at:
www.randomhouse.co.uk/offices.htm

Penguin Random House is committed to a sustainable future for
our business, our readers and our planet. This book is made from
Forest Stewardship Council® certified paper.

Printed and bound in Great Britain by Clays Ltd, St Ives plc

for Helen, Alex and Emma, with love
and
in memory of my mother, Joyce, a true
China Hand

The colophon – – used in this book is of a dragon riding the waves. It dates to the pre-Christian Han dynasty and is thought to suggest that the legends of dragons were based upon saltwater crocodiles then extant in South China but now long extinct.

Gweilo – Chinese slang for a European male – translates literally as *ghost* (or *pale*) *fellow*, but implies a ghost or devil. Once a derogatory or vulgar term, referring to a European's pale skin, it is now a generic expression devoid of denigration. The feminine is *gweipor*.

CONTENTS

AUTHOR'S NOTE

It had never been my intention to write an autobiography.
To do so smacked of arrogance: it was not as if I were a
rock star, an explorer, a footballer or a member of the
miscreant aristocracy. It is true that I have had an interesting and remarkably lucky life, but that is far from unique
and I never thought to document it. I have never kept a
diary, except when travelling, but I do have a very reten-
tive memory, all the more so for its being permanently
exercised by my being a writer.

Then, in October 2002, I was diagnosed with the
nastiest type of brain tumour around. A craniotomy did
little but confirm I was suffering from a curiously named
cancer known as a *glioblastoma multiforma grade IV*. It was
incurable, essentially inoperable and immune to chemo-
therapy. Whilst I was convalescing, with a metal plate and
half a dozen screws in my head, and most of the cancer
still *in situ*, my two children – both in their twenties –
asked me to tell them about my early life.

Having tried, without even a smidgen of success, to
persuade my father to do the same for me, and tell me
about our forebears – he went to his grave in adamant
silence on the matter and I had never thought to ask my

mother, who had died suddenly and at a comparatively young age seven years earlier – I decided I would tackle the task of writing about my childhood, which was spent in Hong Kong.

Once I had set out upon the task, the past began to unfold – perhaps it is better to say unravel – before me. I did have some assistance in the form of a scrapbook and several photograph albums my mother had compiled, yet these did not so much prompt as confirm certain memories, flesh out anecdotes that have spun in my mind for years, rekindle lost names and put faces to them.

If the truth be told, I have never really left Hong Kong, its streets and hillsides, wooded valleys, myriad islands and deserted shores with which I was closely acquainted as a curious, sometimes devious, not unadventurous and streetwise seven-year-old. My life there has been forever repeating itself in the recesses of my mind, like films in wartime cartoon cinemas, showing over and over again as if on an endless loop.

This is hardly surprising. Hong Kong was my home, was where I spent my formative years, is where my roots are, is where I grew up.

Martin Booth
Devon, 2003

1

PORT OUT

FIFTY FEET BELOW, MY GRANDPARENTS STOOD SIDE BY SIDE. IT was a warm spring day, yet my paternal grandfather, Grampy, wore a grey trilby with a black band and an overcoat buttoned to his neck. From far off, he looked like a retired Chicago mobster. His wife wore a broad-brimmed Edwardian hat decorated with faded feathers and wax flowers, which, even at that distance, gave the impression of being on the verge of melting. Her mound of white hair being insufficiently dense to retain her hat pin, every time she craned her neck to look up at me, the hat slid off backwards and Grampy deftly caught it.

It was late on the afternoon of Friday, 2 May 1952, and I was seven.

A deck steward in a white uniform approached. He carried a silver salver bearing rolls of coloured paper streamers.

'Where're you going to, sunshine?' he asked me as he handed me three rolls.

'Hong Kong,' I replied. 'My father's been posted,' I added, although I had not the faintest idea what this meant. As far as I knew, one only posted letters.

'You'll need to grow your hair, then,' he announced,

11

making a show of studying the nape of my neck. 'Far too short . . .'

I asked why.

'Well,' he went on, 'in China men wear their hair in pigtails. You're not going to be able to put a plait in that.' Then he winked at me and moved on down the deck.

Aghast at the thought my hair would be put in a braid, I asked my mother if this was true but her response was obscured by the thunderous blare of the ship's horn, high up on the funnel, announcing our imminent departure.

Further along the rail, my father threw a streamer over the ship's side. I followed suit, hurling mine with all my might into the sky. It arched through the air and, striking the corrugated iron roof of a dockside warehouse, bounced then rolled down to lodge in the drain. It was then I realized one was supposed to keep hold of one end of the ribbon. I threw another streamer. My grandfather caught it and held it firmly until, eventually, it tautened and tore as the ship edged away from the quayside. It was over three years before I saw him again.

The vessel upon which we were embarked was the SS *Corfu*. According to my father, she (not *it*, he impressed upon me) was a twenty-two-year-old liner operated by the Peninsula & Oriental Steam Navigation Company and accommodated 400 passengers.

At first, the ship's movement was infinitesimal; yet, quite suddenly it seemed, my grandparents were minute figures on a dockside far away, indistinguishable from others in the waving crowds. Once well clear of the dock, I watched the land pivot round as the bow gradually turned to face the open sea, the deck beneath my feet beginning to vibrate gently as the engines gathered speed.

My father disappeared to his cabin, but my mother and

I stood at the ship's rail for over an hour. The wind ruffled her short blond hair and tugged at her dress as we passed the Isle of Wight to head down the English Channel. Above us, the funnel pumped out a plume of smoke and the windows of the bridge glistened with the late sunlight reflecting off the sea. Every now and then, a passenger or crew member passed us by but otherwise we were alone with the lifeboats. My mother held my hand, not once letting it go. It was not that she was afraid I might fall overboard but that she wanted to share her exhilaration, too wide for words. As we sailed down Southampton Water, one might have expected her to cry, yet she did not. This was an adventure and one did not cry on adventures. She had told me as much the night before as I lay in the bed in her mother's terraced house in Wykeham Road, Portsmouth, in which she had slept throughout her childhood.

At last, with England a small but thin line on the darkening horizon, she said, 'Let's go and sort out our cabin.'

Ahead was an ocean of sea water and endless possibilities.

My mother and I shared a twin-berth, second-class cabin whilst my father 'bunked up', as he put it, with another male passenger, a forestry officer travelling solo to Colombo. Although attached to the Royal Navy, my father was no more than an Admiralty civil servant, having left school at sixteen to become a clerk in the chandlery offices of Portsmouth Royal Naval dockyard. He never wore a uniform with a rank on it, yet this did not prevent him from assuming naval ways and speech. He drank pink gin, called sausages 'bangers', ate curry puffs and kedgeree, never let a knocked glass chime (for fear it sounded a sailor's knell), referred to his superior as 'the Old Man' and used nautical expressions whenever possible.

The cabin I shared with my mother was fairly basic: two bunks, one above the other, a wardrobe and a small chest of drawers, a steel washbasin the top of which folded down to make a vanity table, two collapsible stools and a chair. I was allotted the top bunk. The ablutions (or, as my father would have it in navy-speak, 'the heads') were communal and a little way down the corridor. The cabin walls were cream-painted iron bulkheads lined with rivets, the ceiling the same but traversed by girders and ventilation pipes. Under an oblong of patterned carpet, the floor was made of iron painted dark green. The furniture was fashioned out of heavily varnished mahogany.

That I was surrounded by metal did not concern me. I somehow accepted that, as houses were made of bricks, plaster and wallpaper, so a ship would be made of iron plates and paint. What was strange was the fact that everything continually quivered, never changing its frequency. It was like living in the entrails of a vast, benign beast, the corridors its bowels, the pipes its arteries and the various cabins its organs or dead-end intestines. What was more, everything smelt of paint, diesel, tar, brass polish and warm lubricating oil.

We unpacked our cases and the steward took them to stow away for the duration of the voyage, then my mother ran me a bath of what I quickly realized, from the taste and sting in my eyes, was hot sea water. On returning to the cabin, I found a silver tray on the table bearing a plate of thin-cut sandwiches, a freshly sliced pear and a glass of milk.

'Supper,' my mother announced. She lifted one end of a sandwich and exclaimed, 'Roast chicken!'

This was opulence indeed. In England, still held in the grip of post-war austerity, chicken was an oft-dreamt-of, but rarely experienced, luxury. So was a pear.

As night settled upon the sea, I climbed the three-step ladder into my bunk, pulled the blanket up to my neck and lay on my side. Next to my pillow was a porthole, closed tight by heavy brass clamps. Pressing my forehead to it, I looked down. The sea was speeding by, the white tops of the wake catching the light from other portholes and the promenade deck above. Now well down the French coast, the *Corfu* rolled gently in the Atlantic swell.

My mother leant up and kissed me. 'We're on our way now,' she whispered with hardly suppressed excitement. 'Aren't we the lucky ones?'

The voyage to Hong Kong took a month, with seven ports of call *en route*. My father, assiduously studying our course on a daily progress map pinned to a notice board in the lounge and maintained by the officer of the watch – whom he accosted whenever he could for a mariners' chat – announced what we might see each day. His first prediction was that we should see Gibraltar 'off the port beam', but it was hidden in sea mist. This upset him greatly. To see Gibraltar was, he considered, a rite of passage.

'You've not lived until you've seen Gib.,' he informed me with an eye as misty as the distance.

'Why not?' I replied. 'It's just a big rock.'

'Just a rock! Did you hear the boy, Joyce? Just a rock . . . What did they teach him in that bloody school?'

15

'To read and write,' my mother answered. 'Well.'

My father, not to be wrong-footed, went on, 'The Romans used to think that if you sailed too far out from Gib., you fell off the edge of the world.'

'But you don't,' I rejoined. 'It's round. You just come back again.'

This piece of puerile logic was met with a brief snort of contempt.

We arrived at our first port of call, Algiers, three days out of Southampton. The city consisted of low buildings encircling a bay into which several moles and pontoons projected. Only a very few minarets poked upwards into the sky, contrary to my expectations, my father having lectured me on Muslims and mosques. There was little shipping in the harbour and almost every vehicle was either of pre-war vintage or ex-military, both Allied and German. All the cars, without exception, were black French Citroëns. The air, warm and dry, tasted of the desert, which I knew from geography lessons covered north Africa.

As soon as the ship was berthed, our steward entered our cabin and, closing the porthole, warned us to keep it shut whenever we were in port in order to deter pole-fishers.

'What's a pole-fisher?' I enquired.

'Pole-fisher's a thief,' he explained in his cockney accent. ''e 'as a long flex'ble pole with an 'ook on it. 'e shoves it through the por'hole an' sees what 'e can catch. But,' he added sternly, 'if you see the pole wigglin' about in the cabin, don't make a grab for it, even,' he glanced at my bunk, 'if 'e's 'ooked yer teddy bear. See, 'e'll've set razor blades in the pole. You grab it an' – zip! – 'e pulls the pole an' you ain't got no fingers.'

I immediately put the bear in the wardrobe, hid it behind my mother's frocks and closed the door.

My mother was eager to go ashore. This was the first time she had set foot outside Britain. I was just as eager to follow. My father, conversely, was not at all enthusiastic. A friend of his had been stabbed to death in Algiers during the war and he considered the place unsafe. That this friend had been in military intelligence, that Algiers had been under the influence of Vichy France and that the war against Hitler had been in full flood at the time did not seem to occur to him. However, my mother prevailed and we set off to see the sights in a small, decrepit bus with some other passengers from the ship. Our ride culminated in the Casbah, the sixteenth-century fortified part of the old Ottoman city. Here, we got out of the bus and, after my father had exhorted us to stay close together and be alert, wandered through the narrow thoroughfares of the *suq*.

Every street and alley was an animated illustration from my grandfather's morocco-bound copy of *The Thousand and One Nights*. Men wearing turbans and baggy trousers passed by, leading donkeys. Some of the women wore burkas, their eyes bright in the darkness of the slits. Dogs scratched themselves indifferently or lay asleep in the shade. Stalls erected under arcaded buildings sold vegetables I had never seen before, quaintly shaped copper jugs, vicious-looking daggers (the better for stabbing British spies with), leather ware and sand-coloured pottery. In coffee shops, men sat around tables drinking from small cups or smoking hookahs, the scent of their tobacco alien when compared to my father's Sobranie Black Russian or my mother's State Express 555 cigarettes. Away from the smokers, I found the air heavy with smells reminiscent of my grandmothers' spice cabinets, of minced pies and apple tart – and the odour of donkeys, camels and human sweat. My mother purchased some fresh dates from a stall and set about eating them, much to my father's alarm.

'How can you tell where they've been?' he remonstrated with her.

'They've been up a date palm,' my mother replied.

'And they picked themselves, I suppose?'

'No,' she responded, in the same tone of voice as she might have used to a dog sniffing at the Sunday dinner table. 'I expect they were plucked by a scrofulous urchin and thrown down to his tubercular aunt who wrapped them in her phlegm-stiffened handkerchief.'

'Well, if you want to poison yourself, at least don't give one to Martin. The last thing he'll want is dysentery.'

'But I want one,' I butted in.

I had no idea what I was being forbidden, but I was determined not to miss out on it or the promise of dysentery. Surreptitiously my mother slipped me a date. Its taste and texture reminded me of solidified honey.

Once through the *suq*, we climbed up to a battlement where I sat on a large cannon. From this vantage point, I could see camels down below, their wooden-framed cargo saddles being laden with sacks. My mother asked me what I thought of the city and was later to write to relatives that I compared Algiers favourably to the outer-London suburb of Woking.

As we retraced our steps through the *suq* to catch the bus, we were beset by a hoard of children, many of them about my age, dressed in flowing rags and the fragrances of warm humanity. They called vociferously for *baksheesh*, their hands out-stretched, their eyes devious and pleading. One or two of the more courageous plucked at my father's tropical-weight linen jacket. He raised his hand as if to strike them and they adroitly retreated.

'What do they want?' I asked my mother, somewhat shocked that my father had thought to hit someone else's child. Smacking me was one thing, but clipping the ear of a stranger was an altogether different matter.

'They want money,' my mother answered. 'They're beggars. Ignore them.'

This seemed callous but I did as I was told.

My mother's first encounter with a camel was more costly. She had an inbuilt attraction to anything of fur or feather. Only a month before sailing, she had narrowly missed having her neck broken by a peeved circus elephant which, bored with being offered currant buns, swung its trunk full force at her. She had just dropped one of the currant buns and, with the timing of Laurel and Hardy, had bent down to retrieve it. The wind of the passing trunk had ruffled her perm.

The camel was sitting on the ground, fully laden, chewing the cud. I wondered if it was dreaming of a wide desert of rolling dunes and a far-off oasis of palms, for its eyes were shut. My mother approached, hand out-stretched, to stroke its muzzle, much as she might have caressed the velvet nose of a placid horse. In an instant, the beast was wide awake and getting to its feet with the alacrity of a sprinter leaving the starting blocks. Its neck arched forward, it sneezed and then it spat. A shower of bactrian spittle lodged in my mother's hair. In the sharp north African sunlight, she looked as if she had been sprinkled with glutinous tinsel. She stepped back sharply, discretion the better part of affection. The camel, thinking it had her on the run, lunged after her but its front feet were hobbled. The camel herder hurried over and struck the beast on its rump with a stout stick, shouting a spate of invective at it in Arabic, for the camel's benefit, and then in pidgin French for ours. The camel lay down again. The camel's owner looked balefully expectant so my father parted with all his loose change, no doubt hoping this would be sufficient for us not to be knifed in revenge on our way back through the *suq*.

When we stepped into the square where we had left the bus, it had gone. Panic entered my father's eyes. He had been to the movies. He knew the cash value of a blond white woman of shapely form and a matching potential catamite. His friend had bled to death in a gutter hereabouts. At this point, my mother disappeared down an alley of tightly packed stalls selling lengths of multi-coloured cloth.

'Joyce!' my father called after her. 'Joyce!' His voice rose half an octave with anger, frustration and fear. 'Joyce! You don't know what you're doing. This isn't Piccadilly . . .'

Yet, in less than a minute, my mother returned, un-scathed by blade or bullet. Following her was an elderly bearded Arab in a flowing blue-and-gold striped robe leading a morose-looking donkey in the shafts of an ancient trap. My mother was ever a resourceful woman.

My parents, Joyce and Ken, were in many ways an in-compatible pair from the very start. My mother was a very pretty strawberry blonde, petite and lithe; my father slim and handsomely dark in an almost Latin-American way. They looked the ideal couple, yet they were not. My mother was full of fun, with a quick wit, an abounding sense of humour, an easy ability to make friends from all walks of life and an intense intellectual curiosity. She was also as determined and tenacious as a bull terrier.

By contrast, my father was a stick-in-the-mud with little real sense of humour and an all-abiding pedantry. Furthermore, he had a chip on his shoulder which insidiously grew throughout his life. He came to hold all relationships at arm's length, considering himself a cut above most of his contemporaries.

My parents' coming together was perhaps unavoidable: born within five weeks of each other, they lived out their childhoods virtually next door to each other in Portsmouth. The marriage, however, greatly discommoded my paternal grandmother who thought my mother and her parents to be socially inferior. Her husband, Grampy, had been a commissioned officer, but his son had married the daughter of a non-commissioned officer from the lower deck. What was worse, my mother was a Modern Woman, had a job as a General Post Office telephonist and smoked cigarettes. In my grandmother's eyes, she was an upstart and could not be more common unless she worked behind the counter in Woolworths.

During the Second World War, my father spent a good deal of his time overseas in south and west Africa and the Middle East. When the hostilities ended, he was employed at the Admiralty in London, his office overlooking Horse Guards' Parade. Although he made himself out to be an important man, he was in fact little more than a superior clerk. Indeed, my mother had had an almost equivalent wartime job provisioning submarines for the Battle of the Atlantic.

After the war, our lives had seemed settled enough. We lived in a semi-detached house at the end of a cul-de-sac in

Brentwood, Essex. My mother was a housewife in the outer suburbs of London, my father a daily commuter into London.

Then, one day, my father came home to announce that he had been posted to Hong Kong, to serve upon a Royal Fleet Auxiliary naval supply ship plying between the British crown colony and the Japanese military dockyard of Sasebo. The Korean War was in full flood and he was, he claimed, to be a part of it.

A debate followed as to what was to be done with me. My father was all for sending me to boarding school in England: I could spend my holidays with his parents. He and my mother, he pointed out, would only be gone three years. The quality of schooling in Hong Kong was an unknown and he would not have me educated in a school for children of military personnel.

'In with Army children?' he declared. 'Out of the question! A rabble of East End brats with snot-besmirched faces and grimy fingernails, the spawn of bloody corporals and squaddies—'

'I'm sure there are local schools,' my mother said, with no foundation whatsoever for her optimism.

'Full of Chinese,' my father announced from an equally strong foundation of ignorance.

'Well, I'm not leaving him here,' my mother pronounced obdurately. 'He'll wind up like some poor child in a Kipling story. Parents in the Orient, boy in—'

'Don't be ridiculous, Joyce! If he's in England, he'll be safe. The Far East isn't Farnham. There are tropical diseases, civil unrest, an inclement climate, native—'

'It's a British colony, Ken. I'm sure they have hospitals and a police force.'

'All the same, we leave him here. In the long run, it's

for the best.' My father's mind was made up. He had clearly worked it all out.

'No, we bloody don't,' my mother exploded. 'I didn't go through nine months of pregnancy and twelve hours of labour – while you were swanning around in the Mediter-ranean – to leave the product behind. I had a child – a son – to raise him, foster him, shape him, not foist him off on a gaggle of minor public school masters, half of them as interested in the contents of his underpants as his mind.'

'Don't be so bloody stupid, Joyce. The masters at Hilsea . . .'

Hilsea College, an insignificant private boys' school in Portsmouth, was my father's Alma Mater, from which he had attained little but a basic matriculation and a few certificates for proficiency in Music.

'Hilsea!' my mother echoed in a voice verging on the falsetto. 'You can have another think coming! Martin's going to be with us. It's a family posting. We're a family. Fix it!'

I overheard this conversation through a closed door and missed bits of it but the gist was clear and the outcome decided. I was going too.

Life aboard ship quickly settled into a routine. It seemed to me that, for many passengers, the voyage was an ex-tended and free holiday, away from the austerity of Britain. Mornings were spent reading in deckchairs, writing letters in the lounge or smoking room, both of which were forbidden to unaccompanied children, or walking briskly in circles round the promenade deck.

Some joined in physical exercise classes on the boat deck. At mid-morning, a steward served beef tea in small china cups. According to my mother, it was supposed to give the white man salt and strength. After luncheon, most passengers either took to their cabins or lay supine in deckchairs. A few participated in deck sports, most of which seemed to involve quoits of tough rope that one threw over a net, shuttled across the deck or tossed from hand to hand frisbee-style. One passenger spent much of his time driving golf balls over the side, from what seemed to be an inexhaustible supply.

As far as I was concerned, the voyage was also a prolonged vacation although, early on, a blot appeared on this landscape of bliss.

Passengers under the age of twelve were expected to attend school lessons every morning in the ship's nursery, a room decorated with poorly executed versions of Disney and nursery tale characters, furnished with chairs and desks of Lilliputian dimensions and overseen by a crabbyfaced woman in a nanny's uniform. The content of the instruction offered bore no relation to any syllabus and my mother, after visiting me shoe-horned into a desk, excused me from all future attendance. Thereafter, she taught me geography and history herself for an hour a day at a table in the lounge, her lessons anticipating the next port of call. My father attempted twice to teach me the basics of geometry but his patience expired before half time and he gave up in exasperation.

The days at sea were euphoric, reading Enid Blyton and Arthur Ransome in a deckchair, playing with the children of similarly educationally enlightened parents and painting watercolours of imaginary volcanic desert islands. A sub-tropical sun beat down from a cloudless sky, its heat deceptively cooled by a stiff sea breeze. I quickly acquired a tan with the aid of a noxious-smelling liquid my mother basted me with at every opportunity.

To amuse the younger passengers, 'diversions' were arranged. The chief engineer conducted a trip to the engine room, a cathedral-sized cavern filled with mechanical noise, spinning fly-wheels and governors, polished copper and brass pipes and brackets, heaving piston rods, levers, taps and the vast propeller shafts which incessantly turned whilst being lubricated by a muscular man with a towelling rag tied round his neck, stripped to the waist and glistening with sweat. The air stank with the all-pervading odour of diesel and lubricating oil, which convinced me that whilst a life at sea might have suited my grandfathers, it was definitely not for me.

Another excursion took us to the bridge, where we feigned interest in engine room telegraphs, radar screens, compasses and assorted nautical navigational aids. We were shown a blip on a green radar screen, then given binoculars, identifying it as another P&O vessel heading west. On passing it at a mile, I was chosen to greet it with a blast on the ship's horn, to which it responded. We were also permitted to steer the ship, keeping her on her bearing with the aid of a large gimbal-mounted compass and the officer of the watch whose hand did not once leave the wheel. This feat accomplished, we were each presented with a certificate to say we had taken the helm of the P&O liner *Corfu* off the north African coast on such-and-such a date.

One morning I awoke to find the ship still and alongside a quay seething with activity. A quaint-looking railway engine passed by, its flat trucks laden with baggage. Men in white turbans mingled round the entrance to a warehouse, chivvied into order by a portly man in a bedraggled suit and red fez. Shouting stevedores pushing hand carts steered around each other with considerable alacrity.

'Port Said,' my mother announced, entering the cabin. 'Egypt,' she added, standing under the ceiling blower and towelling her hair. 'This is where the pharaohs lived. Remember our history lesson?' I nodded. 'Well,' she said finally, 'this is where it all happened.'

After breakfast, four or five elderly Arabs appeared squatting on the promenade deck, each with a lidded basket before him. None of them, it occurred to me, looked as if he might be even distantly related to monarchy. Their loose-fitting robes and turbans were grimy. They were barefoot, the underneath of their feet soiled, cracked and as thick as the soles of military boots. Their toenails were horny and ridged like a tortoise's shell. As I walked past the first, he reached out, his fingers ruffling the hair behind my ear from which he produced a day-old yellow chick, showing it to me with a grin framed by yellow-stained teeth. The little bird cheeped dejectedly and the man dropped it into his basket. As he performed this magic, he muttered, 'Gully-gully-gully,' in a cracked, guttural voice.

'They're called gully-gully men,' my mother explained unnecessarily and she put a coin into the man's open hand. His fingers were calloused, his long, curved fingernails striated like an ancient nag's hoof. He touched his forehead, secreted the coin in the folds of his clothing and produced a hen's egg from inside my other ear. I felt his talon of a fingernail scrape against my ear hole.

My father decreed we could quite safely go ashore. He had been here during the war, had lost no friends to enemy agents or native collaborators and purportedly knew his way around. A decaying landau with faded cream leather seats, pulled by a gaunt pony with a hang-dog look, took us into the centre of town. Once there, we entered a museum of ancient Egyptian antiquities filled with glass display cases containing faded turquoise faience *ushabtis*, scarab beetle amulets, wooden and sandstone carved figurines, framed strips of linen and parchment upon which had been written dynastic poetry in hiero-glyphs, bead necklaces, pottery oil lamps and bronze jewellery. The difference between this museum and those I had visited in England, however, was that everything here was for sale. Captivated by the *ushabtis*, I attempted to persuade my mother to buy me one, even desperately arguing that it might help me with my history lessons, but the price was too high and this was not, she told me in hushed tones, an emporium in which one haggled the price down.

'What does haggled mean?' I asked. My mother's reply was a severe keep-your-mouth-shut look. I complied.

Further along the same street we came upon a low, colonnaded building which seemed to be attracting passengers from the *Corfu* as a picnic did ants. The interior was dark and cool, large wooden and rattan-bladed ceiling fans spinning overhead, blue sparks dancing in their electric motors. This was the Simon Artz depart-ment store, almost as famous in Egypt as the Sphinx or the pyramids, alabaster replicas of both of which it sold in a variety of sizes. In addition, one could buy copies of ancient Greek amphorae; grotesque leather poufs decorated with hieroglyphs, high priests and heavy brass studs; camel saddles (labelled as being *genooine Bedooine*); beaten copper water jugs; wooden boxes inlaid with brass, lapis lazuli or ivory; carved camels, red felt fezes; brass salvers, alabaster ash trays and a working model of a water-raising system called a *shadouf* which I coveted but was forbidden to purchase by my father in case it harboured woodworm. That said, he purchased an alabaster ash tray. Without his knowing, my mother bought me a small wooden camel supposedly devoid of insect infestation.

Wherever we went, my father was addressed as *effendi*, my mother as *Mrs Simpson*. This I found puzzling in the extreme.

'*Effendi* is like saying Sir or Mister,' my mother said when I questioned her.

'But our name's not Simpson,' I went on.

'That's Mrs Simpson, the Duchess of Windsor.'

'Are you related to the Duchess of Windsor?' I enquired wondrously.

'No!' my mother replied tersely. 'She's a tart.'

The look on my mother's face precluded any further discussion of the duchess or her pastries.

We took lunch in a small hotel overlooking the sea, which my father had frequented during the war. The meal consisted of cubes of nondescript gristle immolated on metal skewers and served on a bed of gummy rice mottled with dark brown objects that might have been unhusked grains, mouse droppings or steamed weevils. My mother ate one piece. I masticated another for the better part of ten minutes before swallowing it with difficulty. My father liberally soused his in Tabasco and ate the full portion. His face went red, his brow broke out in a sweat and he drank a number of glasses of pilsner. This, he declared, was an ideal prophylactic for malaria. (Nevertheless, he periodically suffered from a recurrence of the disease, regardless of this occasional medication, until he was in his late thirties.)

As he ate, my father embarked upon a tale of his wartime exploits.

'I was having dinner in this very room in 1942 – er 3 . . . It doesn't matter – when an Arab approached my table. "*Effendi*," he said, "I have some very fine dirty French postcards." He started to open his jacket.'

My father started to open his as if he, too, had something to offer.

'Ken . . .' my mother remonstrated in vain.

' "I have fifty, *effendi*. Just one hundred piastres." '

My father gave me a salacious wink. His eyes were somewhat glazed as if, in his mind, he was back in early-forties Egypt.

'That's enough, Ken,' my mother muttered sternly.

'I bought them,' my father continued unabashed, his voice now quite loud, having gradually increased in volume through the telling. 'And do you know what they were? Fifty grubby identical photos of the bloody Eiffel Tower.' He laughed loudly – a sort of braying sound – and drained his glass of pilsner.

That evening, the *Corfu* left the dock to join a line of vessels waiting to sail in convoy through the Suez Canal; the following morning, she started down it. Along the west bank ran a road and a railway line. It seemed bizarre to be travelling on a ship through a desert landscape dotted with low, square houses and palm trees. Moving at only six or seven knots, it was not long before a train overtook the ship, cars and trucks continually passing it on the road. The only form of transport the ship overhauled were donkeys and camels plodding methodically in the merciless, shadowless landscape.

By late morning, the dry heat was oppressive. My mother insisted I wore a white straw sun hat at all times. As it resembled a cross between a Mexican sombrero and a surrealist's lampshade, I resisted, yet to no avail. Instead, I contrived to forget it whenever possible, eventually managing to engineer for the detestable thing to blow over the side, only to discover the ship's shop had a seemingly inexhaustible supply of them. At least, I placated myself, it was preferable to the absurdly embarrassing knotted cotton handkerchief my father sported, which made him look like a retired London bus driver on the beach at Margate on a Whitsun bank holiday. It gave him little solar protection. The following day, his face was as pink as a prawn. The day after that, it started to peel so that he looked as if he was sloughing his skin.

'It's your own silly fault, Ken,' my mother chastised him as she rubbed calamine lotion on to his forehead, nose and cheeks. The lotion, being coloured faintly pink and drying to the texture of whitewash, did little to alleviate his general over-cooked appearance. 'I mean, what did you do when you were stationed out here?'

'Work,' he replied sullenly. 'I didn't have time to sun-bathe. There was a war on.'

Despite the blowers being on full blast and the porthole wide open, our cabin on the port side (facing the supposedly cooler east bank) still reverberated with heat like the sides of a blast furnace. Luncheon consisted of a green salad in a bowl immersed in a tray of ice. Even the sliced roast beef was served on plates set in beds of ice. Ice-cream, provided in greased paper cups with a wooden spoon like a miniature canoe paddle, melted in minutes into a thick, warm, vanilla drink.

My mother spent the afternoon wallowing in the ship's

minuscule swimming pool or lounging in a deckchair, 'doing a reptile', as she referred to it. She wore tight, brief shorts and a blouse with flounced sleeves: it was to become her informal norm for the rest of her life in the tropics. Meanwhile, my father pretended he was the officer of the watch. He busied himself with his binoculars, watching out for shipping coming the opposite way through the canal and dhows that looked as if they had recently set sail out of the pages of the child's illustrated edition of the Old Testament which Granny had given me the previous Christmas. She was a Salvationist.

Gradually, the *Corfu* edged by the town of Ismailia and entered the Bitter Lakes. The desert receded and the air cooled slightly. Around dusk, the lights of Port Suez twinkled in the hot night air and, shortly afterwards, we entered the Red Sea which, to my disappointment the following morning, was not in the least red.

More on-board diversions were planned to stave off boredom. There was a gala and tombola night for the adults and a casino evening. Every day, a sweepstake was held to guess how far the ship had sailed in the previous twenty-four hours. My father addressed this with mathematical precision, filling several sheets of the ship's notepaper with calculations every day. He did not win once. My mother, by pure guesswork and common nous, won three times, my father taking her success with such bad grace that, at the third win, he sulked and retired to his cabin claiming an upset stomach. We did not set eyes on him again until the following day when he complained my mother had not visited him in his sick bed.

'No, Ken,' she replied, 'I did not. A sick tummy I can fix with chlorodyne but a sick mind's beyond my reach.'

This did not improve matters and my father continued

to brood for another day, his mood only being broken by an invitation from the captain to drinks that evening with a number of other male passengers in or connected with the Royal Navy. Women were excluded. He returned from this party with his plumage puffed up and his head held high.

A fancy-dress tea party was thrown for the children. I was dressed by my mother as a pirate in a crêpe paper cummerbund, one of her head scarves and an eye-patch borrowed from the ship's doctor and painted black with a mixture of indian ink and mascara. A cardboard sword was tucked in the cummerbund and I carried an empty whisky bottle. I took home no prizes. First place was awarded to a tubby boy of twelve whose parents had seized their opportunity in Simon Artz. He wore a pair of round sunglasses, a real cummerbund, baggy pantaloons, Egyptian felt slippers and a fez. A long ivory cigarette holder completed his ensemble. He was King Farouk.

The ocean provided its own diversions. Dolphins cavorted ahead of the bow wave and we were permitted, under the supervision of a parent and a deck officer, to go for'ard to the f'c'sle (as my father would have it) and look down on them. They were sleek and grey, the colour of torpedoes. On occasion, they swam on their sides, the better to look up at us with an almost human eye. Flying fish scudded over the waves, their fins outspread like grotesque, ribbed wings. Occasionally the wind took them and they glided up on to the deck to be spirited away by the Lascars, low-caste Indians who cleaned, painted and polished the ship, who ate them. Off the Horn of Africa, a vast pod of at least fifty whales was sighted, blowing and diving, the huge flukes of their tails rising into the air only to slide under the surface once more.

Every evening, I lay in my bunk watching the sea speed

by and reading or pondering what lay ahead of me. At least I knew the pigtail was unlikely, for my mother had insisted I had a haircut from the ship's barber soon after departing Algiers. But for the rest, I could only let my imagination wander. My father refused point blank to discuss anything about his job, claiming it was top secret. I considered the chances of him being a spy and asked my mother one night as I got ready for bed if this was his role in the Navy.

'A spy!' she retorted. 'In the Navy? What gave you that idea?'

'Daddy said his job was secret.'

'Your father could no more be a spy than I could be a spanner,' she replied, always keen to find an alliterative metaphor. 'He's a Deputy Naval Stores Officer. A naval grocer! It's his job to see ships get fresh supplies of lettuces and eggs. Secret!' She laughed. 'I'm sure the Commies're not interested in how many tins of sardines HMS *Ark Royal* is carrying.'

At seven o'clock – or nineteen hundred hours, as my father preferred – my mother, having seen me into my bunk, would join my father on deck for cocktails and dinner. Although, once in the tropics, the formal evening dress code for the dining room was waived unless there was a dinner dance or the like being held, my father insisted on wearing a lounge suit when all that was demanded was a tie. This greatly embarrassed my mother and, one afternoon between Aden and Bombay, it created an argument conducted *sotto voce* in my cabin. I only heard a part of it, eavesdropping at the door.

'. . . but it's unnecessary, Ken,' I heard my mother say insistently. 'You stand out like . . . like . . . like a daffodil in a daisy field.'

'Just because the mercury touches eighty, Joyce, it doesn't mean we have to abandon all our bloody standards.'

There was a pause.

'You know what they call you, don't you?' She did not wait for a response. 'Commodore Blimp.'

'I don't give a bloody damn,' my father answered, yet I could tell his anger had been goaded.

'And that knotted hankie. I mean! That's setting a standard? You'll be rolling your trouser legs up next. You could at least buy a panama in the shop.'

'I'll wear what I bloody like, when I bloody like, where I bloody like. It's a free bloody country, thanks to the likes of me.'

'Here we go,' I heard my mother say with an air of well-tried boredom. 'Tell me, Ken, I forget: which submarine did you serve on? Which Atlantic convoy did you escort? Which landing craft did you command on D-Day?' She fell silent for a moment. 'None. And whose father was imprisoned for three years in Germany after his ship went down under him at the Battle of Jutland? Mine. And whose mother snubs mine because her husband was only a Chief Petty Officer? And you talk of standards. Double standards in your case, Ken. Double standards.'

There followed a brief scuffling at the end of which there was a loud bang as my father slammed his hand on the wardrobe door. I later saw the dent his signet ring had made in the veneer.

'Don't you ever speak like that to me again, Joyce, or . . .'

'Or? Or what, Ken? A divorce? My! That would look good on your record sheet, wouldn't it? A real blot rather than a splat of ink. Set tongues wagging in the wardroom. And what about Martin?'

'What about him?' my father answered.

It was then I decided to make myself scarce and scurried away down the corridor. An hour later, my father appeared on the deck wearing a straw panama hat with a dark blue band.

Shortly before eight o'clock every evening, and the sounding of the chimes for dinner, my mother would return to the cabin with two silver-plated bowls. One contained salted potato crisps, the other small, pickled gherkins speared by variously coloured satinized aluminium cocktail sticks shaped like arrows and bearing the ship's name. I had never come across either delicacy in England and saw them as harbingers of a new and wondrously strange life to come.

My mother detested Bombay. The streets were dirty, the beggars persistent and frequently mutilated, either by accident, design or disease. Like the beggars, the buildings were in various states of decrepitude. Even the monkeys in the public gardens were a ragged, flea-ridden lot. The liberty with which cattle wandered about, dunging where they chose, also disturbed her, not because they left steaming piles behind them but because no-one bothered to clean it up.

'It would not have happened before independence,' my father declared in hushed tones, perhaps in case the Algerian assassin had a cousin who had migrated eastwards. 'Standards were maintained.'

I asked what cows were doing wandering in the city and sitting in the middle of the road. In my experience, they lived in fields, slept in barns and ate grass.

'They're considered holy,' my mother said. 'People here worship them.'

This struck me as too bizarre to be true. She had to be pulling my leg. Yet, with each port of call, I was realizing the world was not as I had previously anticipated it.

'What about the elephants?' I enquired, having seen several walking sedately down a wide street, their mahouts balanced cross-legged on their necks and armed with a vicious-looking iron spike with which they intermittently jabbed their mount behind its ears. 'They mess in the road, too.'

'That, too, is disgusting, but in India,' she went on, 'elephants are beasts of burden. Like Nanny's milkman's horse.'

By my mother's reasoning mind, this somehow allowed the elephants their defecatory habits and expunged them of all lavatorial responsibility.

'Doesn't anyone grow roses in India?' I asked.

'What?' my father, who had not been following the conversation, responded sharply.

'Nanny puts the milkman's horse dung on her roses.'

My parents exchanged glances and we crossed the road. A passing car ran through a particularly fresh and fluid cow pat which spattered my father's shoes and indelibly stained his socks.

Later, I was shown – from a discreet distance – the Parsee death tower. My father explained to me that the Parsees did not bury their dead but left them for the vultures to eat. No sooner had I been told this than a flurry of plump crows took to the wing from the tower, several of them trailing ribbons of flesh from their beaks. They flew into a nearby park to squabble over their bounty, tugging it between them. One of them tossed a finger into the air for another to catch and fly off with, cawing jubilantly. Meanwhile, the vultures with their vulgar naked necks and hooked beaks perched in the flame-of-the-forest trees laden with scarlet blossoms, preening themselves and letting go pressurized streams of excrement on to the flowerbeds and monkeys below.

Yet the memory of Bombay that was to linger was that of a scrawny cat on the dock. It came each of the two evenings the *Corfu* was berthed alongside. Slinking out of the shadows, it moved with its belly flat to the ground like a leopard stalking a gazelle. Its ribs and shoulder blades protruded through its skin and it had a bloody, torn ear. I tossed it a gherkin which it ignored but it relished the potato crisps. The night before we were due to sail, I spent a long while trying to persuade my mother we should give it a good home but she resolutely refused to cave in. Finally, she allowed me one concession. In the warm dusk air, she led me down the gangway and along the quay where I placed two cocktail sausages and a pile of crisps on the quayside, to keep the cat going at least until its ear healed. I was then given my bath and climbed into my bunk just in time to watch through the porthole as an urchin detached himself from the shadows of the warehouse, ran to the food, crammed it into his mouth and fled.

In contrast, Colombo was paradisiacal. We arrived in the early afternoon, tying up to a mooring about a mile out. In the distance were beaches of coral sand fringed with palms. No sooner were the ship's engines shut down than a plethora of small naked boys no older than I was appeared in the sea off the starboard side. Bronzed and lithe, they must have swum out from the shore, for they had no boat. Like marine nymphs they cavorted in the sea, oblivious to the dangers of jelly fish or sharks. Shouting up to the passengers, they invited us to throw money down to them. As each coin struck the surface, it quickly sank. The boys, thrusting their bare brown bottoms into the air like ducks did their tails, dived after them. They missed not a coin but, as they were stark naked, I could not understand where they stored their booty.

'They put the coins in their mouths,' my mother said.

'What if they swallow them?' I asked, aghast at the thought.

'They don't,' my father said perfunctorily. 'If they do, they get beaten.'

After half an hour, a canoe arrived on the scene sculled by a wizened old Fagin and a girl of about twelve. The passengers, sensing the show was over, drifted away. The boys clambered into the boat, arched themselves forward and either spat out or retched up – I was not sure which – a substantial amount of small change. The old man rowed back to shore, the boys following him like brown porpoises.

That evening, we went ashore in a motorboat to a wooden jetty.

'Who are we going to see?' I enquired as the wavelets lapped against the side of the boat.

'Uncle Bud and Auntie Cis,' my father replied.

'But I don't have any uncles and aunts,' I remonstrated.

'Out here you call a man "uncle" if he is older and wiser than you,' my mother informed me. 'It's a term of respect.'

This seemed to me to be as bizarre as worshipping cows but I decided to keep that opinion to myself.

We were met by my newfound 'uncle' and 'aunt' who were, in fact, my father's cousin Cis and her husband, Bud. They piled us into a vast black Humber saloon and drove us to their home at Mount Lavinia, on the coast south of Colombo. It was, I realized as we made our way along a tree-lined road in the tropical twilight, swerving to avoid potholes, the first time I had set foot in a foreign land at night.

Our destination was a rambling bungalow with a wide veranda on three sides. The pillars supporting the roof were ornately carved with glaring, snarling demons. Upon the veranda stood rattan furniture and a number of collapsible roorkee chairs. Oil lamps hung from hooks or stood on the table. Drinks were served by an almost black-skinned, barefoot man in a patterned sarong. The whites of his eyes shone in the lamplight. My parents drank gin and tonic but I was given a tall glass filled with an opaque liquid in which were suspended small white flecks. I tentatively sipped it. It was exquisite, cooling and strangely sweet. I asked Uncle Bud what it was.

'Coconut juice,' he replied.

'Where do you buy it?' I enquired, hoping I might successfully implore my mother to purchase a supply.

'We don't,' Uncle Bud answered. A ripple of night breeze teasing the lanterns was followed by a dense thud in the darkness. 'There's your answer.'

Uncle Bud called the manservant who led me into the night to pick up a coconut the size of my head.

'Now you know why we don't park the cars under palm trees,' Uncle Bud declared. 'When I first came out, I did so. Once. Didn't think. Had to get a new bonnet shipped out from the UK. Terrible cost . . .'

When we had eaten, I sat on one of the roorkee chairs and looked out into the night. Bats the size of English thrushes wove their shadowy flight through the darkness, issuing barely audible squeaks. Atlas moths as large as my outspread hand, with antennae like feathers and translucent windows in their forewings, fluttered round the lamps. Tiny grasshopper-like insects no bigger than a grain of rice scorched themselves to death on the hot lamp glass while beetles the size of my first thumb joint flew into the circles of lamplight with a whirling clockwork sound but were wise to the heat and avoided it.

The most fascinating creatures to be drawn to the lamplight were the geckoes. No more than a finger long, these tiny lizards gathered round the ring of light to pick off any insect they felt they could handle. They stalked their prey, made a headlong dash at the last moment and delicately chewed on their quarry, a bulbous tongue folding wings and legs into their maws. When they swallowed, one could see the insect they had eaten in their stomachs, sometimes twitching to escape. Fascinated by them, I caught one in my cupped hands. It quickly escaped, however, shedding its tail which, for a minute or so, thrashed to and fro on the floorboards between my feet.

Sitting there, the adults talking in the background, I gradually became aware of someone standing just over my shoulder and turned. Beside my chair stood a beautiful Singhalese girl of about my age. Her eyes were as wide and as black as a starless night, her hair long and cascading like threads of jet upon her shoulders.

'Hello,' I said. 'I'm Martin.'

Her response was to put her hands together as if in prayer and bow to me. This formality over, she sat on the floor by my side and remained there unspeaking until we left for the ship. I tried several times to take her hand for I was utterly smitten by her, but she demurely shunned any physical contact with me.

Returning to the *Corfu* in the motorboat, I watched

the shore recede with a curiously heavy heart. The quayside lights rippled on the sea with a clarity that I had never before seen. It was as if the balmy tropical air transformed it into something magical and I was leaving behind a singular, mystical place I knew I would never find again.

Two days out of Colombo, we sailed past the Great Nicobar Island, changed course, skirted the northern tip of Sumatra and headed east across the Strait of Malacca, bound for Penang. A small British colony founded in 1786, it consisted of an island bearing the main settlement of Georgetown and a parcel of the Malayan mainland opposite. Once again, we went ashore to walk along an esplanade, drink a lemonade that was ubiquitous east of Gibraltar and look at a number of sedately squat nineteenth-century colonial buildings, one with a tower, the only building above three storeys in the town. Sated with colonial architecture, my parents then decided we should take the funicular railway to the summit of Flagstaff Hill from which, my father declared, one was afforded a panoramic view of Georgetown. Quite why one should particularly seek out this vista escaped me but my father had his binoculars round his neck so perhaps he intended to ensure that the Imperial Japanese Navy was not poised for a sneak attack, as – he informed us several times – it had been in 1941.

The funicular consisted of a single carriage resembling the hybrid of a horse-box and a guard's tender with open windows. Moving at not much more than a walking pace, it took twenty minutes to arrive at its destination, passing over viaducts and through dense expanses of jungle.

Halfway up the mountain, the carriage slowed. As it did so, a troop of several dozen macaques materialized out of the luxuriant undergrowth and invaded it. The first we knew of this simian assault was the patter of their hands and feet on the roof: then they swung in through the windows into the carriage. Pandemonium broke loose. The monkeys grabbed what they could with the well-rehearsed proficiency of an experienced pirate boarding party. One seized on my father's binoculars and, finding them attached to him by a strap, proceeded to chew through the leather. My father batted it away with the back of his hand only to have a second monkey take its place. Another, to my considerable gratitude, grabbed my sombrero lampshade hat and made off with it into the tropical undergrowth.

'Let him have it!' my mother wailed. 'Let him have it!'

I willingly complied.

'Don't resist! Don't let them bite!' one of the other passengers from the *Corfu* yelled whilst at the same time lashing out with a black furled umbrella at a large male, and swearing in what I took to be a local language.

'They'll be rabid!' shouted the umbrella lunger's wife, a plump, middle-aged woman in a sun dress. She turned to my mother. 'I lost my firstborn to rabies at a tin mine up-country from Ipoh.'

My mother hugged me to her bosom in much the same fashion as a female monkey balancing on the window frame clutched its own infant. As she did so, nimble fingers skilfully plucked a handkerchief from her blouse pocket not two inches from my eye and I found myself face-to-face with a big-eared monkey. It bared two rows of yellowed teeth at me and promptly vanished.

Meanwhile, my father was engaged in his own tussle, retaining his binoculars only because, being wartime Royal Navy issue, they were too heavy for the monkey to carry off. Another man was not so lucky and watched as a monkey snatched his Kodak camera and started to rip open the bellows. Throughout this attack, the monkeys uttered not a sound. It was as if they were working with military precision to a set plan requiring no orders.

In less than a minute, the raiding party of hirsute imps retreated into the jungle to be followed by a hail of pebbles hurled inaccurately and far too late by the funicular brakeman. Once in the cover, they chattered and screamed and howled. Victory was theirs and they knew it.

On our way back down the mountain, I caught a brief glimpse of my detested sun hat hanging from a thorny creeper, shredded. There were, I subsequently discovered with ill-disguised glee, none left in the ship's shop.

Whereas the monkeys' ambush had been pure pantomime, our next excursion ashore lacked any potential to degenerate into farce.

In Singapore, our next port of call, we were greeted by a friend of my father's who whisked us off in a large black Cadillac, through Singapore to the causeway crossing to Johor Baharu, where we had to halt at a military checkpoint. Once through it and across the causeway, our host drove at breakneck speed. It was then I noticed, with a certain quiver of excitement, that there was a submachine-gun propped against the front seat between the driver and my father, with a number of spare magazines on the top of the dashboard. Tucked into the crease of the seat was an automatic pistol. At intervals along the road

GWEILO

were stationed Bren gun carriers or armoured scout cars with soldiers sitting in them.

After half an hour of driving through serried rows of what I knew from my mother's shipboard lessons were rubber trees, we turned off down a gravelled drive at the gates to which were posted several British soldiers in a sandbagged emplacement. They wore steel helmets covered in camouflage netting stuck through with leafy twigs, the muzzle of a heavy machine-gun protruding through a gap in the sandbags. To one side, a soldier in his shirt-sleeves was boiling a dixie of water over a tiny solid-fuel stove.

I asked why there were so many soldiers. I thought it impolite to enquire why we had a veritable arsenal in the car.

'It's the Emergency,' our host told me.

'What's the Emergency?' I replied.

'It's a war between the British and the Malayan Communist Party,' came the reply.

I wanted to ask why but my father cast me a keep-your-mouth-shut look so I kept quiet.

We had arrived at an extensive bungalow raised on brick piles under a wide tiled roof and surrounded by trim gardens of huge, fan-like travellers' palms, elephant-eared banana trees and what I later discovered were cycads, a plant dating back to the times of the dinosaurs. Thorny bougainvillaea bushes grew supported on bamboo trestles. By the veranda was a virtually leafless tree in full blossom, the exquisite perfume unlike anything I had ever come across. When I asked what it was, my father abruptly told me not to interrupt and our host informed me it was called a frangipani.

The entire garden was surrounded by intermeshing

44

coils of barbed wire. We had a hurried lunch, after which I was permitted to play in the garden – so long as two Chinese men oversaw me – and an equally hurried tea and then we were driven once more at speed back to Singapore and the *Corfu*.

'Why did we have guns in the car?' I asked my mother that night as she brought me my gherkins and crisps.

'We could have been ambushed by terrorists,' she answered matter-of-factly.

At that moment it dawned on me that what I had previously taken to be a safe existence was quite possibly going to be anything but from then on.

The following night, my parents attended a formal end-of-voyage dinner, my mother dressed in a long evening gown, my father in a tuxedo. They cut a dashing couple. If there had been an adults' fancy dress party, he could have gone as a thirties matinée idol or a jazz band leader.

The next day, the steward returned our suitcases from the store and we spent the day packing. I realized all I had to show for my voyage halfway around the world was a collection of multi-coloured cocktail sticks, the small wooden camel and a coconut. My mother persuaded me to abandon the latter which I did with reluctance, but not until the cabin steward had drained the juice from it which I sipped slowly, as if it were ambrosia.

The morning of 2 June dawned overcast. I woke to find the *Corfu* barely vibrating, the sea outside my porthole hardly moving by. I dressed quickly and went up on deck to find my mother standing at the rail. A hundred yards off, a red and white launch bobbed on a low swell, the word *Pilot* emblazoned on its hull. As we watched, it edged alongside the *Corfu's* hull, a rope ladder was flung over the side from one of the gangway ports and a man in a white uniform clambered up it. A short time later, the *Corfu* picked up a little speed and sailed slowly into a channel only two or three hundred yards wide. On the starboard side were scrub-covered mountains descending to a treacherous rock-strewn shore against which a light swell broke. To port were more steep hillsides covered in grass and intersected by several bays containing sandy beaches. The shoreline otherwise consisted of more sharp rocks. On a stubby headland was a small village and some low houses set apart in trees beside, to my astonishment, a golf course. The summits of the mountains were lost in a thick fog. The air was warm and humid.

'That's Hong Kong,' my mother remarked. 'Our home for the next three years.'

My father joined us wearing starched white shorts and a white shirt with long white socks and brown brogues. It was tropical kit for a naval officer save that his shoulders were not adorned by 'scrambled egg', as my father termed gold braid.

'And who are we today, Ken?' my mother enquired amiably.

Ignoring her, my father raised his binoculars to his face and scanned the shore for dangerous rocks and under-water sand bars.

'Which one?' I asked.

'Which one what?' my father replied, lowering his binoculars and peeved by my mother's gentle sarcasm.

'Which one?' I repeated. 'Mummy says this is Hong

Kong where we're going to live for three years. Which of the houses is ours?'

'You blithering idiot!' my father responded, yet he typically made no attempt to elucidate.

'No,' my mother said tenderly, 'we aren't living in one of those exact houses. We don't know where our quarters are yet. Just wait and see.'

The *Corfu* steamed slowly to port round a headland lined with warehouses, a shipyard and a large factory complex with the word *Taikoo* painted on its roof.

'What does *Taikoo* mean?' I enquired.

'I have absolutely no earthly idea,' my mother replied. 'Not the foggiest.'

I crossed to the starboard rail. A peninsula of land culminating in some docks, a large cube of a grey stone building and a railway station with an ornate clock tower jutted out towards the ship. Behind them was a city of low buildings. In the distance was an undulating range of mountains, free of mist. One of the summits was, in profile, vaguely like the lions around the base of Nelson's Column in Trafalgar Square. Rejoining my mother at the port rail, I discovered the *Corfu* was moving slowly past a city which extended up the slopes of the mountains close behind. In the centre were two tall buildings and a Royal Naval dockyard, the basin and quays lined with grey-painted warships.

'That's HMS *Tamar*,' my father said.

'Which one?' I asked.

'What do you mean?' my father snapped back.

'Which ship is HMS *Tamar*?'

'None of them. That's the name of the dockyard,' he answered tersely. 'That ship there', he pointed to a grey vessel devoid of armaments, 'is a Royal Fleet Auxiliary. An

RFA.' He lowered his voice in case there were any shiv-carrying Communist Chinese spies loitering near us. 'I'll be on one of them. She's called RFA *Fort Charlotte*.'

Aided by nudging tugs, the *Corfu* very gradually eased round to moor alongside a substantial jetty on the western side of the peninsula. Immigration and health officials came on board and we were obliged to congregate in a passenger lounge to go through the disembarkation formalities. These completed, my father met a naval officer dressed as he was in a tropical white uniform but with his rank in black and gold braid epaulettes on his shoulders. He also wore a peaked cap with a white cover on it and the naval anchor and crown badge. Our cabin baggage was collected from our cabins by two naval ratings. Both were Chinese. Neither, to my relief, had his hair in a pigtail: similarly, none of the Chinese stevedores or the men pulling rickshaws along the jetty, laden with baggage, had theirs plaited either.

At exactly noon, as signified by the dull boom of a cannon somewhere across the harbour, we walked down the gangway and into a large, dark blue saloon car with the letters *RN* painted on the side in white.

We had arrived.

2

THE FRAGRANT HARBOUR

THE DRIVE TO OUR LODGINGS, THE SOMEWHAT OSTEN-
tatiously named Grand Hotel, took but minutes. My room
was on the third floor next to my parents'. It had a narrow
balcony on to which I stepped the moment the door was
opened, to look down upon a street lined with wrist watch,
jewellery, camera, curio and tailors' shops. Directly below
me was a rickshaw stand, the coolies who pulled them
squatting or lying between the shafts of their scarlet-
painted vehicles. Those not asleep smoked short pipes, the
sweetly pungent, cloying fumes rising up to tease my
nostrils.

Before I could begin to unpack my suitcase, my mother
entered. She ran a damp flannel over my face and a wet
comb through my hair, then hustled me down to the hotel
lobby and out into the dark blue saloon once again.

'BB,' my mother whispered as I got into the car. It was
her code for *Best Behaviour*.

'Where are we going?' I murmured.

'Lunch,' my father replied sternly. 'And mind your Ps
and Qs.'

The saloon drove through a gateway guarded by two
army sentries and pulled up in front of a large, long

Nissen hut with very un-military gingham curtains hanging in the windows. Along the walls were prim flowerbeds of low, pendulous scarlet and orange blossomed bushes being watered by a barefoot Chinese man in a conical rattan hat with two watering cans suspended from a bamboo pole balanced over his left shoulder. His hair was not tied in a cue either.

Inside the building was a large dining room with a bar at one end. The tables and chairs were made of rattan, the cushions, tablecloths and napkins matching the curtains. We were joined by the officer who had met us on the *Corfu*. He handed his peaked cap to a Chinese waiter and we sat at a table. Another waiter dressed in loose black trousers, a white jacket fastened with cloth buttons and black felt slippers took our order for drinks. I requested the usual east-of-Gibraltar lemonade, but this was countermanded by the officer who ordered me a brown-coloured drink in a green fluted bottle with a waxed paper straw in it. The glass was running with condensation.

'What is it, sir?' I enquired, heedful of the Ps and Qs – whatever they were – and my father's previous instruction that I was henceforth to address all men as *sir* unless I knew them very well indeed. Or else . . . That veiled threat implied a succession of brief consecutive meetings between the sole of his slipper or the back of my mother's silver hairbrush and my nether regions.

'It's called Coca Cola. If you don't like it,' the officer replied, 'you don't have to drink it and I'll get you that lemonade.'

He was not to know it but that first day in Hong Kong, he started me on a lifelong addiction as effectively as if he had been peddling dope.

The same thing happened when we came to order our meal. To be on the safe side, I asked for an egg and cress salad. What appeared before me was a salad with, arranged around it, some bizarre, pink, curled objects with long feelers, a battery of legs and black shoe-button eyes. Each of these weird creatures was about four inches long.

'Prawns,' the officer said, leaning across the table to me in a conspiratorial fashion. 'Have you ever eaten crab?'

I nodded, a little overwhelmed at his paying me so much attention, not to mention his forthcoming and amicable manner: to him I was not a child so much as an adult-in-training. My father certainly never treated me in such a fashion.

'These are first cousins to the crab,' the officer went on. 'Much nicer and without the stringy bits and chips of shell.' He picked one up and deftly stripped off its carapace with his thumbnail, dipping it in a ramekin of mayonnaise and holding it out to me. I bit it in half and another addiction was given its first rush. He then showed me how to shell one, rinsed his fingers in a bowl of warm water with a segment of lime floating in it and turned his attention back towards my parents.

At the end of the meal, which was punctuated by steam locomotives periodically hauling trains along a railway track not thirty feet from the Nissen hut, the officer shook my hand.

'A word of advice, my lad,' he said. 'So long as you are in Hong Kong, whenever someone offers you something to eat, accept it. That's being polite. If you don't find it to your fancy, don't have any more. But', he looked me straight in the eye, 'always try it. No matter what. Besides,' he went on, 'Hong Kong is the best place in the world to eat. Promise?'

My mother listened to this counsel with an ill-suppressed look of maternal anxiety but she did not protest: assuming the officer to be superior to my father, she was perhaps afraid to speak out for fear of disregarding naval protocol. I never knew the officer's name, nor ever saw him again, but I was never to break my promise.

As dusk fell, the street below my balcony at the Grand Hotel underwent a remarkable transformation. Drab hoardings and shop signs erupted in numerous shades of neon colour. Peering over the balcony was like looking down on a fairground: even the lights of the circus or the seaside funfair in Southsea could not compare. There, the lighting had been provided by ordinary light bulbs. These were fashioned out of thin neon tubes shaped into Chinese characters, English letters, watches, diamonds, suit jackets, cameras and even animals. Just down the road was a restaurant bearing a red and yellow dragon ten feet high. The illuminated words were strange, too: Rolex, Chan, Leica, Fung, Choi, Tuk . . .

That evening, my parents were invited to a welcoming cocktail party and I was left in the care of the hotel child-minding service, which consisted of a middle-aged Chinese woman with her black oiled hair severely scraped into a tight bun. I was introduced to her by my mother.

'This is Ah Choo,' she said.

I collapsed into paroxysms of laughter which were promptly silenced by a stern maternal grimace.

'Ah Choo is the hotel baby amah,' my mother went on.

'What's an amah?' I enquired to defuse the situation, ignoring the deprecatory implication that I was a baby.

'A female servant,' my mother replied, 'and you'll do exactly as she tells you. Exactly!' She turned to the amah standing in the door. 'Ah Choo, this is my son, Martin.'

'Huwwo, Mahtung,' the amah replied, then, looking at my mother, said, 'You can go, missee, I look-see Mahtung. He good boy for me.'

'Behave yourself,' my father said pointedly as my parents bade me goodnight. 'If I hear from Ah Choo that you've been monkeying about . . .' He left the rest unsaid. I caught a brief vision of a leather slipper.

The first thing Ah Choo attempted to do after my parents had departed was undress me. I had not been undressed before by anyone in my life save my mother and grandmothers and I wasn't going to let this diminutive, alien stranger called Sneeze be the first.

As soon as she unfastened one button and turned to the next, I did the first up again. Finally, unable to undo more than three shirt buttons at a time, she gave up, informing me, 'You bafu w'eddy.' Going out of the room, she left me to disrobe and wash myself.

I gave her a few minutes, wet the bar of foul-scented hotel soap, pulled the bath plug and glanced outside the bathroom. I had expected to find her in my bedroom. She was not there. The door to the corridor was open. Leaving the room, I headed nimbly along it and down the stairs, into the lobby and out on to the street. I knew this excursion came under the 'monkeying about' heading yet I could not resist it. The street called to me as a gold nugget must beckon to a prospector. Until then, my life had been bounded by my parents' small suburban garden, a nearby playing field, an ancient tractor and, more recently, a ship's rail. Now, it was colourfully lit, boundless, un-known, exciting and throbbing with adventurous potential.

No-one paid me any attention. The hotel doorman completely ignored me. Reasoning that I would not get lost if, at every corner, I turned left and would therefore end up where I started, I turned left.

Buzzing with the frisson of an explorer stepping into unmapped territory, I made off down the street. The first shop I stopped at was a jeweller's. In the brightly illuminated window, gold bracelets, necklaces and chains glistened enticingly. Strings of pearls glowed with a matt marbled lustre. A black velvet-lined tray of diamonds sparkled like eyes in a jungle night. Inside the shop stood a sailor, his arm round the waist of a young Chinese woman wearing a very tight dress that shimmered under the shop lights. The sides of the garment were slit from the bottom hem to the top of her thigh. When she moved, almost her entire leg was visible. I had never seen anything like it – the dress or the female limb.

The sailor's uniform was very different from a British naval rating's. It was all white with thin blue edging and insignia, topped off with a pill-box-shaped hat that made me think of Popeye. His sleeves were rolled up tightly to his armpits showing the tattoo of an anchor, a palm tree and the words *San Diego*. As my grandfather had several faded tattoos, these did not surprise me. What did take me aback was that, as I watched him, he slid his hand in one of the slits in the dress and squeezed the young woman's buttocks. She made no sign of complaint and I wondered if this was how one greeted all Chinese women.

I was still contemplating the social manners of the Orient when the shop door opened and the pair came out, the young woman admiring a gold bangle on her wrist.

'Hey, kid!' the sailor addressed me. 'How yah doin'?'

Not quite understanding him, I answered defensively, 'I'm not doing anything, sir.'

'Why you out late time?' the young woman asked. She

stroked my hair. Her fingernails were long and painted vermilion. So were her toenails, visible through the ends of her high-heeled sandals.

'Where d'yah live, kid?' asked the sailor. I pointed down the street. 'Well, y' come along now, y' hear? Ain't right for yah to be out so late.'

They took a hand each and walked me back to the Grand Hotel, passing me into the custody of the desk clerk who was given an earful of invective by the young woman. A brief but heated argument ensued at the end of which the hotel doorman arrived. An uncharacteristically burly Chinese, the sailor took a swing at him. It did not meet its intended target. More invective followed before the sailor, holding the young woman's hand, grinned at me and said, 'Stay lucky, kid!' and with that they were gone.

Back in my room, Ah Choo had run another bath. I closed the door, undressed, washed and put on my pyjamas. I had just pulled up the bottoms and was tying a bow in the cord when Ah Choo came in without so much as a brief knock, bending down to gather up my clothing. I seized the moment to test my rudimentary understanding of local etiquette and squeezed one of her buttocks. It was soft and pliable like a semi-deflated balloon.

She stood bolt upright as if a lightning shaft had run along her spine.

Turning sharply to face me, she exclaimed, 'You v'wy lautee boy, Mahtung!' Yet, behind her castigation and indignation there lingered a smile.

She put me to bed, switched on a pedestal fan, lowered the slatted blinds and left. I slid out of bed and went on to the balcony. The rickshaw coolies were sharing a saucepan of rice on top of which was a complete boiled fish – head, fins and all. I watched as they dissected it with their chopsticks, spitting the bones on to the street. Opposite my balcony was a tenement building which housed a work-shop over a tailor's establishment. Under the blaze of strip lights, a dozen men deftly cut and sewed suits. Next door, four Chinese men shuffled what looked to me to be cream-coloured dominoes. They rattled loudly on the metal table top as they were mixed up, sounding with a report as they were slammed down. From a window higher than mine, a small boy was peering out through metal bars. I waved to him but he did not respond: instead, he disappeared and I heard him calling out. A shirt on a hanger hung from the bars of another window. In yet another was a dark blue glazed pot holding a single, red lily. The illuminated windows reminded me of an advent calendar except that this was secular and alive.

I climbed into bed. My cotton pyjamas were sticking to me with the heat so I removed them and fell asleep to the staccato rattle of the game tiles, the passing traffic, the occasional raised voice or laugh from the rickshaw coolies and the drone of the fan.

The next morning, I woke with a nagging headache. So did my parents.

Sitting at breakfast in the hotel dining room, my mother remarked, 'I only had two G 'n' Ts last night. I hope we're not all coming down with something.'

'You didn't sleep well, Joyce,' my father observed. 'Tossing and turning . . .'

'Well,' she answered, 'what with the whine of the fan, the clatter of that infernal mahjong game opposite and the stench of the rickshaw coolies' pipes, is it any wonder? I really don't think, Ken,' she went on, 'we can go on staying here.'

I was not a little dismayed at this turn of events. I

wanted to explore more of the streets. Furthermore, Ah Choo had not ratted on me. I wondered why until it dawned on me that to do so would have been to bring her job into jeopardy.

'I like it here,' I chipped in. Then, hoping to justify my statement, added, 'I like the smell of the coolies' pipes.'

For a long moment, my parents looked at each other.

'That does it!' my father agreed. 'We move as soon as we can. Another week here and we'll all be ruddy opium addicts.'

3

SEI HOI JAU DIM

THE NEXT SEVEN DAYS WERE FILLED WITH ACTIVITY. MY father prepared to join his ship at the Sasebo naval base in Japan. I was enrolled in Kowloon Junior School, and kitted out with several pairs of khaki shorts and white short-sleeved shirts, on to the pockets of which were attached a chocolate-brown and yellow school badge, held in place by press studs. My mother frantically wrote letters to inform her many correspondents of our change of address.

During this time, we stayed with a colleague of my father's in a spacious bungalow at Mount Nicholson half-way up a mountain on Hong Kong Island, which I was told was known as Hong Kong-side, the peninsula upon which we were to live being referred to as Kowloon-side. Indeed, many places were suffixed with -side: I'm going shopping was I go shop-side, beach-side (swimming), office-side (work), school-side (school) and so on.

A car collected us from the Grand Hotel and drove us over the harbour by way of a vehicular ferry. *En route*, we saw the *Corfu* departing on its return journey to Southampton.

'Just think,' my mother said, 'in a month that'll be back in England.'

I could not tell if she was wistfully yearning for England's shores or horrified at the thought of returning to austere, drab British towns filled with dowdy-looking people, strikes, grey skies and snow.

The air was much cooler at the bungalow. The only sounds were birdsong and, in the evenings, the metallic click of the geckoes encircling the ceiling lights to pick off mosquitoes, gnats and small moths. The proliferation of mosquitoes demanded we sleep under mosquito nets: the bungalow was above the Wong Nei Chong valley, an infamously malarial area in the early days of the colony. One could pick up the high-pitched whine of these minuscule insect fighter bombers approaching only to hear it abruptly halt when they hit the netting. This would then agitate as a gecko ran down the muslin to consume the insect, returning to the top of the net to await the next one. My mother wondered aloud that if evolution moved any faster, geckoes would soon learn to weave webs as spiders did.

The lantana bushes on the edge of the lawn were in full multicoloured blossom and frequently visited by black-and-emerald-green butterflies the size of sparrows. The verdant undergrowth of the hillsides coming right down to the edge of the bungalow garden and a border of azaleas and bougainvillaea bushes did more than encourage merely insects into the house. On our third morning, the houseboy entered my bedroom and woke me with a gentle shake.

'Young master,' he addressed me in hushed tones, 'you come. Slowly, slowly. No makee noise.'

With that, he took me by the hand and headed for the french windows to my bedroom. Cautiously, he led me out on to the veranda where everyone else in the house – servants and residents – were gathered in a silent group.

'No talkee,' he whispered. 'No makee quick.'

To lend weight to his instructions, the man who lived in the bungalow with his wife and a son six years my senior, muttered, 'Don't make a sound or move a muscle, old boy.'

In the sitting room, the gardener and another Chinese man seemed to be rearranging the furniture. Suddenly, one of them darted behind a rattan settee and scrabbled about unseen on the parquet flooring. When he stood up, all the Chinese muttered *Ayarh!* in unison.

In his hand, held by its neck between a long thumb nail and index finger, was a cobra over four feet long, its hood expanding and contracting against the man's palm. He carried it out on to the lawn and killed it by cracking it once, like a whip. The tenant of the bungalow gave the gardener and his companion a purple dollar bill each before the former walked off with the reptile's carcass.

'That'll make a nice purse,' my mother remarked.

'I doubt they'll take the snake to a tanner,' came the answer. 'They'll cook it. The Chinese'll eat anything that can move under its own locomotion.'

Remembering my promise, I decided to assiduously avoid the gardener until after the next main meal.

Five days after arriving in Hong Kong, we booked into two adjacent rooms with a connecting door on the third floor of the Fourseas Hotel at 75 Waterloo Road, Kowloon.

Built on one of the main thoroughfares running down the Kowloon peninsula, it was a modern, E-shaped three-storeyed block with a flat, tiled roof, modest gardens and a short, sloping, crescent-shaped driveway leading to a covered entrance. Beneath the front lawn and giving directly on to the pavement was the hotel garage. My parents' room had a balcony: mine did not. On either side of the hotel were low-rise apartment buildings whilst opposite, across the wide road, was the steep bare dome of a hillside rising about a hundred feet from the street. It contained a deep fissure I was sure, in my romantic imagination, was an old volcanic vent just waiting to erupt.

'This is definitely a leg-up,' my mother declared as, for the third time in a week, she unpacked our cases.

'How long will we be staying here?' I asked, having grown used to a peripatetic existence.

'At least until Christmas,' she replied. 'Now,' she continued, 'if you ever get lost, this hotel is called *sei hoi jau dim* in Cantonese. It means *four seas hotel*. You say that to a taxi driver and he'll bring you home safe and sound and the receptionist will pay him. Repeat it.'

These were my first words in Cantonese and I was not slow in realizing that as many Chinese did not speak English, if I wanted to explore as I had on my first night, I would need a command of their language. In next to no time, I possessed a substantial vocabulary ranging from a polite *Nei wui mui gong ying mun?* (Do you speak English?) to such commonly used colloquialisms as *Diu nei lo mo* which, I discovered, implied anything from You don't say! to Well, I never did! to Bugger me! to Don't bullshit me, you sonofabitch! And worse. Much worse . . .

Early the following Monday, my father reported to Kai

61

Tak airport to depart for Japan. My mother was very anxious, not because my father was in effect heading for a theatre of war – Korea – but because he was flying out of Hong Kong. According to my father, who was never loath to dramatize if it boosted his ego, the wind direction was crucial to a successful landing or take-off. If at all possible, he declared, aircraft took off towards the south-east, the runway aiming for the sea. However, rarely, aircraft had to take off facing inland. This meant that as soon as it was clear of the ground the aircraft had to veer sharp left to avoid crashing into the Kowloon hills. These rose to nearly 1,900 feet at a distance from the end of the runway of not much more than two miles. Pilots regarded it as one of the most dangerous and demanding airports in the world.

Standing at the steps of an RAF twin-engined MacDonald Douglas 'Dakota' DC3, my parents atypically hugged each other for several minutes. My father then bent down, gave me a cursory embrace and shook my hand.

'While I'm away,' he ordered, 'look after your mother. You're the man of the family now.'

It was a pure Hollywood moment, my father handsome enough to have been played by James Stewart, his wife petite and blond enough for the part to have gone to Doris Day. I suppose I would have been played by Mickey Rooney: it would have been my luck.

'Yes,' I replied noncommittally but, as usual with my father, I had been instructed to do something without any guidance as to how to do it. Was I, for example, to see my mother across the road, ensure she washed behind her ears, went punctually to bed and so on? I was about to enquire but my father was already at the aircraft door and stooping to step aboard. A moment of fear swept through me. I had been given a serious task, yet how could I, in my ignorance, hope to do it efficiently? There was, I saw, only one outcome – a slippering for failure. Even before the DC3 took off, I was already dreading my father's return.

The engines started with billows of black smoke and the plane moved away. My mother crossed her fingers. The gesture failed. The Dakota turned right and taxied to the very south-eastern extremity of the runway. It was to be a take-off into the mountains.

At this point, my mother noticed a main road crossed the runway at about three-quarters of its length, the traffic controlled by a set of lights. This added hazard unsettled her further. I saw her watching avidly to ensure the traffic lights were working and the drivers obeying them.

The Dakota rumbled forwards. As it passed by us, its tail wheel lifted off the runway, the plane taking to the air at the road crossing. Its ascent seemed excruciatingly slow. For a moment, I was quite certain it was heading straight for the mountains and followed its progress with terror mingled with fascination.

'I can't watch,' my mother declared and she studied her shoes. Her hands shook.

At what seemed the last minute, the DC3 banked so sharply to the left I could see both wings as if I were looking down on top of it. It flew along the face of the hills, climbing slowly, levelled out and began its gradual ascent until it disappeared in the haze of the day, the sound of its engines suddenly dying.

'What's happened?' my mother asked, almost in tears and still not daring to look.

'Nothing,' I said, exercising my licence as head of the family for the first time. 'It's flown so far away we can't see or hear it.'

A Royal Navy saloon car took us back to the Fourseas Hotel.

'When does Daddy come back?' I enquired.

'In about twelve weeks,' my mother replied. 'On his ship,' she added with evident relief.

'What happens if I don't look after you very well?' I said anxiously.

'Don't you worry,' my mother answered, sensing my concern and putting her arm around me. 'You'll do just fine.'

A telegram arrived that evening from my father. Opening it, my mother visibly relaxed. It had been an uneventful flight. She poured herself a gin and tonic.

The Thursday after my father's departure, I started school.

Kowloon Junior, as it was known, bore as much resemblance to my previous school as a cat did to a caterpillar.

Since beginning my education at the age of five, I had attended a small dame school in Brentwood, Essex. Owned and operated by a kindly, elderly spinster called Miss Hutt, Rose Valley School provided a very sound basic schooling from the huge, dark front room of a mid-Victorian terraced house. A noxious lavatory, the floorboards irredeemably stained by years of small boys with a poor aim, was in the basement and the rear garden had been flattened, surrounded by a picket fence and covered with cinders to make a playground of sorts. Beyond the fence were vegetable allotments in which the citizens of Brentwood attempted to supplement their rations. Every lunchtime, the pupils – there were about a dozen of us aged from five to twelve – were marched in single file to Brentwood High Street where we were fed in a café with oil-cloth-covered tables. The monotony of the menu never varied – scrag end of beef or mutton stew with boiled potatoes, mashed swedes and cabbage, helped down with a glass of milk. Dessert was invariably a bowl of semi-liquid, lumpy custard. Sometimes this was supplemented by an apple or, on one occasion, a banana the skin of which was turning black.

By contrast, my new school was a long, two-storeyed building with veranda corridors, bright, airy classrooms with ceiling fans and individual desks: at Rose Valley, we had hunched round two old dining tables. Everyone wore a uniform which somehow gave the place an added appeal. Outside, the playground was beaten earth with patches of grass surrounded by a six-foot chain-link fence on the other side of which was a steep drop to the dusty football field of another school. In one place, the fence stopped at a vertical earth bank into which the boys had cut mountain roadways for Dinky cars.

The school was less than a mile from the Fourseas and so I walked there most days, my mother at first seeing me across Waterloo Road. If it was raining, I was sent in a scarlet-painted rickshaw with a green pram-like hood and two huge spoked wheels with solid rubber tyres.

Riding in a rickshaw was a strange sensation. The coolie lowered the shafts to the ground, one stepped between them on to a footboard in front of a padded seat covered in a loose white cloth and sat down. At this stage, the whole contraption was sloping forwards and downwards. I had to hold on to the sides to stop sliding off – the cloth didn't help. The coolie then picked up the shafts, his elbows bent at right angles. This meant the rickshaw suddenly tipped backwards and the passenger fell to the rear of the seat.

The coolie set off at a walk, building to a steady

trot. His bent arms acted like leaf-springs on a vehicle, reducing the shock of the road bumps for his body.

The coolies were usually bare to the waist, except in winter, and one could see their muscles flexing across their shoulders, the tendons tightening and relaxing under their skin. Most of them were sallow, with sunken chests, gaunt faces and drawn skin on their necks: and when they sweated, they exuded a faint, strangely sweet body odour. They all looked old enough to be Confucian sages, but they were almost all certainly no older than their late twenties. A rickshaw coolie's lifespan seldom reached thirty-five. It was not long before I realized virtually every one of them was an opium addict.

They wore small, domed rattan hats with numbers painted in scarlet on them: it was from these I learnt to count and read numbers in Cantonese – *yat, yee, sam, sei, ng, lok* – and the coolies were called by their number. Of the half dozen who lingered near the hotel, I always chose number 3, hailing him by shouting, 'Ah Sam!' I never knew his real name.

What really fascinated me about him were his legs. First, he was barefoot, the slap of his soles on the road as distinct as the sound of a shod horse. In the hot weather, this was accompanied by the suck of warm tar as he took the next step. Every varicose vein stood out, the sinews like cables, his calf muscles huge and powerful. One day, I witnessed an altercation between Ah Sam and a taxi driver. With one kick, the coolie stove in the taxi door, deforming the panelling and frame to such an extent the door would not close.

In a letter to her mother, my mother wrote, *Ken gone to Japan. Lonely.* She was also anxious, even though she knew my father was not going into the actual line of fire.

To counteract her solitude, if not her apprehension, she turned to me and I found myself exploring Kowloon with her.

We started after school one afternoon by going to the Peninsula Hotel for tea. Known locally as the Pen, the hotel was considered one of the best in the world. We sat in the grandiloquent entrance lobby, surrounded by gilded pillars and serenaded by a string quartet. Silver pots of Indian, Earl Grey or jasmine tea, cradling over methylated spirit lamps, were served with wafer-thin sandwiches and delicate little cakes. The bread and butter came with four different jams. My mother was in seventh heaven. To her, this was a film star's existence. When the bill was discreetly presented, she blanched.

'Martin, go outside and wait round the back of the hotel. I'll be out in a moment,' she said abruptly.

'Where are you going?' I enquired.

'For a pee,' she replied.

I did as I was told. Five minutes later, my mother appeared, walking briskly along the street. Taking hold of my hand as if I were a baton in a relay race, she headed for the nearest bus stop.

Yet my mother was a woman of honour. Returning the following afternoon, she made straight for the head waiter's desk. Holding out the previous day's bill and payment, she blushingly explained the situation. He consulted the *maître d'hôtel*. I am sure my mother was anticipating the view from the nearest police lock-up. The *maître d'hôtel*, a Frenchman, stepped over and said, 'Madame, these accidents may happen.' He closed her fingers over the bill and money in her hand. 'Please, be our guest for tea for yourself and your son this afternoon.'

And we gained more than four free teas from this escapade.

Leaving the Pen, my mother made her way down Hankow Road, one of a grid of back streets, window-shopping the jewellers' shops. She paused outside the Hing Loon Curio and Jewellery Company. In the window was something that caught her eye and we entered. Thereupon began a friendship that was to last decades.

The interior of the shop was like a treasure cave. Heavy Chinese furniture stood piled piece on piece to the ceiling, layers of cardboard protecting them from marking each other. Glass cabinets contained cloisonné trinkets, ebony carvings, ivory figures and beads, trays of gold rings set with multicoloured stones, displays of unmounted gems, gold chains, pendants and brooches. One display case was filled with netsuke, another with jade miniatures and Chinese snuff bottles, Siamese silver and enamel fingernail covers and models of junks.

The proprietor, Mr Chan, approached my mother, smiling. 'You like a drink? Very hot today. You like a Coke, Green Spot, San Mig.?'

My mother, not knowing one from the other and feeling it impolite not to accept such a kind invitation, went for a San Mig. At this, Mr Chan poured her an ice-cold beer. I, being adventurous, asked for a Green Spot and was passed a bottle of sickly orange juice.

Whilst well intentioned, the drink was of course a means of keeping a would-be customer in the shop. For twenty minutes, we sat on leather-topped stools in front of a glass-topped counter. My mother bought a curio or two to send 'home', which meant Britain. When she was done, Mr Chan asked me, 'What year you born?'

'Nineteen forty-four,' I replied.

'What mumf?'

'September.'

'You *mahlo*.'

From a jam-packed cabinet behind him, he produced a small, crudely carved ivory monkey.

'For you,' he said, handing it to me. 'I see you again.'

Mr Chan was to be my mother's jeweller for the rest of his life and his two sons thereafter until the end of her life. She never bought a single item of jewellery from any other Hong Kong shop, declaring to all who would listen that Mr Chan was the only man of his trade who had not once attempted to swizzle her. For years, she directed friends, acquaintances, visitors and even tourist strangers who accosted her for directions in the street to his shop – 'Just mention my name – Joyce Booth – and you'll not be done,' she would tell them.

It was not long before my mother acquired a social life. The wives of my father's colleagues began to invite her out during the day, and to dinner or cocktail parties in the evenings. When this social whirl began in earnest, she delegated the job of seeing me safely to and from school to one of the hotel room boys. Tall for a Chinese, he was handsome, in his late twenties and spoke English without the usual Cantonese accent or pronunciation. His full name was Leung Chi-ching, but we called him Ching. In a very short time, I came to love this man as if he were a favourite uncle. Every morning, he guided me across the traffic on Waterloo Road, Chinese-style. This meant crossing to the central white line and lingering there as vehicles zipped by on either side, waiting for a gap in the traffic to complete the journey to the far pavement. He insisted on carrying my rattan school case – an oblong sort of picnic hamper-cum-briefcase known as a Hong Kong basket –

containing my books and some sandwiches wrapped in translucent greaseproof paper. Some of my fellow pupils were taken to school by an amah; some came by car. I stood out, accompanied by this imposing but obviously gentle man who acted like a bodyguard.

One day, I asked Ching where he lived. He was reluctant to inform me. However, he embarked upon his life story, which he told me over the next few days, walking back slowly from school with the warm, late-afternoon sun in our faces, little eddies of wind lifting miniature dust tornadoes off the road surface.

His father had been a wealthy landlord in Kwangtung province, not far from Canton. I asked how he came to speak such good English if he had lived in China. He replied that his father had been rich enough to send him to a Christian missionary school.

'It was a very good school. The brothers were trained teachers, men of learning. I was taught by them, not only English but mathematics, geography, history. One, a Chinese brother, also taught Cantonese and Mandarin. Then, one day when I was eight years old, there was much fighting. People were shot in the street and the paddy-fields. It was Japanese fighting Chinese. Then, when I was seventeen years old, there was more fighting. This time, it was Communist Chinese fighting Kuomintang Chinese.'

'What are Kuo—' I began.

'Nationalist Chinese,' Ching explained. 'The army of Generalissimo Chiang Kai-shek.'

'What happened?' I asked.

'They lost,' Ching said candidly. 'Then the Communist soldiers came, and the officers, and they took away my father's land and our house. Our belongings were taken, our farm animals killed. My father had a motor car. They burnt it. We had horses to ride. They shot them.'

'Were the horses ill?' I enquired. I knew sick horses were shot: I had stayed for a holiday on a farm in Devon the year before when a dray horse broke its leg and was put down.

'No.' Ching shook his head. 'They just shot them.'

It seemed incomprehensible that anyone would deliberately set fire to a car and barbaric that they should shoot a perfectly healthy horse.

'What happened to you?'

'We were told to go, so we went. If we had not they would have killed us. They killed our friends who refused to go. I came to Hong Kong.'

'If your father is so rich,' I ventured as we waited to cross at a busy junction, 'why do you work as a hotel room boy?'

'I have no money,' Ching answered. There was no regret in his voice. 'All I have are my clothes. When the Communists drove us away, we could only take what we could carry.' We crossed the road and started walking slowly along the pavement towards the hotel. 'There are many, many people like me in Hong Kong.' Ahead of us, the Fourseas Hotel transport, a cream-painted, American shooting brake with varnished wooden bars on the side, drove out of the hotel garage and across both lanes. 'You see Mickey, the hotel driver?' Ching asked. 'He is one who escaped from the Communists. At least half the room boys have escaped from China. Some with their families, some, like me, alone.'

I felt a terrible sadness for Ching and took hold of his hand.

'You've got me and my mum,' I said comfortingly.

I never discovered where Ching laid his head, but I

71

found where others did. A week or so later, my mother was invited out to a dinner party on Hong Kong-side.

It was already dark before she left in the Studebaker shooting brake for the Star Ferry to cross the harbour to Hong Kong island. I waited a respectable time, got dressed and walked out of the hotel tradesmen's door, a steel gate that gave on to a street called Emma Avenue. I turned left and headed for Soares Avenue, a fairly busy thoroughfare used by traffic taking a short cut to the next main road, Argyle Street.

At the time I was not to know it, but these streets were to be my patch, my playground, and I was to become as well-known in them as any of the shopkeepers.

The streets were warm, the air heavy with the unfamiliar scents of exotic food cooking in the tenements. Traffic fumes fought to suppress these smells but failed. Above the sound of passing cars was a trill of argumentative birdsong from the trees. Finches in bamboo cages, hung outside the tenement windows for an evening airing, joining in the conference with their free-living brethren.

Walking along the streets was mildly hazardous. First, one was periodically peppered with bird seed and desiccated droppings as a finch had a scratch-about in the bottom of its cage three floors above. Second, one was dripped on from laundry hanging out to dry over the street on bamboo poles. Third, and less benign, was the fact that one could be hit by a chicken bone or other detritus from a completed meal. This I found curiously incongruous. The Chinese were a fastidious race and yet here they were throwing their garbage out of the window and into the street. Without looking first. From some way up. When I passed my thoughts on to Ching, he explained that it was habit: in China, one threw waste food into the street and the local pigs or dogs ate it. That there were no pigs wandering the streets of Kowloon seemed immaterial to the residents. At least there were pi-dogs – stray mongrels – although none of them looked porcinely overfed.

In Soares Avenue, there was a line of shops. I crossed the road and started to inspect them. They did not have front windows, being more like square caves giving directly on to the pavement. One sold everyday kitchen utensils, but even some of these were alien to me. Shallow, cast-iron cooking pots, which I subsequently learnt were called woks, hung from hooks overhead, a shelf bore what I was to discover were rice steamers and there were sets of woven baskets, one inside the other. Packets of chopsticks, rice bowls, serving dishes, quaint porcelain spoons tied together with string, minute bowls, soy sauce dispensers, teapots decorated with red and gold dragons and handle-less tea cups and bowls with lids stood or lay in profusion on a table board balanced on trestles. Near by were displayed wooden cutting blocks bound by steel hoops, meat choppers and knives of medieval ferocity.

Moving on, I came to a fruit seller whose stock, spread out under bright lights, was even more unusual. He sold oranges, lemons, bananas and apples, but the remainder of his offerings might well have been picked on another planet – waxy-looking star-shaped fruit reminiscent in texture of my grandmother's hat flowers only not as dusty; huge grapefruit-like fruits, split open to show pale citrus-like segments within; knobbly custard apples; deep sea-green watermelons bigger than footballs; spiky ovals I discovered to be durians; and what appeared to me to be short lengths of leafless tree branch.

The shopkeeper, seeing me standing admiring his stock,

came round the front and spoke to me, picking up the grapefruit-like pomelo and holding it out. By now, I had picked up more than a smattering of Cantonese and said, '*M'ho cheen.*' To emphasize my impecuniosity, I patted my pockets. He laughed, stroked my blond hair, took out a sharp knife, sliced open the pomelo and offered me a segment. It was time to keep my promise.

I accepted it, said, '*Dor jei,*' and put it in my mouth. It was sweet and tart at the same time, the cells of the segment erupting upon my tongue. '*Ho!*' I said and I meant it. It was very good.

The fruit seller smiled and picked up one of the lengths of branch. It was pale silvery-green and about an inch thick. He shaved the bark from all of its length but a few inches at one end, with which he handed it to me like a truncheon. I had no idea what to do with it. Seeing this he prepared another length, bit some off the end and chewed it. I followed suit. It was sugar cane, saturated with syrupy sap. When he had sucked the stringy cane dry, he spat it out on the pavement. I copied him. Then a fish head hit me on the shoulder. I was, I considered, now at one with the streets, duly initiated and baptized.

I made friends at school but rarely visited my friends' homes or spent time with them away from the classroom or playground. My life was centred on the Fourseas and the adjacent streets and alleyways.

In one fetid passageway, I came across a family of four who lived in a large crate that had been used to ship a Heidelberg printing press from Germany. They had improved their abode by nailing a sheet of tin to it to protect against the elements, putting a plank across the entrance to stop any rubbish drifting in and standing the crate on four short blocks to keep it clear of the ground and rainwater that cascaded down the alley. Inside, some planks had been erected to pass as shelving. Otherwise it was still a packing crate. My Cantonese was insufficient for me to converse with the family, but they smiled at me when I passed and greeted them. When the hotel started to redecorate some of the public rooms, replacing the venetian blinds with curtains, the manager agreed to give me one. I gave the blind to the family to hang over the crate entrance. They were delighted with it but, a week or so later, they had vanished. It was not just that the family had gone. So had the crate. Their departure left a hole in my life, even though I had only known them for a fort-night. I never saw them again.

My primary circle of acquaintances consisted of the shopkeepers to whom I was introduced by the fruit seller. His name, I came to discover, was Mr Tsang. It was from him that I picked up a knowledge of pidgin Cantonese – it was commonly referred to as kitchen Cantonese, because it was what the European lady of the house spoke with her domestic servants. In exchange, Mr Tsang learnt pidgin English from me.

Next door but two or three to Mr Tsang was a tiny shop squeezed into the sloping space under a staircase. It consisted of a single display counter with a pigeon-hole arrangement of shelves behind it made out of fruit boxes courtesy of Mr Tsang. Owned and operated by an elderly man and his teenage son, it sold plastic biros, ten-cent notebooks, rubbers, plastic rulers, toy guns that spat sparks, tin rocket ships with the same sparkling mechanism in them, playing cards, glass marbles, combs, nail clippers and files . . . It was Soares Avenue's equivalent of a department store. It also sold something that at first bemused me. Packed into small cardboard boxes and surrounded by fine sawdust were what appeared to be clay marbles. I picked one up and put it between my thumb and forefinger as if to flick it marble fashion. The store owner quickly cupped my hand in both of his and shook his head vigorously. Then, taking the clay ball, he waited for a break in the traffic and tossed it into the road. It exploded loudly with a drift of clay dust. He gave me another and gestured for me to throw it into the road. I did so. It too went off with a loud report. A flock of birds rose from one of the trees and a passing rickshaw coolie volubly cursed me. I returned in minutes with a dollar and bought a boxful. They were confiscated the following morning by the teacher on playground duty, who informed me they were called cherry bombs, they were illegal and if I ever brought one into school again I would be expelled. A letter was sent home to my mother and I was roundly chastised and stripped of that week's pocket money. Yet, at the same time, I felt with that innate seventh sense of childhood that my mother did not entirely disapprove. From that moment, I knew she was not unduly averse to my wandering the streets and I began ranging more widely.

Five hundred yards down Waterloo Road from the Fourseas was a railway bridge beyond which were the streets of Mong Kok. This was almost another land, the railway a national border. The streets contained few shops. Instead, there was a large hospital and a good number of factory units that turned out belt lengths, sandal parts, brightly fluorescent coloured plastic twine, plastic flowers and metal-framed hand trolleys. Other workshops manufactured metal buckles, cheap tin pad-locks, trouser waist catches, metal buttons and washers. Most of these items were pressed out of sheets of metal. The air reverberated with the hiss of hydraulics, the ring of hammering and the whine of the cutting or sharpening of metal. Brilliant oxy-acetylene torches lit up the interiors and the sparks of welding guns spattered on to the pavements. On one occasion, I found a fifty cent coin on the pavement outside one of these metal workshops and, no-one looking, pocketed it. Later, Mr Tsang refused it in payment for a pomelo and showed me why. When he dropped it on the pavement it made a dull clunk: the coin was made of aluminium. There were, additionally, several car repair shops, their concrete floors thick with black oily grime, the pavements scattered with discarded ball-bearings and wadges of multicoloured cotton waste. I was addicted to the smell of these garages, of warm oil, rubber, leather and newly sprayed paint: it was like none other I had ever encountered.

As the weeks passed, I grew bolder and – more con-fident in facing traffic – I traversed Nathan Road, the main artery running up the spine of Kowloon, to enter the district of Yau Ma Tei, an area that was more residential than Mong Kok. Many of the three- or four-storey build-ings were old, with arcades, their balconies lined with green-glazed railings patterned to look like bamboo. The roofs of some were covered in green-glazed tiles and curved upwards at the eaves. A few bore ceramic ridge tiles of dragons and lions in faded blue, red or gold. I felt an added excitement coming upon old rusty signs at the entrance to some side streets declaring *Out of Bounds to Troops*. It was as if I was the first explorer of my race to tread these urban jungle paths. Even soldiers had not come this way before.

The shops here were more traditional than those in Soares Avenue. A bakery sold soft bread buns with red writing stamped on them. Dried fish shops displayed desiccated shrimps, squid, cuttlefish, scallops, mussels, sharks' fins (hanging from the ceiling like triangles of light grey leather) and other unidentifiable seafood. Butchers offered raw meat hanging from hooks under 100-watt bulbs beneath red plastic shades. Poultry shops sold chickens, ducks, quail, exquisitely plumaged pheasants and geese but, whereas the butchers' fare was slaughtered, the live poultry was crammed into bamboo cages. No self-esteeming Chinese housewife bought fowl that was not still breathing and it was commonplace to see someone walking down a street with two trussed hens clucking with avian irritation.

One afternoon I wandered into a back-street butchery thinking that I might watch the meat being portioned. Unlike British butchers who carefully shaped specific cuts, Chinese butchers merely chopped the carcass up with razor-sharp cleavers. Turning a corner in the shop, out of sight of the street, I was suddenly confronted by the corpse of a black chow dog hanging by a hook that had been thrust through the tendons of a hind leg. Its black tongue hung down from its mouth. There was a massive wound on the back of its head.

No sooner had I seen it than the butcher arrived, grabbed me by the neck and, swearing volubly, turfed me out into the street. Subsequent questioning of Ching ascertained that the Chinese ate dogs – black ones, pref-erably – and they killed them by pole-axing them. However, he added, dog-eating was illegal in Hong Kong because the *gweilos* liked dogs as pets and that was why I had been given the bum's rush out of the shop.

Rice vendors were also prevalent in Yau Ma Tei, displaying different types of rice in open sacks or, if they were of especial quality, in dark polished barrels with brass hoops. The variety and price were displayed on a tablet of dark wood with the information painted on them in red calligraphy. To me, one rice grain looked much like the next but there were several dozen strains, types and grades available. The tops of the unopened rice sacks were invariably the resting place of sleeping cats which doubtless earned their place keeping vermin down in the early hours.

I was fascinated by the egg shops too, where fresh duck and chicken eggs were on offer alongside dried egg yolks and 100- (or 1000-) year-old eggs. These preserved duck eggs were prepared by soaking them in strong tea then rolling them in a coating of wood ash, salt and lime. They were then stored in a huge earthenware jar and surrounded by fine soil rich in humus. In this state, they were left for just over three months during which time the yolk hardened and turned grey-green, the white of the egg turning into a semi-transparent black jelly that looked like onyx. Another preserved egg was made by coating it with red earth and ash, salt and lime bound together with tea and rolled in rice husks. They were then stored in an airtight jar sealed with candle or beeswax. When consumed, they were not cooked and were usually taken raw as an hors-d'oeuvre.

Several streets were lined by food stalls known as *dai pai dongs* from which exotic and enticing aromas wafted. One evening, much to the consternation of the stallholder-cum-chef who was cooking over a charcoal brazier, I hoisted myself on to a stool, passing cars inches from my back and, ordering by pointing, asked for one of the preserved eggs. It was served sliced on a plate with a small bowl of pickled sweet vegetables and a dipping bowl of Chinese vinegar, rice wine, soy sauce and thinly sliced ginger. I picked up the chopsticks. A crowd gathered. The spectacle of a blond European boy sitting at a *dai pai dong* alone of an evening was more than most could resist. The traffic slowed. Then stopped. A jam began to form.

Tentatively, not because I was suspicious of the egg but because I was aware that I was the centre of attention and not yet fully proficient at using chopsticks, I picked up a piece of yolk, dipped it in the sauce and ate it, following it down with a nibble of ginger. The taste was unique, savoury and rich and not at all egg-like. I ate a piece of pickled cabbage. The stallholder put a bowl of steaming green tea before me. I held it up as if giving a toast. The crowd applauded, laughed and gradually dispersed, not a few of them touching my head in passing. I then tackled the problem of eating egg jelly with chopsticks. When I was done, the stallholder refused payment. I tried to press him. He refused again. I then saw why. I had brought him good luck. He had not a vacant stool.

My excursions into what my mother referred to her friends as Darkest Kowloon were, during term time, limited to the late afternoon and early evening. This was an exciting time of metamorphosis. Pawnshops vied for electric space with restaurants and shops. The *dai pai dongs* commenced a vibrant trade, steam or charcoal smoke redolent with the odours of frying rising from them to glimmer in the neon above. Stalls appeared selling clothes – anything from children's vests to ladies' frilly knickers, all piled haphazardly under canvas awnings – or shoes, kitchenware or bolts of cloth, or offering services such as grinding knives or cutting keys. The streets, busy in the day with people going about their work, now filled with shoppers or those merely out for a stroll. Men walked by promenading their birds in cages. In a few places, people gathered to read the daily papers pasted to a wall or congregated at a street library where they could read books for a minimal charge but not take them away.

Just off Nathan Road, there stood a large temple dedicated to the deity Tin Hau, also known as the Queen of Heaven and the protectress of seafarers. Next to it in the same complex of buildings were smaller temples to To Tai, the earth god, Shing Wong, the city god, and She Tan, a local god without, it seemed, a celestial portfolio.

Tin Hau was a major goddess of the first league: this I learnt from a book in the minute hotel library – contained within one glass-fronted case in the first-floor residents' lounge – called *Chinese Creeds and Customs*. I frequently consulted it.

According to legend, Tin Hau was born in Fukien province in the eleventh century. One day, her father and brothers went out to sea to fish. She fell asleep and dreamt their junk was foundering in a typhoon so she flew to their aid on the clouds and rescued them from drowning. It is also said she could predict rough weather and was deified on her death at the age of twenty.

In keeping with her position in the heavenly pantheon, her temple was ornate. The roof ridge was lined with glazed china figurines and all the interior woodwork painted deep red. A little way in front of the altar stood four very tall effigies. They represented the goddess's bookkeeper who tallied up mankind's sins and virtues, the keeper of her seal and two generals of yore called

Favourable Wind Ear and Thousand Li Eye who could help to foretell the weather for those going to sea. Elsewhere in the temple were the goddess of mercy, a small altar to Shing Wong whose role it was to intercede with Tin Hau on behalf of the dead, a green-glazed china horse god, a tiger, several deities of prosperity, a god of beauty, a heavenly dog and the effigy of Tong Sam Chong, of whom I had heard at school. He was a Buddhist monk who had brought the Buddhist scriptures from India to China in a sort of Chinese odyssey which had become a famous fairy tale.

Tin Hau's idol sat on her altar wearing a Ming dynasty headdress hung with pearls. The effigy's face was expressionless, painted a garish flesh pink, the same colour as prosthetic limbs, her own appendages out of sight under a red cloak embroidered with gold dragons. Before her were brass candlesticks, offerings of oranges, small china effigies and a brass bowl of sand for worshippers to stand their joss-sticks in. Every so often, a drum or bell sounded, the former so resounding it caused sound waves that were visible in the joss-stick smoke.

In the evenings, the area in front of the temple attracted me as a magnet does iron filings. Crowds flocked there to consult fortune-tellers, necromancers and phrenologists who had their charts of the human head spread out on the ground.

The fortune-tellers would invite their customers to cast small elliptical pieces of wood or shake numbered bamboo splints out of a bamboo cup, which they would then interpret according to the way they fell or the number written on them. One had a tortoise with a highly polished shell which seemed to possess the powers of divination. In their midst, an old man, a four-inch-long wisp of grey hair sprouting from a mole on his cheek, sat at a small lectern writing letters for illiterate coolies at five cents a time. A black silk skullcap that had seen better days, topped off with a red soapstone finial, lent him the air of an imperial scholar down on his luck.

They all fascinated me in their way but one of them held my attention every time. He was employed in the most bizarre occupation I had ever seen. Seated on a stool, his client – man or woman – perched on another before him. He plucked their eyebrows with tweezers, then either pulled out or clipped their nasal and ear hair. The high point of his service came when he produced a tiny steel spatula and assiduously scraped out his customer's ear wax which he put in a tiny bottle. What he did with this disgusting gunge was left to my vivid imagination.

On the western edge of Yau Ma Tei was the sea and a typhoon shelter, a large artificial basin surrounded by a sea wall of massive boulders, behind which fishing junks and other small craft took shelter during storms. It was also where fishermen landed their catch. Some Saturday mornings, I would go to the shelter to watch the night's haul landed – green and blue-backed crabs and azure lobsters, sea bass with electric-blue scales and black lines, gold and black mottled grouper, thin, silver needlefish, octopi that slid their tentacles across the quayside, squid, sea cucumbers, long-spined sea urchins, eels, rays and sharks ranging in length from a few feet to such as it took four men to lift them, their eyes sunken and their mouths bloody. Nothing, it seemed to me, had been thrown back: everything was up for sale as edible and women jostled to buy the entire catch. Even the seaweed snagged in the nets sold for ten cents a bundle.

On one occasion, I squatted down to look closely at a

large shark when it spasmed, opened its mouth wide and slammed it shut within inches of my hand. Before I could leap away, a fisherman grabbed me by the armpits and hauled me rapidly backwards.

'He lo dead!' he warned me. 'Sometime liff long time lo wartar.'

He picked up an iron bar, smote the shark on its head, rammed the bar in its mouth, twisted it to and fro and, breaking off some of the shark's teeth, scooped them up and gave them to me. They had a sharp, serrated edge. When the bar struck the fish, it sounded like someone hitting a semi-inflated football with a cricket bat.

Three types of vessels predominated in the typhoon shelter. The smallest and most numerous were sampans, ranging from little more than skiffs to boats about fifteen feet long. Constructed of wood, they were propelled by a single stern oar, although some had a short mast with a square-rigged sail. Most had arched canvas awnings that ran their length, beneath which lived a complete family. There was even a place for a charcoal cooking stove. The majority of sampan dwellers were fishing folk who cast gill nets or fished with sleek, long-necked cormorants.

I was intrigued by cormorant fishing, a typically devious and clever method the Chinese had developed. The cormorants were black sea birds about the size of small geese. When a sampan reached a shoal of fish, the fisherman would let the bird go. It would dive into the sea, catch a fish and swallow it. However, the fish could not reach the bird's stomach because of a ring affixed round its neck. Once the fish was caught, the cormorant returned to the sampan and, unable fully to swallow its prey, spat it out; with its wings clipped, the cormorant could not fly off. When it had caught a few fish, the fisherman would remove the ring, let the bird have a fish as a reward, re-affix the ring and wait for another shoal to pass.

At night, the sampan fishermen caught their quarry with the aid of a bright hurricane lantern. This was hung over the stern, the fish being attracted to it only to be taken in dip nets.

The next boats up in size were the walla-wallas. These were motorboats that operated round the harbour as water taxis. They acquired their name from the puttering sound their exhaust pipes made when a wave momentarily covered them, although I was given an alternative explanation of the name by one of my mother's friends who claimed they were named after the town of Walla Walla in the USA. Curious about this, I looked the place up in an atlas. It seemed improbable to me: the town, little more than a pinprick on the map, was in the state of Washington, at least 170 miles from the Pacific coast.

Third, and most impressive of all, were the huge ocean-going and long-distance coastal fishing or trading junks. Three-masters, they lay alongside the typhoon shelter quay like the remnants of the lost age of sail, prehistoric maritime monsters inexorably creeping towards extinction. Made of seasoned teak, some over eighty feet long and twenty wide, they were not only boats but family enterprises. Infants to grandparents lived upon them, as did cages of chickens and ducks, dogs, cats and even baskets with pigs in them. The poultry and pigs spent much of their lives suspended in mid-air over the stern, their droppings falling to the sea, not the deck.

Not infrequently, I was invited aboard one of these wooden leviathans. My blond hair, considered by the Chinese to be the colour of gold and therefore likely to impart wealth or good fortune, was my passport to many a nook and cranny of Chinese life. It was also the reason why, whilst walking down the street, a passer-by would often briefly stroke my head. I was a walking talking talisman.

At the stern of the junk were the living quarters for the captain or owner and his family, low-ceilinged compartments that smelt of snug humanity, soap, sandalwood incense and paraffin. Weighted oil lamps hung from hinged brass mountings; two boarded-off *kangs* – traditional Chinese beds – were made up with thinly padded quilts and hard headrests the size of building bricks but made of lacquered papier mâché and painted with flowers or dragons. In one bulkhead, a cubby-hole contained maps, brass and steel dividers, a navigator's ruler and a sextant. Upon a bulkhead was a small shrine to Tin Hau, the effigy seated demurely behind a tiny offertory bowl of rice wine, four kumquats arranged as a pyramid and a smouldering joss-stick.

Below the main deck was the hold which, according to the usual cargo, smelt of fish or a mixture of cloth, rice and, for a reason I never understood, dry earth. In the fo'c's'le were the crew's quarters: up to thirty men crewed the biggest junks. Every junk occupant was deeply tanned, almost the colour of the vessel's hull, and as sinewy as a rickshaw coolie but with a healthy glow to their skin. The junk children were lithe and sharp-eyed, like maritime gypsies. Even the dogs seemed to have a spring to their step, unlike those on the dock that just slept curled up in a convenient patch of shade. Other than to trade or buy supplies, the junk folk seldom stepped ashore and considered themselves a cut above land-dwellers.

Perhaps because she was lonely, perhaps because she missed our cat Gunner (so-called because he had been born in a cannon on HMS *Victory*) who had been left behind in England with my grandparents, or perhaps simply because her love of animals was getting the better of her, my mother decided she wanted a pet. As we lived in a hotel, a cat or a dog would be impractical and were, in any case, prohibited by the management. This did not, however, deter her.

'What animal would you like?' she asked me.

'A monkey,' I replied. It would, I considered, be like owning a little caveman whom I could teach to be civilized or, like those in Penang, criminal. The possibilities for entertainment were boundless.

'One monkey in this family's quite enough,' she retorted. 'What else?'

'A snake.'

'No!'

'Why not? They're not all poisonous.'

My mother thought and said, 'Because it would be stolen and eaten.'

It seemed a good enough reason.

'A pangolin, then,' I suggested.

I had seen one in a market a few days before, curled in a defensive ball with its scales capable of protecting it against every enemy save the butcher's knife. I had wanted to buy it then, to save it from pride of place on a menu, but the asking price was fifty-five dollars and I only had three.

'No.'

Lee Chun Kee and Company at 646, Nathan Road offered, according to their business card, to 'procure strange animals from all countries', a claim I found highly suspect. What if, I wondered aloud, I had the money and wanted a hippopotamus? An elephant? A tapir? A platypus? Best of all, a panda . . . ?

'They could probably get you one of those,' my mother remarked. 'I don't think you could keep it on the balcony, though. And every day you'd have to get several hundredweight of bamboo shoots for it to eat.'

The walls of the shop were lined with cages containing a multitude of song birds, most of them species of finch. Other cages were occupied by guinea pigs, terrapins, rabbits, white sulphur-crested cockatoos, kittens with their eyes barely open, macaws, love-birds, mynahs, mongrel puppies with eager tails, budgerigars and canaries. My mother drooled longingly over the kittens and puppies with all the emotion of a child peering in the window of a well-stocked confectioner's shop. At last, we were approached by a man we assumed was Mr Lee. He smiled ingratiatingly, displaying a solid gold canine tooth.

'You wan' baby dog, missee?' he enquired, swiftly opening a cage door and depositing a puppy in my mother's arms, from where it immediately proceeded to furiously lick her face. I could almost see her heart melting.

'Fifty dollar,' Mr Lee said, 'but for you, firs' customer today, speshul p'ice forty-fi'e dollar.'

As it was mid-afternoon, I found his salesman's pitch to be dubious in the extreme, but said nothing. Reluctantly, my mother returned the dog and, after much soul-searching, she purchased a budgerigar, a bamboo cage, a porcelain water bowl, a tin seed bowl, a mirror, a bell and two pieces of cuttlefish. These accoutrements cost over three times as much as the bird despite my mother beating Mr Lee down by fifteen dollars.

'What shall we call him?' my mother suggested as we

retraced our steps through the back streets. 'How about *Sai Juk?*'

As this translated as Little Bird, I was not impressed. My mother's desire, which lasted the rest of her life, to give everything – dogs, cats, cars – a Cantonese name did not always show imagination or an extensive vocabulary.

In the end, we settled for Joey. He was happy in his cage, trilling to the wild birds outside, kissing his image in the mirror, ringing his bell, hopping from perch to perch and nibbling at his cuttlefish to keep his beak sharp. This, my mother deemed, was insufficient exercise, so every afternoon she switched off the fan, closed all the windows, locked the doors and gave Joey the freedom of her hotel room. With a flutter of wings, he darted about the room depositing birdshit wherever he went. This continued for two months until the day my mother omitted to close the fanlight window. Joey hopped out of his cage, chirped once and was out the window like a ballistic missile. My mother was devastated and we returned to Mr Lee bereft of a budgie but the proud owners of a miniature aviary with all mod. cons. except running water.

Despite being fully equipped, my mother decided not to get another bird because, she declared, 'You can't cuddle a bird or talk to it like you can a cat or dog. And it's cruel to keep them in cages.'

So she bought a terrapin, a glass tank to keep it in and a stone for it to sit on out of the water.

About two inches in diameter, its carapace was grey on top with a yellowish-green underside. Its head was yellow and black striped with bright red flashes by the ears. My mother, being new to terrapin ownership, asked Mr Lee what it ate.

'He eat w'ice, missee.'

'Rice?'

'Yes, missee. Plenty w'ice. An' dis one.' He reached under the counter to bring out a container of writhing bloodworms.

My mother recoiled but it was too late. She had paid for the terrapin.

On the walk back, we determined to call it Timmy, my mother not knowing the Cantonese for terrapin.

'It's a shame we couldn't have a puppy,' she mused. 'I don't like to dwell on their fate . . .'

'They'll be all right,' I said to placate her. 'The Chinese only eat black dogs.'

My mother stared at me. 'How do you know that?'

'I just heard it. One of the room boys . . .' I replied innocently. 'Besides, it's against the law in Hong Kong to eat dogs.'

My mother looked relieved. I did not admit to having seen the black chow.

Timmy and his tank were delivered an hour later. Convinced that terrapins did not exist on a diet of rice and bloodworms, my mother telephoned the University of Hong Kong Biology Department to get the truth, which was that red-eared terrapins were carnivorous and ate fish. They could also grow to twelve inches in length. Our tank was about fifteen inches by ten. My mother hung up with a thoughtful look on her face. Luckily for us, but un-luckily for Timmy, he was dead in three months despite a diet of fresh boiled fish which stank out my mother's room, even when the tank was placed on the balcony so, as my mother put it, he could feel the warmth of the sun on his back. Her reptilian consideration may have been what put paid to him. In the wild, terrapins avoided the sun and took to deep water. Timmy's tank water was barely an inch deep and contained pieces of uneaten fish and terrapin droppings.

Timmy's death did not, however, occur before my father's first return from Japan and his presence, when discovered, caused ructions.

On the second morning of his shore leave, my father stepped out on to the balcony of my mother's room to be confronted by Timmy the terrapin.

'Martin!'

I came running.

'What, for Pete's sake, is this ruddy thing?' He pointed at the noxious tank in which Timmy was perching on his rock.

'It's Timmy,' I replied.

'I didn't ask what its bloody name was. Get rid of it.'

'He's Mum's,' I said defensively.

'What?' my father replied.

'He's Mum's,' I repeated. 'She bought him in a pet shop in Nathan Road.'

At that moment, my mother entered the room.

'Joyce, what is this benighted thing?'

'That's Timmy.'

'Dad doesn't want to know his name,' I said.

'Timmy the terrapin.'

'Get rid of it. It smells to high heaven.'

'That's only because his tank needs cleaning. I'm doing it later. He doesn't smell at all.'

She reached into the tank, picked Timmy up and held him level to her face. His head came out from under his shell, his legs treading air.

'Get rid of it,' my father again commanded.

My mother looked from him to the terrapin, as if she were a young girl deciding which suitor to date.

'He means no harm,' she remarked and tickled his throat with her fingernail. 'Do you, Timmy?'

'I'm going back on board,' my father declared, bringing the argument to an abrupt conclusion. 'You've got the ship-to-shore number.'

With that, he left, not to return until nightfall.

'We could sell Timmy back to the pet shop,' I suggested.

'I don't think we would make much of a profit on a second-hand terrapin,' my mother said. 'Besides, he isn't going anywhere and your father sails back to Japan in a week.' She paused. 'Maybe I should've listened to you and bought a snake. On the other hand, one poisonous viper in this family is, I think, sufficient. Don't you?'

Despite the escape of Joey and the demise of Timmy, fortuitously before my father's next return, my mother had still not learnt her lesson. On another trip to Mr Lee, she purchased a cute lop-eared rabbit, naming it *To Jai* which, entirely predictably, meant Rabbit. It too succumbed in a matter of months. By then, my mother had made a number of new friends amongst the members of the United Services Recreation Club and no longer felt lonely. The cavalcade of pets mercifully ceased.

I had only been at school a matter of weeks when the summer holidays began, which posed my mother a problem. She was loathe to take me everywhere with her but, on the other hand, she was just as loathe to leave me to my own devices. Consequently, a compromise was reached. I was given a crossing-the-road examination and restricted to the areas bounded by Nathan Road in Mong

Kok to the west, Prince Edward Road to the north and the far side of the hill opposite the hotel to the south. To the east, where there was no obvious boundary, I was told to use my discretion. From my mother's viewpoint, there was little risk involved – except from the traffic – for Hong Kong was famously street-safe. Muggings were unheard of, child molesters non-existent and street violence usually restricted to a territorial fight amongst hawkers and stall-holders. The nearest a European was likely to come to crime was when he had his pocket picked.

In exchange for this liberty, I was to accompany my mother at any time she requested without 'whining, whingeing, binding or generally being a little bugger'. I consented with alacrity. The restriction cut off Yau Ma Tei but I felt I had seen all there was on offer there: and there were *dai pai dongs* in Mong Kok.

A day or two into the holidays, my mother tested my submissiveness. She was going to Tsim Sha Tsui that afternoon and I was going with her.

'Are we going to tea at the Pen?' I asked hopefully as we waited for a number 7 bus at the stop opposite the hotel.

'No,' she replied. 'Somewhere far better.'

The Pen, I considered, would take a bit of bettering.

The bus pulled up, the gate of silver-painted bars slid open and we boarded. The conductor rang the bell twice by pulling on a cord running the length of the roof and we set off. We disembarked in Tsim Sha Tsui, an area at the tip of the Kowloon peninsula filled with watch and camera shops, restaurants and tailors who would make a three-piece suit in twelve hours. This was where the tourists from the big liners or staying in the better hotels unwittingly mingled with touts, pickpockets and other ne'er-do-wells.

When we alighted, it was to head through the streets behind the Pen and into a small baker's shop with a display bow window such as one might have found on any Edwardian street that had survived the Second World War. The window glass was flawed, the frame darkly varnished. Above was the establishment's name – *Tkachenko's*. Inside were a number of rattan chairs and tables, also darkly stained. Along one wall ran a glass-fronted cool cabinet which contained a cornucopia of cakes and pastries the likes – and sumptuousness – of which I had never seen: gateaux covered in flaked dark chocolate, puff pastry slices filled with fresh cream and cherries, white chocolate-coated éclairs with segments of glacé fruit and angelica embedded in them and tortes containing fresh fruit slices.

My mother and I sat opposite each other at a table. The rattan scratched the backs of my legs. She ordered a pot of Assam tea, a tumbler of cold milk and four cakes.

'What is this place?' I asked in tones of wonderment.

'A long time ago,' my mother began obtusely, 'there was an uprising in Russia called the Bolshevik Revolution. Many people were killed. Others lost their homes and businesses and had to flee.'

'Like Ching?' I suggested. My mother glanced at me, surprised I knew of his past.

'Yes, much like that,' she confirmed. 'Some fled to France, a few to London even, but most came east, through Siberia to Manchuria and on to Shanghai, always being forced to move along by war. Finally, they settled here in Hong Kong. And where they went, they took their skills with them. And the Russians are famous for their cakes and pastries.'

An elderly European woman, her grey hair in a

dishevelled and disintegrating bun at the back of her neck, approached our table with a tray.

'Herrre iss your orderrr, madame,' she announced in a thick accent, sliding the tray between us.

The milk was fresh, chilled and tasted quite unlike that served in the Fourseas. The cakes were summed up by my mother, her upper lip moustachioed with cream.

'If God was a baker,' she said, 'this is what he'd bake.'

When the bill came, she ordered a box of cakes to go and paid with ease.

As we walked to the bus terminus at the Star Ferry, I felt somehow uneasy. It was not that I had over-indulged at Tkachenko's but more a feeling of unaccountable foreboding, as if something was not quite right, not just with me but with the whole world. The air seemed heavy, more humid than usual. Blustery breezes blew along the street, peppering my legs with fine gravel. An old man who usually made lucky grasshoppers out of woven bamboo strips by the fire station had packed up his pitch and gone. Glancing down Salisbury Road towards Signal Hill, I could see the observatory tower on its hill. From the signal mast hung a black symbol like an inverted T. In the harbour, the sea was choppy. The sampans and walla-wallas were conspicuous by their absence and the ferries were having difficulty coming alongside their pier.

In fifteen minutes, we were back in the Fourseas. Even in that short time, the sky had darkened. When we arrived, the room boys were busy in the first-floor lounge, fitting strips of towelling into the french window frames whilst the gardener was occupied removing the pots of flowers from the lounge balcony and the sides of the driveway.

'There's a typhoon coming,' my mother told me.

'What's a typhoon?' I asked.

'The word is English but it comes from the Cantonese, *tai fung*, which means a big wind. It's the Chinese equivalent of a hurricane.'

Throughout the evening, the wind increased. When I went to bed, it whistled through the window frame. Ching came in just before I fell asleep and stopped it with lengths of rag. At intervals during the night, I woke to the sound of the wind but fell asleep again. Just before dawn, the pelt of rain on the windows finally woke me. I got out of bed and raised the venetian blinds. The street lights were still on, the thirty-foot-high concrete lampposts swaying like saplings. The rain came by in sheets. Under an overhang in the wall separating the Fourseas from the next building was gathered a crush of small birds, different breeds all huddled together. The bushes lining the hotel drive thrashed and shed leaves as if an invisible hand was stripping them. Across Waterloo Road, a waterfall was roaring down the fissure in the hillside, gushing on to the road in a torrent of orange, muddy water. No traffic drove by, no pedestrians were about. I wondered where Ah Sam and the other rickshaw coolies might be sheltering.

By noon the rain had abated somewhat, so I sneaked out of the hotel rear gate and made my way to Soares Avenue. The streets were strewn with paper, twigs, leaves and a sheet of galvanized steel. The shops were all boarded up. Pressed against them were the rickshaws in a line, their awnings raised, the shafts of one fitted under the rear of the next. The coolies were hunched up inside, with the tarpaulin covering that protected the passengers' legs pulled tight. Only the drift of smoke eking out from under the tarpaulins alerted me to their presence. By mid-afternoon, the sun began to break through, the wind dropped and life slowly returned to normal. The flower-pots reappeared, the waterfall ceased and the buses started running. So did the rickshaws.

'It didn't last long,' I observed to my mother.

'That wasn't a direct hit,' she replied laconically. 'The centre passed over seventy miles away. All we had was a tropical storm. You don't want to see a direct hit.'

But I did.

The residents of the Fourseas were a mixed bunch. There was a small contingent of British forces wives with their children, whose spouses were either involved in the Korean War or waiting to be allocated permanent quarters. There was a fluid population of troops temporarily billeted in the hotel whilst in transit to the war. On the rear top storey of one of the wings, four rooms were occupied on a rotational basis by a dozen Chinese whores who worked a twenty-four-hour shift pattern. The rest of their floor was taken up by itinerant American or Canadian salesmen who visited Hong Kong from time to time to buy cheap goods to ship home.

It was not unusual to see boxes of samples in the corridor outside the salesmen's rooms. When they had decided what to buy, they gave the remaining samples to me and another boy of my age whose father, like mine, was in Japan. I quickly became the proud owner of three torches that changed colour, a pair of magnificent six-guns and an eight-bladed penknife with a multitude of hidden tools. It was only a matter of time before I took to trading my surplus and was involved in selling torches, cap guns, penknives, manicure sets, nail clippers, pocket staplers, plastic hair clips set with paste diamonds and Zippo-style cigarette lighters to the shopkeepers of Soares Avenue at well under the wholesale price. This led one day to my having a stand-up row with a real wholesaler, from which I was rescued by Ching, who pointed out to the man that Hong Kong survived on free enterprise and always would.

The expatriate wives were not always a docile clientele. Under my mother's leadership, they forced the hotel manager, a tall, inoffensive and highly educated Chinese man called Mr Peng, to instigate a special children's menu, and to place a large Kelvinator refrigerator in the third-floor lobby for their use: my mother kept New Zealand butter, jam and Tkachenko's cakes in it. She also tried to have the whores evicted, but in vain. They paid well over the going room rate, the troops in transit keeping them busy twenty hours a day at what I came to know as *bouncey-bouncey* or *jig-a-jig*, although I did not know exactly what this entailed. Mr Peng no doubt received a percentage not to report their presence to the hotel owner, a stern, grim-faced Chinese who appeared monthly with his accountant and hovered behind the reception desk as the books were checked in the back office. Even if he had known of the whores, it was unlikely they would have been removed: an occupied room was an occupied room. So long as they turned a buck, the owner was satisfied and probably regarded them as an asset, for they kept the troops in the hotel buying beers and eating food there rather than wandering off to bars on Hong Kong-side. In short, they were an in-house attraction.

This disparate community was catered for by the room boys. By and large, they were happy young men despite the fact that many, like Ching, were refugees from Communism and had had to abandon their families back in China. They were efficient, thorough and paid a pittance. Yet they were grateful for a job. Thousands had none and they each knew only a tweak of fate's tail lay between them and sleeping on the pavement. Or pulling a rickshaw.

My mother befriended them all. Perhaps because she was an expatriate like them, perhaps because she had lost her father and her widowed mother lived 7,000 miles away, she identified with them and, over the years, as they improved their lot, she remained in touch with them, attending their weddings, becoming godmother to their first born, giving them advice and loaning them money.

One member of the hotel staff was my especial friend and not infrequent enemy. My mother called him Halfpint (abbreviated to Halfie) because he was short and wore a white uniform with a pillbox hat that made him look like a bottle of milk. His real name was Ah Kee and he was the bellboy. I learnt much from Halfie: how to roll tight, aerodynamic (and therefore accurate and painful) rubber-band-propelled pellets and fold paper planes out of PanAm timetables, flying them off the hotel roof to see if we could get one over the hill opposite. We never did succeed.

Halfie also played on my *gweilo* gullibility. One day, he persuaded me to eat a chilli from one of the ornamental bushes growing in the hotel grounds. I thought he had eaten one first but, by sleight of hand, he had avoided it and secreted it in his pocket. I spent three hours eating sugar lumps, drinking cold water, chewing on ice cubes and, ultimately, retching my stomach inside out. For a week, we were sworn enemies. Mr Peng was of a mind to sack him but my mother interceded on his behalf. A week later we were friends again, our camaraderie cemented by our jointly dropping a dead Atlas moth covered with stinging ants into the jacket pocket of a passing coolie then following him to see how far he went before the ants started in on him. As they abandoned the moth for living flesh, he began to prance and cavort along the street, a man with St Vitus's dance and no way to relieve himself of it.

The third-floor captain was Ah Kwan. My grandfather would have described him as a leery fellow. He spoke English and Cantonese fluently and was the *de facto* manager of the whores' rooms. He also collected their rent, paying it into the front desk after doubtlessly taking a cut. Although married with several children, Ah Kwan had a favourite trick. He would think himself up an erection, placing his penis along the inside of his thigh in his trouser leg. Then, seated on his stool behind the floor captain's desk, he would invite the hotel children to try to squeeze it to judge how firm it was. It was some time before any of us realized exactly what it was he kept in his trousers. We did not report him to our parents. It seemed a harmless activity, did not occur frequently and, besides, we liked him. He was funny.

Every fortnight or so throughout the second half of 1952, drafts of Australian servicemen passed through the Fourseas *en route* for Korea. They arrived by sea or military transport aircraft and marched from Kai Tak airport to the hotel, carrying their kitbags over their shoulders. Once there, they were 'processed' by officers seated in the lounge. I hung around the door and fell into conversation with them. They were mostly in their late teens or early twenties, wore the ubiquitous Aussie cocked hat and had a kangaroo on their brass badges. Some gave me pennies with kangaroos on them. One gave me his hat badge and address in Japan. A few years older than most of his comrades, his name was Frank Martin and he was a Flight Sergeant in the Royal Australian Air Force. I wrote to him every month: he replied with stamps for my stamp collection until, late in 1953, an official communication arrived. My mother opened the envelope while I was at school. On my return that afternoon, she took me aside.

'Your Aussie friend who writes to you . . .' she began. 'He's been lost in action.'

She handed me the letter. It was succinct in the extreme and gave no details other than to assure me he had been courageous and honourable. It was signed by his unit officer.

I thought for a minute and said, 'What does that mean?'

'It means he's dead,' my mother explained solemnly.

I did not cry. It somehow seemed like an inevitability. You went to war, you died.

American troops passing through the Fourseas were mostly non-commissioned and junior commissioned officers. They were aloof, handing out packets of Wrigley's PK chewing gum with almost divine largesse. I was never a chewing-gum person. It seemed pointless to me to chew on a sweet then spit it out to stick to the side of the waste-paper bin or lavatory pan in which if it did not hit the water first go, any number of flushings would not shift it.

Regardless of nationality or rank, they all visited the third-floor in-house entertainment area.

The system ran like this: one innocent would be given a 'ride for *kumshaw*'. In other words, a free ten-minute tumble. This was a loss-leader and the whores took it in turns to provide it. Once the word got round, those seeking servicing waited in the hotel bar to be ushered discreetly upstairs to their fifteen minutes of carnal release. I, of course, had no idea what went on in the rooms but I was aware that it was secret, private and out of bounds. Ah Kwan had said as much and that was good enough for me.

The bar, where I chatted to and drank Coke with the soldiers and, on occasion, flyers while they waited, was a vaguely art-deco counter in the reception lobby to the left of the main entrance. The back wall – and the ceiling above – consisted of lime-green plastic panels with strip lights behind them. To the right was the entrance to the hotel dining room. Grandly named *Grill*, it had clearly been designed by the architect with a penchant for art deco and lime-green, back-lit plastic. Next to that were the main stairs: there was no lift. On the other side of these was the reception desk and back office with a reception lounge area.

It was not long before I knew every corner of the Fourseas. The minuscule gardens drew little interest other than to provide a place to play and a supply of tart kumquats which I occasionally ate. The fire escape staircases to the rear of every floor were a mild distraction but only for their contents.

Had there been a fire, we would all have been burnt to death, for the staircases were piled high with stores. Catering-size tins of fruit, tomatoes and peas, drums of cooking oil, packs of Heinz sauces, boxes of jars of jams and marmalades, cans of Brasso, Mansion House floor polish and shoe blacking were balanced on the steps, five or more high. The passing space beside them was at best one thin person wide. What's more, the hotel gardener had made the tiny landing at the top of one flight of steps his own. Every night, he went on to the hotel roof, washed himself at the tap from which he watered the rows of plants he nurtured there, then spread out a quilt on the landing and laid his head on a large tin of fruit which he tucked into his neck shot-putt fashion.

He was fiercely territorial about the top of his staircase. The same applied to the kumquat bushes and a stand of paw-paw trees in front of the hotel. If he caught me or one of the other child residents even approaching them, he came at us with a vicious-looking curved pruning knife, moving with the mobility of a mongoose. He did not shout but grunted unintelligibly at us in a bestial language all his own. Had he caught us, we were certain he would have maimed or killed us. His face like that of a skull, the skin drawn tightly over the bones and his eyes sunken, he had the temper of a demon. There were effigies of him in temples, guardians of the underworld.

Some way down Waterloo Road from the hotel, a dirt track ran up behind the hill opposite. It was rutted from rain water and unsuitable for motorized vehicles. Despite this fact, people always seemed to be going up and down it, laden with bundles. Coolies with heavy loads suspended from their poles were frequent pedestrians. Rickshaws went up empty but returned loaded with packages. Curious, I followed the track one sweltering day in August.

For a few hundred yards, it rose steeply before coming out on a mildly sloping plateau upon which there was an area of about fifteen acres crammed with shanties. Most were made of wood with tin roofs constructed of flattened oil drums and any other metal to be had, whilst a few had scraps of tarpaulin patch-worked over them in lieu of metal. Doors fitted loosely and windows were shuttered without glass. A thin pall of smoke hung over them.

At first, I thought they were residential shacks for there were dogs wandering about, laundry drying on poles, women attending to domestic chores with babies strapped to their backs and infants staggering here and there with no seats to their pants as was the Chinese way. However, I soon found out at least half the shacks were thriving industrial units. Men and women toiled over paraffin or charcoal stoves. In one shack, a man was cooking up what smelt like Brylcreem hair tonic. In another, a woman was stooped over a vat of bubbling sugar making boiled sweets. A third was steaming the flesh off fish to shape into fishballs. I saw two men roasting a whole pig over a pit of charcoal, turning it on a spit and cooking it in its own fat, which fell spitting into the fire, bursting into puffs of flame like tiny meteors hitting the surface of a burning star. By the time I arrived on the scene, the pig was almost done, its whole carcass, including the head and feet, golden brown and shining.

I sauntered on through what I now realized was officially called a squatter area. These people were on the bottom rung of Hong Kong's social ladder, only the street sleepers below them. All of them refugees, they were setting out to rebuild their lives and here was where they were starting.

My presence caused no little curiosity. Men laughed a greeting, women smiled and the boiled-sweet maker offered me one of her wares. I took it. It was flavoured with cinnamon and was a cough sweet. The infants generally took one look at me and fled, screaming. To them I really was a *gweilo*.

The shanties had no sewage. That flowed away down the hill in a network of shallow ditches to soak into a stinking gully. The only water supply was provided by a standpipe down near the school on Waterloo Road and had to be fetched in a bucket. That one tap had to cater for several thousand people.

I continued through the squatter area and up on to the ridge of the hill. The ground was dry and covered in loose volcanic gravel which glittered like discarded gemstones. It sloped steeply like a dome down towards Waterloo Road, with very little plant life other than a few nondescript bushes. I kept well back from the edge of the slope. One slip would certainly have been fatal.

On the far side of the plateau, as far away as it could have been from the squatter area, was a small cemetery. The graves were unlike those in a Christian graveyard, being low, oblong stone plinths with a headstone at each end bearing inscriptions that were in neither English nor Chinese. They were old and looked untended. Desiccated grass grew between them. I was pondering these when a strange pattern materialized in the soil beside one of them. I knelt to discover, half buried, the skeleton of a snake about three feet long.

It was exquisitely beautiful, delicate and graceful. With my penknife, I carefully excavated it but as soon as I tried to lift the bones, they broke. All I was able to retrieve was the skull and mandible but these, cosseted in my cupped hands, shattered into white dust before I had gone twenty steps.

When I returned to the Fourseas, I asked Ching about the graveyard.

'The graves are those of people of Islam,' he informed me. 'They did not worship God or Buddha, but Allah. Many of them were Indian soldiers in the British Army a long time ago when the soldiers camped on the hills of Kowloon. Some were merchants. It is a very unlucky place,' he continued. 'You see how the squatters do not build near there? There are many restless ghosts.'

Over the summer, I frequently went up the hill, sitting on a huge boulder that must have been its summit. From there, I could see most of Kowloon, the Kowloon hills, Kowloon Bay, the island of Hong Kong and the western harbour. It was a breathtaking panorama and always set me humming one of my mother's favourite songs, 'I'm sitting on top of the world'.

Early one afternoon as I was sitting on the boulder, I heard a faint droning coming from the direction of Lei Yue Mun, the narrow strait of water the *Corfu* had sailed through to enter Hong Kong harbour. As the sound grew in volume, I could make out a dot in the sky. It became bigger and descended until its shape was obvious: it was a Short Sunderland flying boat like the ones I had watched with Grampy, taking off from Poole harbour not thirty miles from my grandparents' homes.

Very slowly indeed it lost altitude, its four engines by now thundering. Had it not been for the noise that echoed off the mountains, it could have been taken for a huge lumbering sea bird. Its flight almost horizontal, it dropped slowly but surely to the water, a huge spray suddenly clouding out behind it as it touched down. At last, it settled on the sea, a hatch opening near the nose. A crew member moored the aircraft to a buoy even as the propellers were still turning under their own momentum. In a minute or so, a motor launch pulled alongside and the passengers started to disembark. It was, I thought, strange to think that just five days before, it had been in England.

For a moment, I felt homesick for England. I wanted to be back in my grandfather's garden shed with him, surrounded by worm-eaten, Gallipoli souvenir Turkish rifles, a huge pedal car my father had owned as a boy, biscuit tins of straightened nails and rusty, obsolete tools. I wanted to go with Nanny to the fish 'n' chip shop in Powerscourt Road and order a plaice and six penn'orth. It soon passed. Here the sun shone, you could buy cherry bombs and go to Tkachenko's: no-one made cakes like that in Portsmouth.

Dissatisfied with the rudimentary hotel laundry service, which really only catered for bed linen, my mother decided to employ a wash amah. This entailed a new experience for her: interviewing for a servant.

'I want you to be with me, Martin,' she declared. If she used my Christian name in such a way I knew something serious was going on. Just before the first applicant arrived, my mother grinned nervously and said, 'Isn't this funny? Nanny used to be in service. She was a maid in a big country estate in Sussex. Now here's me, a proper madam of the house—'

There was a knock on the door and a middle-aged Chinese woman entered. Her black hair was scraped into a bun and she wore a white tunic jacket and baggy black trousers – the same uniform as the hotel room boys and amahs. On her feet were black slippers.

'Me name Ah Choy,' she said softly. 'I good wash-sew

amah for you, missee.' She saw me standing by the window. 'You young master?' My mother introduced me. 'Ve'y han'sum boy,' Ah Choy replied, no doubt perceiving my blond hair and anticipating many brief daily encounters with good fortune. 'Good, st'ong boy. Be plentee luckee.' At that point she produced some sheets of paper bearing references from previous employers dating back to the late 1930s with a gap from 1941 to '45.

'Where did you go in the war?' my mother enquired.

'I go quick-quick China-side,' she replied. 'Master go soljer p'ison Kowloon-side. Missee and young missee go war p'ison Hong Kong-side. Japan man no good for Chinese peopul.'

She got the job, my mother paying her $100 (about £6) a month.

A gentle soul, Ah Choy arrived at nine in the morning, collected the laundry and took it on to the hotel roof where the wash amahs of other long-term residents congregated around the tap. They chattered like hens as they worked, squatting at basins with their sleeves and trouser legs rolled up and their shoes off. When the laundry was done, they hung it to dry from lines strung across the roof. At midday, they vanished in the direction of Soares Avenue, returning at two o'clock to collect the laundry. This was bundled up and taken away, I never knew where to but it returned three hours later ironed, starched, as pristine as the day it was made. Missing buttons had been replaced and rents sewn. A pair of shorts I had torn in the school playground returned invisibly mended. My mother couldn't believe it.

Ah Choy was one of a group known as *saw hei* amahs: *saw hei* meant *combed* and referred to the way they kept their hair in taut buns. Originally from Kwangtung province, they were members of a sorority of single Chinese women who had sworn to each other strictly to maintain a vow of celibacy. Traditionally, they were silk factory workers from the Three Districts of the Pearl River delta but, in the thirties, they had been displaced by the advancing Japanese forces during the Sino-Japanese War, most fleeing for British Hong Kong, where they became servants, particularly to Western families.

During the Japanese occupation of Hong Kong, many *saw hei* amahs remained in the colony, at very great risk to themselves. It was not unknown for them to smuggle food into their former employers in prisoner-of-war camps, sometimes tossing it over the wire by night. Others fled into China, crossed north of the Japanese lines and some-how eked out an existence. When Japan capitulated in 1945, they returned to Hong Kong, sought out their former employers and took up where they had left off.

It was not long before Ah Choy started to assign herself other duties than washing and sewing. She insisted on seeing me over the road to school, even though Ching had long since given up the task as I was now considered traffic-wise. At the end of the day, or if I returned home at lunchtime, she would waylay me halfway to school in order to carry my Hong Kong basket for me. I found this agonizingly embarrassing. Should I not feel well, she would come into my room and curl up on the floor by my bed. If I woke in the night, she would too, to fetch me a glass of milk from the Kelvinator or call my mother. Many years later, my mother told me how Ah Choy had once walked in on her and my father as they were making love in the middle of the night. Not fazed in the least, she walked straight to the bed, shook my mother's shoulder and said, 'Come quick, missee. Young master . . .' She then did a passable imitation of vomiting and rushed back to my room.

I came to love Ah Choy and even permitted her to undress and wash me. She was kind, tolerant and loyal. Yet, in three months, she was gone, employed by someone with an apartment and servants' quarters. We could hardly blame her.

There followed a succession of interviews, culminating in the appointment of Ah Fong. She was the antithesis of Ah Choy. A young, smiling woman, she wore her hair in a perm and lacked the devotion to service of her celibate compatriots. She could be brusque and determined to brook no nonsense from me. I consequently led her a merry chase, especially at her evening call of 'Barfu, Martung!'

It was a matter of principle.

Beneath the main hotel staircase was a snug hideaway in which Halfie and the luggage porter huddled whilst waiting for their services to be called upon. In this little den was a telephone, a shoeshine box, a shelf of telephone directories, three stools and an electric ring on which they boiled tea for themselves and the office staff.

Returning from school one September afternoon not long after the beginning of the new academic year, I walked up the hotel drive to see Halfie twirling something round his head on the end of a six-foot length of cotton. When he stopped swinging it round, it flew of its own volition.

'I wan' one,' I said.

Halfie tantalizingly hid the object in his pocket and, pointing to the lobby clock, answered, 'You wan', you get. Light-time, I show you.'

At six thirty that evening, I met him and the porter in their den and followed them out into Waterloo Road. We stood under one of the neon street lights and waited. Twilight fell. We were joined by several more people. Beneath the other street lights, small groups of three or four were gathering. I was about to ask what we were waiting for when the street lights came on. In a few minutes, once they had reached full brilliance, something hard hit me on the head. Before I could react, Halfie ran his fingers through my hair and showed me a beetle nestling in his palm.

The insect was the size and shape of a large plum stone, its glossy carapace smooth and a dark green which was almost black. A bright yellow stripe lined the edges. Its underside was deep yellow, its two hindmost legs at least as long as its body and jointed in the mid-point.

'What is it?' I enquired.

'Wartar bee-chew,' Halfie answered.

Suddenly, more began to fall around us. They were attracted to the street light, flew into the bulb, knocked themselves senseless and fell to the pavement. Halfie and the porter collected the dazed water beetles and put them in a saucepan. As soon as they gained consciousness, they took to the wing inside it, banging against the lid and sides. In thirty minutes, we must have collected a hundred.

'What do we do now?' I asked.

'Tomowwow,' Halfie answered.

The following morning, as I left for school, Halfie presented me with my beetle-on-a-line. He had tied a length of cotton to the insect's two hind legs and showed me how to swing it round.

'No too fas',' he warned. 'You do too fas', leg b'okun.'

I gently swung the beetle round my head. It took to the wing and flew above me like a miniaturized motor-powered kite. All the way to school, I was accompanied by its whirring flight as it kept ahead of me. It was a wonder to behold. Inevitably, however, it was confiscated and given its liberty the moment I entered the school premises. My liberty that lunchtime was sequestered and I was given a hundred lines to write on the topic of cruelty to animals.

As soon as I reached the Fourseas that afternoon, I went straight to the niche under the stairs. Halfie and the porter were hunched over a pan on the electric ring.

'Bee-chew gone,' I said, miming its supposed escape. I was loathe to lose face by admitting what had actually happened.

'Lo ploblum,' said Halfie. 'Can get wung more light-time.'

He opened the lid on the pan. Inside, the remainder of the water beetles were gently simmering. 'You wan?'

This was, I considered, the severest test of my promise to the naval officer so far. Halfie removed a beetle from the pan with a spoon, blew on it to cool it then split the carapace open with his thumbnail, flicking the wing casing, wings and legs into a rice bowl already containing other beetle parts.

'You eat . . .' Halfie made a kissing-cum-sucking noise '. . . lo go down.' He pointed to his throat then mimed spitting the bits into the bowl.

I put the beetle in my mouth and chewed it thoroughly, swallowing the mushy liquid of its innards mixed with my own saliva. It tasted slightly muddy, yet the overriding flavour was like the smell of stagnant freshwater ponds mixed with smoked fish. I spat the bits out, ate another just to show willing, accepted a toothpick holder and a bowl of jasmine tea, the contents of which were more than welcome. Every tooth in my head had a bit of bee-chew wedged against it. Expecting to be violently sick at any moment, I went to my room and sat on the bed to await the advent of regurgitated beetle and tea but it never came so, half an hour later, I went down to the hotel bar and ordered a cold Coke. In the cubby-hole, all the beetles had been consumed.

4

THREE LIVES ON THE EDGE

IN THE FOURSEAS, WITH ITS PREDOMINANTLY NOMADIC POPU-
lation, only the staff, the whores, one other expatriate
woman and her son, a European man who lived in a single
room at the back of the hotel and my mother and I were
more or less permanent over the winter of 1952.

My father came back from Japan on the *Fort Charlotte*
for Christmas, bearing gifts. I received a battery-powered
wooden motor boat and a superb model of a Chinese junk
with hand-sewn sails and windlasses that worked. The
hotel did its best to become seasonally cheerful, with
decorations in all the public rooms, gifts of bottles of
VSOP brandy in each occupied room (including mine) and
Christmas dinner of an American turkey and Australian
roast potatoes, brussels sprouts and carrots. The Christmas
pudding was brought in fiercely burning but was inedible:
it turned out the cook had set it alight with paraffin
instead of brandy. One kindly old Chinese, who did not
speak English and was the night watchman and odd-job
man, went around wishing everyone a 'Happee Kiss-Mee'.

My father's return was not the happy occasion it should
have been. After delivering his largesse, for which he
demanded expressions of deep gratitude, he soon slipped

into his old short-tempered ways which he had presumably had to keep in check whilst he was on board ship. He was enough of a sailor to know that one pain in the arse in a wardroom was enough to unsettle an entire ship's crew.

The day before the ship sailed back to Japan, we were invited aboard the *Fort Charlotte* for lunch. I was shown my father's cabin, the wood- and brass-work polished, his clothes neat in the drawers, his bunk immaculately made. Lunch was taken in the wardroom with the Chief Engineer and the Captain, both of whom wore uniforms with gold braid. The meal was beef curry and rice to which were added 'bits' consisting of crisp-fried onion, croutons, diced cucumber and pineapple, grated coconut, currants, chopped tomatoes, mango chutney, hot lime pickle, poppadoms, chipattis and flaky Bombay duck which, I was surprised to discover, was not duck at all but dried fish. When it was over, we were given a tour of the ship which did not impress me. I had seen bridges and engine rooms before.

Leaving the wheelhouse, my father muttered, 'Show some interest. The Old Man doesn't have to show you round.'

I had an answer to that but wisely kept it to myself.

Returning to Kowloon across the harbour on a naval launch, my father set upon me.

'You are a rude little ingrate,' he said irately.

'What now, Ken?' my mother wanted to know.

'Martin,' my father answered. 'Taken all over the bloody show. Might just as well've left him behind.'

'Well, Ken,' my mother replied, 'he did see it all on the *Corfu*. Let's face it, unless you're a marine engineer, one ship's boiler looks very much like the next.'

GWEILO

'Neither the *Corfu* nor the *Fort Charlotte* have boilers,' my father retorted irritably. 'Not in the accepted sense. They're diesel driven. That's what I mean. The two of you. Blind as bats to life's opportunities. As inquisitive as a building brick. Curious as a dead cat.'

For the remainder of the day, my father sulked. That evening, I asked my mother – foolishly in my father's hearing – why the other men on the ship wore gold braid but my father did not.

'Go to your room!' he shouted at me. 'Put your pyjamas on.'

'I was only being curious,' I defended myself.

'Get out!'

I went.

Ten minutes later, he entered my room. I was bent over a chair and hit twice across the buttocks with the flat of my mother's silver hairbrush.

'That's for your bloody insolence,' my father said spitefully as I wiped my tears away and rubbed my running nose against my pyjama sleeve.

I had hit a raw nerve.

One afternoon early in January, my mother took me to Tsim Sha Tsui. She was going to Hing Loon to collect a ruby and gold pendant she had ordered and I was to have a new pair of shoes. It was a cold day, the wind had an edge to it and I wore a thick pullover.

As usual, we boarded the number 7 bus across the road from the Fourseas and set off. As it slowed for the last stop before turning left down Nathan Road, a face surrounded by rats' tails of dishevelled, filthy grey hair appeared at the window next to me.

I instantly recognized it. It was that of an old European woman who lived in a cockloft – a sort of semi-permanent shanty – on the flat roof of a tenement block in Liberty Avenue. I had often seen her wandering the back streets of Mong Kok, scavenging from restaurants, buying (or stealing) fruit from stalls and eating at the cheapest *dai pai dongs* where she swore volubly in fluent Cantonese at the coolies beside whom she sat. Most shop and stallholders kept an eye open for her, shooing her away with a broom or stick as if she were an alley-cat or pi-dog. I saw one or two Buddhists who were honour-bound to give alms to the poor taking pity on her but almost everybody else was hostile.

She ran along the side of the bus as it slowed, banging her hands on the panelling. I broke into a sweat. This old woman knew me, in a manner of speaking. Whenever she saw me in the street, she would run towards me, an animated pile of old rags that stank of urine, sweat, rice wine, tobacco, opium and garlic. And, on occasion, shit. I avoided her and fled but, with an alacrity one would not credit her with, she would stagger after me, shouting, 'Alexei! Alexei!'

The bus stopped, she boarded it and headed straight for me and my mother. On the way down the aisle, the conductor accosted her for her fare. She snarled at him, muttered incomprehensibly and elbowed him into an empty seat.

As the bus set off, the woman stood next to my mother, swaying to the motion of the bus and alcohol.

'Gif me one thousan' dollaire!' she demanded, holding out a filthy hand.

My mother looked over my head and out the window.

'Ignore her, dear,' she instructed me, *sotto voce*.

I was only too glad to obey. Any second now the old crone was going to recognize me.

'Gif me fife hundred dollaire,' she insisted, holding her hand out close to my mother's chin. Her nails were split, the skin of her hand ingrained with dirt. Her face was made up but badly, the lipstick smeared around her mouth, rouge heavy on her cheeks, the remainder pancaked with powder in which was etched a map of sweat, the contours highlighted by grime. Over her shoulder hung an expensive leather bag in good condition, almost certainly a recently filched acquisition. On her feet were a pair of common Chinese felt slippers.

My mother ignored her.

The bus stopped.

'Gif me two hundred dollaire!' the old woman insisted, her voice growing louder.

'Would you mind going away?' my mother said through gritted teeth. We were becoming the object of much curiosity from the Chinese passengers and she was getting embarrassed.

'Gif me one hundred dollaire!' the crone insisted, her voice louder still and even more insistent.

My mother opened her handbag on her lap, unclipped her purse and removed some dollar bills. The old woman snatched at them and, as she did so, dropped something wrapped in pink lavatory tissue into the handbag. At the next bus stop, she got off and swiftly disappeared, pushing her way through the pedestrians, moving with the gait of a practised drunk. We carried on to Tsim Sha Tsui and went into Tkachenko's. When it came time to settle the bill, my mother opened her purse. In with the coins was the tissue paper. She took it out, felt it, unwrapped it, studied the contents for several minutes, replaced it in her purse and paid the bill.

When we entered his emporium, Mr Chan was sitting behind his counter reading the newspaper. He stood up, welcomed my mother, poured us each a Coke and produced the ruby pendant set in rose gold my mother had commissioned from him. He tutted disapprovingly at it. Rose gold had a high copper content. The Chinese preferred 24 carat, 99.99 fine gold which was brassy and looked almost fake.

As he put the pendant and matching chain into a small brocade bag, my mother took the pink tissue out of her purse and placed it on the counter.

'What is this, Mr Chan?' she asked, adding, 'It's probably paste.'

He unwrapped the tissue and tipped a colourless stone on to the counter, rolling it about on the glass top with his finger. He then picked it up with a pair of tweezers, held it against a bare light bulb in a desk lamp and placed it in a velvet-lined tray.

'Is a good quality diamung,' he said. 'Little bit damage, no too much. Can recut, make maybe t'ree, four nice stone. For ring maybe for you?'

'How big is it?' my mother wanted to know.

'Maybe two-half carat,' Mr Chan replied.

For a moment, my mother was silent before asking, 'How much is it worth?'

'Is damage,' Mr Chan repeated, 'but maybe fife t'ousan'd dollar.'

My mother stared at him. At the current exchange rate, the sum approximated to £312.

For the next fortnight, my mother caught the same bus

at the same time every day in the hope of coming across the woman again and either returning the stone to her or giving her the *fife hundred dollaire* she had demanded. It was the highest sum to which my mother could go. She never saw the woman again. The diamond was duly re-cut and my mother had the resulting three stones set in a ring as Mr Chan had suggested.

I, of course, could have told my mother exactly where to find the old woman, but I did not for fear that, had she discovered some of the more insalubrious haunts I frequented, my freedom to roam would have been severely curtailed.

The Chinese in the streets called the old crone the Queen of Kowloon. Bit by bit, I came to know her story, or what it was perceived to be. The truth would be some-where near it.

She was a White Russian, the wife of a high-ranking army officer who was also possibly of minor nobility. When the Bolshevik Uprising occurred, he was killed and she headed east with the White Russian diaspora. After some time, she reached Shanghai, settling there and making her living as a courtesan and piano teacher. She became the mistress of a Chinese gangster or warlord – the story varied on this point and may have been a romantic fictional episode – and lived very comfortably for a while. Then war intervened again and she moved on, drifting ashore in Hong Kong in the mid-thirties. In those days, she lived comfortably if frugally in a tenement apartment where, once again, she gave piano lessons. However, it was not long before she took to the bottle and pipe which were the start of her decline into beggary.

Her looks now gone, she no longer had any steady source of income. Or had she?

From time to time, she appeared at pawn shops in Mong Kok and Yau Ma Tei with pieces of jewellery, valuable gems and the occasional gold coin, most of them of tsarist origin. Her tenement was burgled several times and thoroughly turned over, as once was she, but the thieves found nothing despite knocking down internal walls. Clearly, her stash was hidden elsewhere, so the thieves began to tail her but she was as sly as a leopard. Years of living on the edge had honed her senses to feline acuity. All that anyone could deduce was that, at irregular intervals, she disappeared for hours at a time into the foothills behind Kowloon.

What had happened to her during the Japanese occupation of Hong Kong was unknown. Those who stayed behind and suffered the atrocities never saw her. Some thought she ran for neutral Macau, others that she had a Japanese 'protector' although that was unlikely as, by 1941, she could no longer have been a beautiful woman. Some thought she ran a bordello for Japanese officers but that was improbable as they had rounded up any women as and when they wanted on the street.

In later years, as her mind began to slip and opium fumes befuddled it, she claimed to be Princess Anastasia, who had survived the assassination of the Russian Royal Family, but no-one believed her. She still came up with jewellery but at less frequent intervals and the local Chinese just tolerated her rantings in the street, her foul mouth and her stench.

One day, a month or two after my mother's reluctant audience with the Queen, I was trapped by her in a dead-end alley. She advanced on me slowly, her every step measured as if she were tiptoeing from stone to stone across a river. All the while, she was muttering incomprehensibly. Finally, not two yards away, and certainly close enough for me to be swathed in her odour in the windless alley, she stopped and studied me closely.

'Why do you run, Alexei?' she asked in English.

'My name's not Alexei,' I replied.

She smiled at me. Her teeth were grey. For a moment, a shard of the beauty she must once have been shone through her decrepitude.

'One day, you will be the Tsar,' she prophesied.

I looked round her to see if I might make my escape. She glanced over her shoulder.

'Are they coming?'

Terrified, I shook my head.

'If they come,' she went on, wagging her index finger at me in an admonishing manner, 'you will tell me. Yes?'

I nodded, having no idea who might be coming – thieves, the police, a man from the Lai Chi Kok mental asylum . . .

'I liff herre.' She pointed vaguely to the sky and, stepping forward, stroked my hair before I could do anything about it. She then moved past me, her rags brushing against my face. I sprinted for the Fourseas and, to my mother's consternation, for it was the middle of the afternoon, immediately ran myself a bath and shampooed my hair twice. It was one thing to have the Chinese touch my golden hair for luck. They were clean. She was a different matter altogether.

A week or so later, I joined a gang of Chinese boys pelting her with gravel from the railway line. I felt no pity for her. She had defiled me.

In 1952, The Bank of China building on Hong Kong island was the tallest in the world between Cairo and San Francisco. As for the remainder of Hong Kong, most buildings were over fifty years old. The streets of Kowloon could have changed little in that time, the arcades bustling with shoppers then as they had at the time of the Q'ing empire when men really did wear their hair in waist-length cues and pirates were executed by the sword on the beach in Kowloon Bay.

True, Hong Kong was just beginning its meta-morphosis into one of the financial powerhouses of Asia, but it was still essentially a very Chinese city with bicycles and a non-interventionist British administration.

Men in pigtails may have vanished but little else had changed. Rickshaws were commonplace. Coolies carried extraordinarily heavy loads on bamboo poles over their shoulders. Conical rattan hats were widely used whilst the Hakka women wore hats with black cloth fringes like curtains hanging from the rim. People ran like hell across the street through fast-moving traffic to shake off the demons they believed were perpetually following them: sometimes, someone walking along the pavement would suddenly dart into an alley, slip into a shop or board a departing bus at the last minute, in the hope of giving the slip to these malevolent supernatural entities. For the same reason, many Chinese assiduously avoided having their photo taken for fear the demons would see the picture and be able to track them down. Unlicensed street hawkers sold sweetmeats, sugar cane, melon seeds and *wah mui*. These were plums soaked for several days in sea water then dried in the sun. When one sucked them, they puckered the inside of one's cheek, the salt and the fruit sugars mingling together. Others carried braziers on poles, selling roasted peanuts or chestnuts, slices of hot roast pork with the crackled skin still on the meat, cut from a whole pig such as I had seen cooking in the Ho Man Tin squatter area.

These were everyday sights in the streets around the Fourseas. What were much less frequent were itinerant street entertainers. Few had survived the war years and the advent of Radio Hong Kong, but one who did was the plink-plonk man: and I was there for his final act.

My mother based his moniker upon the rosewood xylophone he played. His pitch was in Emma Avenue, directly behind the Fourseas, where he occasionally appeared to place his instrument on the pavement under the shade of the trees, squatting on his haunches behind it. After striking a few of the keys as if tuning up, but in fact to alert those in the buildings around to his arrival, he invariably launched into a Chinese classical arrangement of 'Tipperary'. Once this was over, he opened a wooden box he carried over his shoulder from which pranced a small monkey dressed in the clothing of a Ming dynasty mandarin. To prevent any escape, the monkey was tethered to the box by a long leather leash.

The plink-plonk man's second tune was usually a rendition of the Japanese song known in English as 'Rose, Rose, I love you' followed by 'Marching through Georgia' in an arrangement possibly conceived for a Cantonese opera. He finished with an embellished version of 'Swing Low, Sweet Chariot'.

As he played, his monkey cavorted about in a

haphazard jig that bore no rhythmical relationship whatsoever to the music, while people threw down ten-cent coins from windows and balconies. At the end of each tune, the plink-plonk man pitched a hard olive on to the balconies or through the windows of those who had tossed down money and at the end of the whole performance, musician and monkey collected up the coins.

All went well until one day when, halfway through 'Marching through Georgia', the monkey finally managed to bite through its leash. I was on the opposite side of the road and watched the whole drama unfold.

In a flash, the monkey was up the nearest tree. The music stopped abruptly and the plink-plonk man stood up to survey the situation. The monkey was out of reach, the tree too stout to bend and the remnant of the leash too short to be grabbed.

At first, the musician tried to sweet-talk the monkey down, holding up a piece of a bun. The monkey just peered down through the branches. Not to be hoodwinked by this, it then slowly, strip-tease fashion, divested itself of its ludicrous costume, letting each piece drift to the ground where the musician collected them up, folding them as he might those of a child. His attention taken by this task, the plink-plonk man's eye was briefly off the monkey which, holding on to its little cock, gave it a few masturbatory tugs before proceeding to urinate upon its erstwhile master.

It was a moment or two before the musician realized what was happening. He unwisely looked up to be hit in the face by the full stream. This not surprisingly drove him into an irate frenzy, cursing the monkey at the top of his voice, throwing the clothing at it and then pelting the monkey with unripe olives, some of which it caught and returned with considerable accuracy, the hard fruit bouncing off the musician's head.

Tiring of this game, the monkey headed off down the street, swinging Tarzan-like from tree to tree, always keeping just out of reach of the musician who ran below, jumping up to attempt to grab the dangling leash.

It was pure pantomime and, by now, had gathered a crowd far greater than any the plink-plonk man could ever have hoped to collect through his music. He ran along behind the escaping monkey, his face wet with urine, his fists clenched, pleading, cussing, cajoling and threatening the creature by turns. His swelling audience, meanwhile, hooted with laughter, shouted spurious advice and encouragement to the escapee.

At the junction of Emma Avenue and Soares Avenue, a network of electricity wires spanned out from a junction box. The monkey, blithely swinging through the foliage, was unaware of the danger. The plink-plonk man saw it and tried in desperation to turn the monkey back. Enjoying its liberty, it ignored him. There was a violent blue flash accompanied by an equally brief high-pitched squeak. The lights in the shops flickered. A few bulbs exploded. The monkey was instantly immolated. All that was left was a charred corpse stretched between two wires, a drift of smoke and the acrid smell of burnt hair.

The plink-plonk man sat on the curb, his feet in the gutter, and broke into tears. The crowd, now subdued, dispersed.

I never saw him again.

The single European man who lived in the cheapest room in the Fourseas was universally known as Nagasaki Jim.

My mother emphatically warned me against him. So did Ching, Ah Kwan, Halfie and all the other hotel staff with whom I was friends. Even the manager, Mr Peng, who was usually aloof unless remonstrating with me for misbehaving, told me to avoid him.

He was British, in his mid to late thirties, of average height with ginger-ish hair cut short and badly. His face and arms were freckled and he had watery blue eyes. Like the Queen of Kowloon, he also reeked of tobacco, alcohol and, not infrequently, opium. His clothes were always just the clean side of filthy although he laundered them himself once a week on the roof. He did not eat at the hotel but went every evening to a *dai pai dong* – always the same one – in Mong Kok.

I knew this because I followed him there on several occasions, keeping to the shadows, stalking him as one might a wild beast.

Indeed, he was like one. He could fly into a fit of anger at the drop of a chopstick, rushing at the object of his ire, his arms flailing. He seldom swore or shouted but breathed heavily. If he caught someone when in one of his rages, as I saw him do with one of the room boys, he would beat them about the head with clenched fists or slap them hard in the face. His assault over, he would speak rapidly and incomprehensibly in a high-pitched, faltering voice. Only later did I come to understand from my mother that Nagasaki Jim spoke Japanese in his raging.

He did not spend his whole time in the Fourseas but, when he was there, he tended to keep to himself in his

GWEILO

room, looking out of his door every so often to peer down
the corridor. His actions were tentative, guarded, like a
hermit crab periodically glancing out of its shell to check
there were no predators about. Where he went apart
from the Mong Kok *dai pai dong* and the shops in Soares
Avenue, I never discovered. His life was a mystery, closed
behind his hotel-room door.

Over time, I gleaned the story of his past, as exotic
and romantic and brutal as any of those of the other
Europeans or White Russians who had run ashore in
Hong Kong.

Nagasaki Jim was said to be the heir to a famous British
biscuit manufacturer but the family had disinherited
him save for a small monthly stipend. He had joined the
British Army at the outbreak of war and, by 1940, was
stationed in Hong Kong with the rank of Captain. When
the Japanese overran the colony on Christmas Day 1941,
Nagasaki Jim was taken prisoner and incarcerated in the
Sham Shui Po prisoner-of-war camp.

Life in the camp was harsh in the extreme. Food was
insufficient and barely edible. Diphtheria, dysentery and
cholera were endemic and medical supplies exceedingly
scarce. Escape was virtually impossible: of the few who
managed to get away, most were rounded up, hideously
tortured then shot or bayoneted to death on the seashore,
in full view of the mustered lines of their comrades.

In September 1942, the Japanese prepared to take a
draft of 1,800 Allied prisoners to Japan to use as slave
labour in their war effort. The men, along with 2,000
Japanese soldiers returning on leave, were loaded aboard a
cargo vessel, the *Lisbon Maru*. The prisoners were accommodated in the locked-down holds, the Japanese soldiers
making do with the main deck spaces.

Early on the morning of 1 October, an American submarine called the USS *Grouper* came across the ship off the Chusan Islands. Seeing all the Japanese troops on board, it was assumed to be a troopship. The submarine torpedoed and sank it. The Japanese battened down the hatches. Hundreds of PoWs drowned in the holds. Some succeeded in getting out but were machine-gunned in the water by Japanese gunboats. In all, 846 perished. Nagasaki Jim was not amongst them.

Along with other survivors, he was trans-shipped to Japan and put to work. Conditions in the mines and factories were worse than they had been in Sham Shui Po but he still survived and was somehow to end up near Nagasaki when the Americans dropped the second atom bomb on the city on 9 August 1945. It was said Nagasaki Jim was near the city and not only saw the bomb fall but witnessed its horrific aftermath. This experience, I was told, turned his head.

When prisoners-of-war in Japan were repatriated, he wound up in Hong Kong and, upon his discharge from the Army, did not return to Britain. Quite why was unknown.

Of course, I knew little of this at the age of eight and yet I was well aware that Nagasaki Jim had more than a few loose screws: as my mother put it, he only had one chopstick. I was street-wise, too. What with Princess Anastasia and various deranged beggars who wandered the streets – not to mention the crazy hotel gardener with his pruning knife – I knew there were boundaries in life and roughly where they lay. Yet if, playing in the hotel corridors, one of us strayed in the direction of Nagasaki Jim's abode, one of the hotel staff would run towards us and admonish us.

'You lo go dis place. Dis Nagasaki Jim place.' A finger would sternly shake in our faces. 'You lo go! You savee? Lo go!'

One day in the spring of 1953, I was playing cowboys and indians with friends along the corridors of the Fourseas. Or cops 'n' robbers. Whichever. The salient point was that I was carrying a cap gun six-shooter and strayed towards Nagasaki Jim's place, intending to dodge down the stores-packed staircase to the floor below and come up on my enemies from behind. There were no hotel staff about: they were attending the monthly staff meeting with Mr Peng in the dining room.

Just as I drew level with Nagasaki Jim's door, it opened. I was not a yard away from it.

'Hello,' he said pleasantly. It was the first time he had ever spoken to me.

'Hello,' I replied cautiously. If needs be, I was ready to run.

'What's your name?' he went on and, not awaiting an answer, added, 'That's a nice gun you've got. Would you like to see my gun?'

Were I a year older, the innuendo and ambiguity of this question would not have been lost on me, but I was eight and a half and a bit.

'Yes,' I said.

He disappeared into his room. There was the sound of a scuffling about in drawers.

'Come in,' he called amicably.

'I'll wait here,' I answered. My seventh puerile sense was tingling like a high-tension cable.

Nagasaki Jim came to the door and knelt down, his face level with my own.

'Here you are,' he announced and, from behind his

back, he produced a British Army .38 service revolver. The gunmetal shone with a parade-ground lustre. The wooden butt was as polished as my grandmother's dining-room table.

All my fears of Nagasaki Jim evaporated at the sight of this wondrous object. It was the first time I had ever been close to a firearm with the exception of the rusting Turkish rifles in my grandfather's garden shed, a heavy brass First World War Verey pistol he let me play with and the guns in the car in Singapore.

'Would you like to hold it?'

He held the revolver out to me by the barrel, took my six-shooter and put it on the floor between us.

The .38 was much heavier than I had expected. I could not hold it up to aim, even with both hands. The metal was warm and smooth and smelt of gun lubricating oil. Whilst my hands were occupied with the revolver, Nagasaki Jim leant forward and, hooking his index finger under the leg of my shorts, said, 'Show me your winkle and I'll buy you a gun like mine.'

Letting the revolver go, I was off like a startled hare. Naïve I may have been, stupid I was not. As my mother would have put it, I was not as green as I was cabbage-looking.

With the fluidity of a rat, Nagasaki Jim was up and after me. He threw my six-shooter at me but it missed and hit the wall ahead of me, smashing into pieces. I kept going, to be saved by two hotel guests turning a corner into the corridor. Nagasaki Jim retreated into his room like an earthworm down its burrow.

I did not report this incident to my mother for the same reason that I had kept tight-lipped concerning the where-abouts of the Queen of Kowloon. However, I did tell Ah

Kwan. That night, he and three other room boys let themselves into Nagasaki Jim's room on a pass key and lay in wait for him. When he returned from the *dai pai dong*, they gave him a sound working over.

Two months later, under threat of eviction for non-payment of rent, Nagasaki Jim hanged himself.

5

FIRECRACKERS, FUNERALS
AND FLAMES

IN 1953, CHINESE NEW YEAR FELL OVER THE END OF JANUARY
and the beginning of February. Dependent upon the lunar
calendar, the date varied from year to year. All that could
be counted upon were the keen northerlies which blew
down across China from the steppes of Siberia, the skies
blue and more or less cloudless, and the astonishing
spectacle of the festival. Friends advised my mother to
leave the Fourseas for the duration of the main festivities,
and we were invited to the bungalow at Mount Nicholson,
but my mother declined. She wanted to be in the thick of
it.

Over the weeks leading up to the festival, firecrackers
had been on sale in practically every shop. Even the fruit
shop owner sold them. Mostly, they came in square cardboard boxes the size of a paperback book, sealed with a
label printed with images of laughing children letting
them off and crude drawings of demons or dragons. In the
boxes, the fuses were plaited together so the individual
firecrackers had to be shaken loose from what was otherwise a short string of them. Always coloured red, they
varied in size from those not much fatter than a thick

pencil lead and about an inch long – and named by us tom thumbers – to others three inches in length and thicker than a cigarette.

I bought a box of fifty cigarette-sized crackers for a dollar and, with several of the other expatriate children who lived in the hotel at the time, went up on to the hill to let them off. We put them in holes in the ground or under rocks, lighting them with a small joss-stick. When they exploded, they made the holes bigger and one rock as big as a football split open. We had also taken an empty Coke bottle with us as a finale. I held the firecracker in the mouth, lit the fuse, dropped it in the bottle and ran. The others stood at a safe distance. There was a muffled sort of *thoomp!* behind me, quickly followed by a searing pain in my upper leg. I looked down. Blood was beginning to ooze out of a cut in my thigh as neat as a surgeon's incision. I staggered back down the hill, my sock becoming glutinous with the stream of blood running down my leg. I was scared but, within a few moments of reaching the hotel lobby, the porter had staunched the flow. My mother arrived, decided I did not need stitches and bandaged me up. In an hour, I was being taught by Halfie how to let off a tom thumber whilst holding it.

Although tiny, these firecrackers packed a punch sufficient to blow a five-inch-wide, two-inch-deep crater in the earth of a pot of the chrysanthemums that decorated the hotel front lawn. It was easy once you realized that the gunpowder was concentrated in the middle of the fire-crackers. If you held one by the base, gripping it between two fingernails, you could light it and let it explode with no danger – so long as you kept your eyes closed. The first I held as it went off left a tingling feeling in my fingers. The second hurt but machismo demanded I did not show it and lose face. Thereafter, we embarked upon tom thumb fights, hurling them at each other. No-one was hurt. It was good seasonal fun.

The first day of the fortnight-long, but not continuous, festival was quiet. All the shops in Soares Avenue were shut. The hotel room boys who were my friends gave me *lai see* and I returned the compliment, having been tipped off to do so. *Lai see* was a small red paper packet containing a small amount of money. It was not so much a gift as an omen of good luck and prosperity for the year ahead. I was warned by Ching not to swear, not to mention death, illness, bad luck or anything of that ilk, even in passing. Our amah refused to take anything but Chinese New Year's Day off, despite my mother's protestations; yet she did accept a thirteenth month's salary as was common practice.

On the second day, the celebrations started in earnest.

Across the road from the rear of the Fourseas was a pro-Communist secondary school which occupied a triangular plot between Emma, Julia and Soares Avenues. Every morning, the pupils gathered in the school yard behind twelve-foot-high stone walls like those of a prison and sang patriotic songs about labouring in the fields, striding ahead for liberty, equality and fraternity under the red flag and in the footsteps of Mao Tse-tung. The accompaniment was provided by a phonograph with a set of well-worn records.

Shortly after dawn, the school staff had hung strings of firecrackers over the walls. In all, there must have been two hundred of them, the walls looking as if they had suddenly been festooned with vermilion ribbons. And these firecrackers were by no means the little bangers such as might have graced a British Bonfire Night party. These were the size of a grown man's index finger, the fuses woven together around a core of hessian twine. What was more, they were grouped in threes down the twine. The aim was not to provide a display but to create as much noise as possible to drive off devils, demons and the pantheon of other supernatural ne'er-do-wells which every Chinese believed occupied every spiritually inhabitable niche.

I went into the street to watch. One of the teachers appeared at the corner with Soares Avenue, another at the corner with Julia Avenue. Both held large joss-sticks, the smoke drifting away on a keen breeze: it was cold enough to wear a padded jacket. There was no-one else in the street. A whistle was blown in the school yard. The teachers ignited the end of the first string of firecrackers, moving immediately on to the next. After a brief fizzle, the explosions began in the first string, then the second, then the third . . . In a matter of seconds, my head was filled with the report of the explosions. They echoed off the walls of the buildings as they might have off the sides of a canyon. The air went blue with smoke, and the acrid smell of gunpowder was suddenly inescapable and almost choking. A dense blizzard of paper blew along the street, thicker than snow. The explosions continued uninterrupted for at least twenty minutes.

I re-entered the hotel with a blinding headache but a feeling of elation. This had been an exhibition of raw power, the elimination of demons, the establishment of good fortune and the cleansing of the underworld.

Over the next few days, Kowloon sounded as if it were a war zone. In some places the streets were inches deep in fragments of acrid-smelling paper. The traffic stopped to allow fifty-foot strings of firecrackers to explode down the front of the taller buildings. Some of these, every two or three feet, contained an extra large firecracker the size of a tin can which went off with an ear-splitting detonation. Gradually, the firecrackers died down and a semblance of peace returned. On either side of many shops and doorways, new red scrolls with black writing upon them were pasted over the previous year's, presaging good fortune.

When I visited the temple to Kwun Yum (or Kwan Yin), the goddess of mercy, it was doing brisk business. The temple was always in semi-darkness, even on the sunniest day. At the rear of the altar, mysterious in the half-light of guttering red-wax candle flames and a few bare, low-wattage light bulbs, the deity's effigy sat demurely, with attendant gods to either side, leering through the twilight. The altar was hung with an embroidered cloth in imperial yellow, red and gold. From the tarnished brass incense burner rose a column of smoke.

In front of the altar was a throng, mostly of women and children, making offerings, praying or casting fortune-telling sticks. Amongst the offerings being made, mostly of fruit and food, was money. I was amazed to see otherwise poor-looking women dropping fistfuls of banknotes into a brass cauldron of hot embers. In a flare of flame, they were incinerated to a drift of ash rising on the hazy heat of the fire below. It was not until a partially scorched note escaped the fire that I came to see the currency. It was not dollars issued by the Hongkong and Shanghai Bank but Hell's Banknotes in vast denominations – $100,000, $1,000,000, $10,000,000. This was celestial, not terrestrial, cash.

As all this went on, a low-toned bell sounded, striking once every time a worshipper made a donation of real money to the idol. The temple staff hurried between the devotees, removing the burnt-out joss-stick and candle splints, pushing aside the last round of offerings, the food by now inedible as a result of the cascade of ash falling from the incense coils. One man replaced candles on the altar, two others trimmed wicks and cursorily removed ash from the effigy with a duster made of ginger cockerel's feathers fixed to a long bamboo cane.

Pushing through the crowd of worshippers, I purchased a fifty-cent pack of joss-sticks from an elderly man by the door, lit them all from a candle and stuck them in the urn full of sand provided. It was not that I was a devotee of Kwun Yum but that I was bent on doing what everyone else present was – hedging their bets for the coming twelvemonth by getting on the good side of the gods.

The general stores in Soares Avenue opened on a self-agreed rota throughout the first five days of the festivities. There was a purpose to this: not only did they open for the convenience of their customers but also to collect debts and settle tabs unaddressed before the new moon. By the time the new year started in earnest, all outstanding debts should have been paid. The day before the holiday commenced, Ching and I went into one of the shops to buy a packet of *wah mui*. The shopkeeper and his family were standing before a shrine positioned in a scarlet-painted box at the rear of their shop. I watched for a while in silence.

'What are they doing?' I whispered to Ching.

'This is the shrine of the kitchen god,' he explained.

The family kow-towed several times to the shrine then the shopkeeper's wife smeared the god's face with something in a bowl.

'What is that?' I murmured.

'Sweet food,' Ching replied. 'Soon, the kitchen god will go to heaven and tell the Jade Emperor if this has been a good family for a year. To make sure he says good words, they give him rice and honey. Make him talk sweet.'

This done, the shopkeeper tore out from the shrine the picture of the god, printed on red paper and faded over the year. He then took it outside on to the pavement and set light to it.

'Now the god goes to heaven,' Ching said.

This act smacked to me of writing a wish list to Father Christmas, whose non-existence I no longer questioned, and sending it up the chimney, but I kept my thoughts to myself. When the ashes had drifted down the street to mingle with the firecracker confetti, a new picture was pasted into the shrine and the shopkeeper stepped back behind his counter.

The lighting of firecrackers was not restricted to Chinese New Year. Whenever a new shop or business opened, the front of the building was decorated with bamboo scaffolding covered in paper flowers and characters propitiating good fortune. Long strings of firecrackers suspended from roof to pavement would be lit, the street soon filling with choking smoke and the continuous cacophony of explosions. If the building was over five storeys high, they could last an hour.

At only one event were firecrackers not let off – funerals.

When I saw my first Chinese funeral procession, I thought the circus had come to town. The initial indications of the approaching funeral procession were the muted sounds of inharmonious music. I went out on to the communal balcony of the hotel to watch.

Soon, a small truck appeared further down Waterloo Road. A large bamboo frame had been fixed to the front of the truck and adorned with paper flowers, gold and scarlet bunting and, I presumed, the name of the departed in huge characters. In the centre of this was a large monochrome photograph of the deceased. This vehicle was followed by a two-hundred-yard procession containing delivery tricycles similarly decorated. Interspersed between these were men carrying tall poles topped by Chinese fringed umbrellas, a large paper orb with a ladder rising through it and a number of other incomprehensible ceremonial items. At the rear of this came the coffin. I had expected a hearse but it was in fact carried in a sort of palanquin between eight perspiring coolies. The sides were decorated with white and yellow flowers. The coffin itself was highly polished and of a curious shape, in section rather like a four-leafed clover. To the rear of the coffin walked the relatives of the deceased, the foremost being a small boy of about my age wearing a white cloak. Every so often, he wiped his eyes and nose on the sleeve of his coat.

'Who is he?' I asked a room boy standing beside me.

'He dead man son. Now he Number One man for him family. Big job for him.'

The other primary mourners also wore white cloaks whilst everyone else was soberly dressed, with the men sporting black arm bands. It was all most dignified – except for the music.

Just behind the leading truck walked a small classical Chinese band of about eight musicians. They wore white bandsmen's uniforms with peaked caps and looked like a rather run-down English seaside town band. The music they played was doleful, the woodwind instruments high-pitched and keening, the small gong cracked and discordant. Not far behind them came a band equipped with Western brass instruments. They played 'When the Saints Go Marching In' – badly. Three other bands in the procession played 'Doin' What Comes Naturally' (from *Annie, Get Your Gun*, a recent cinema hit), 'Greensleeves' and finally, on the correct instruments, Chinese classical music once again. Each band played in apparent ignorance of the others so the whole musical contribution to the event was a raucous medley of disconnected tunes from three cultures.

My mother, who watched this procession with me, remarked that she preferred firecrackers to the assassination of music but she had by then forgotten the five-day migraine that marked Chinese New Year.

My father returned for good from Japan in the early summer of 1953. The Korean War was winding down, truce talks had been held and his job at the Sasebo naval base near Nagasaki was becoming redundant.

Immediately after my father's return, moves were put underway for us to leave the Fourseas. It was deemed an unsuitable billet for a family. There was, however, a shortage of quarters due to the pull-back from Japan, so we were tabled to move temporarily into a flat on the top floor of a building in Boundary Street, pending a more suitable quarter falling vacant.

Although less than a mile or two from the Fourseas, I was, at first, reluctant to go. I had many friends and acquaintances amongst the hotel room boys and in the streets of Mong Kok, with which I was as familiar as a rickshaw coolie or a pedlar. It would seem strange living in a self-contained home once again, without them around.

As the name implied, Boundary Street marked the periphery between British Kowloon and the hinterland of the New Territories, ceded to the British for ninety-nine years from 1898. As our flat was on the northern side of the street, this worried me. We were being housed in a no man's land that was only provisionally British. For several weeks, I had nightmares of being overrun in my sleep by Communist Chinese troops, bayoneted in my bed or sent to a slave labour camp, nevermore to see my mother.

In spite of my misgivings, I was beginning to feel excited by the impending move. It meant new horizons, new challenges and, more importantly, a new area to explore. Yet, two weeks before the move, the most dramatic event of the months I lived in the Fourseas occurred on Ho Man Tin hill.

Late one afternoon, I was walking back from school alone when I saw a thin wisp of smoke rising from over the hill. I gave it no thought and trudged on down Waterloo Road. As I reached the hotel, I saw the wisp was now a column. People were running down the track by the school and spilling out on to the main road, blocking the traffic. In a few minutes, the smoke was denser, rising faster with sparks glimmering in it, despite the sunlight. Then I heard the far-off bells of fire engines.

I ran into the hotel garage, dumped my Hong Kong basket and headed for the hill. Hordes of squatters were pouring off it, every one carrying something. Even toddlers, one hand held by their mother, clumsily dragged a cooking pot or enamel basin. Adults laden with bedding – men with complete beds – struggled down the track, slipping on the loose gravel. Laden rickshaws wove between them. The exodus was orderly but noisy. Everyone was shouting.

The police and the fire brigade turned up simultaneously. In minutes, hoses were snaking up the track and the police had instigated a cordon to prevent squatters returning to the fire to rescue more belongings. This, however, was soon considered futile so they took to directing the flow of people and getting the traffic moving again.

I hurried to the bottom of the track. The smoke was by now hundreds of feet high but, the squatter area being over a ridge, I could not see the seat of the blaze. Consequently, I joined the throng of people returning to save their belongings.

Cresting the ridge, I was so shocked by the scene before me I just stood still in stunned wonderment. In my naïvety, I had assumed a squatter shack had caught fire and those running away with their belongings were simply being cautious. What lay before me was an inferno. At least half the squatters' shacks had been reduced to piles of smouldering ashes with, here and there, uprights burning brightly. The conflagration was moving through the area like a forest fire through a plantation of pines. The noise was terrifying, with tin sheeting cracking as it warped, explosions caused by tinned food and the incessant hiss and spit of burning wood accompanied by the crash of shacks caving in. A strong wind blew towards the fire, sucking in paper and scraps of cloth, feeding it with oxygen and peppering my legs with fine gravel. As the fire progressed, it instantly ignited whole shacks at a time. One moment, a flimsy building looked intact, the next it was alight. Before my eyes a shanty exploded as if an artillery shell had hit it. A fountain of flame rose from it only to die in the rising smoke.

Ahead of the fire, people were running in and out of

their shacks, piling their belongings on the ground, on handcarts, on their children. I circumnavigated the blaze, upon which the fire brigade were preparing to play their hoses, and started to gather up armfuls of clothing from a pile, folding them in on themselves to make a tight bundle. A young Chinese man ran out of a shack to accost me, stopped and went back in. I tumbled the rest of the pile into a sheet, tying the corners together, using them to pad out some rice bowls and other crockery. The young man appeared and added a framed sepia photo to the bundle. It showed a family group seated on upright chairs. In the centre sat an ancient woman with a baby on her knee, her feet tiny where they projected from under an old-fashioned long gown.

I waited. The fire was moving nearer, and quickly. I could feel its intensity on my bare arms and legs. My eyes began to weep from the heat and smoke.

'*Wei!*' I shouted. '*Ché! Ché! Fide! Fide!*' (Hey! Go! Go! Quick! Quick!)

My pronunciation and the grammatical accuracy of this dog-Cantonese were doubtless atrocious but more than sufficient. The man came out of the shack followed by a woman carrying a babe-in-arms. He was laden down with a very battered suitcase and a wooden box. I gathered up the pile of linen and crockery and, hugging it to my chest, started down the track. I could not see my feet and frequently stumbled. Once, I fell, but my burden broke my fall. In a crowd of others, I reached the police line and was allowed through by an English inspector.

'Got a squatter hut, have we?' he enquired with a wry smile.

'I'm just helping,' I answered.

He looked at me for a moment and said, 'Where do you live, son?'

'Down the road, sir,' I replied, jutting my chin in the direction of the Fourseas and hoping my politeness would deflect the ticking off likely to be coming next.

'Well done, son,' he said and he patted my head. 'Go up that road over there.' He indicated Soares Avenue which, closed to traffic, was now a sort of squatter holding pen.

Once there, the young man gave his name to an official and we were guided into Emma Avenue where the pavements were filling up with groups of squatters. They sat chattering and tidying their belongings. To my astonishment, no-one was looking miserable or crying or showing any real sign of distress.

There was a touch on my head. It was the young man.

'You luckee boy for me,' he said in pidgin English. 'T'ankee you plentee plentee.'

'Martin,' another voice remonstrated, 'you're filthy.'

My mother stood before me, arms akimbo. I put the pile of clothes and bedding down at my feet and studied myself. My legs and arms were covered in ash: no doubt my face and hair were, too.

'What have you been doing?'

'Dis you littul boy?' the young man asked my mother. 'He plentee good littul boy. Plentee good for me. You no beatee, missee. No beatee.'

At this point, it came to my mother what I had done. She hugged me, ash and all. The young man touched my hair again, either for luck or in gratitude. His wife did likewise. I was sent in for a bath and my mother offered her assistance to a Red Cross worker.

Lying in the warm water smelling of my mother's perfumed salts, I realized just how fragile life was, that

everything one counted upon could come crashing down
in less than the time it took for a double maths class. I also
learnt that whilst it was one thing to live in a large box, a
shack, a cockloft or between the shafts of a rickshaw, it
was quite another to lose everything.

6

DENS, DUCKS AND DIVES

133 BOUNDARY STREET HAD BEEN BUILT IN THE 1920S AS A bijou residence on the edge of the countryside. By the time we moved in, it had gone down in the world. The exterior stonework was blotched with dead lichen and algae, the kitchen was dark and dank, the servants' quarters smelt of mould and the flat roof leaked into the bathroom. The city had reached out to it and the countryside was no more, although the barren foothills of the Kowloon hills did come down to within a hundred yards of the garden of the ground-floor flat.

Moving to a flat necessitated my mother employing more servants. As it was usual to employ a husband and wife wherever possible, the wash amah who had replaced Ah Fong was let go. She was genuinely sad at leaving us but my mother secured her a good job with an Army major and his wife who preferred to do her own cooking so only required an amah. That they had a blond-haired daughter no doubt helped to sweeten the bitterness of parting.

After an in-depth culinary interview, my mother took on Wong and his wife, Ah Shun. With them came their four-year-old son, Chan-tuk, to whom my mother took an instant liking and nicknamed Tuppence.

So far as we knew, Wong – whose references gave his name as Hwong Cheng-kwee – was a Shanghainese who, like so many others, was a refugee from Communism. He and Ah Shun had several other children whom they lodged in the New Territories or had had to leave with relatives in China. A tall, round-faced man, Wong had apparently worked in a top-class hotel in Shanghai as a pastry chef. At least, that was what one of his well-thumbed references stated. My mother gave him a month's probation. This ended after a day when he made his first sponge cake. It did not so much sit on the plate as float over it. We had never tasted anything like it. He had a permanent job from my mother's first mouthful. Ah Shun became the wash and sew-sew amah and the two of them shared the chores of keeping house.

To say that Wong was a one-in-a-thousand cook-houseboy was not to be guilty of hyperbole. He was utterly superb, with the attentiveness of a high-class butler, the culinary skills if not of Escoffier then certainly of his *sous chef*, the attention to detail of a water-colourist and the mien of a true gentleman's gentleman. He and Ah Shun wore the customary *sam fu* white jacket and black, loose-fitting trousers with felt slippers, in which they glided across parquet floors they had so highly polished you could see the reflection of the windows in them. They also served at table, which at first I found most peculiar. I had been served in restaurants, on the *Corfu* and the like, but in our own home . . . It was like being a member of the aristocracy.

There were some teething problems. Ah Shun starched my father's white shorts which he wore to the office. The hems chafed his legs raw. Thereafter, she artfully starched only the crease. When the monthly provisions bill came, my mother found Wong had used six dozen eggs, which accounted for the levitatory sponges. My mother asked him to cut down: then she saw he had used nine bottles of Heinz Salad Cream. As Wong did all the basic shopping, only discussing the matter of provisions or menus with my mother if she were holding a drinks or dinner party, this wanton purchase of salad cream seemed not only extravagant but suspicious. Wong was called into my mother's presence. It was not long before I was summoned too.

'What is this?' my mother muttered, glowering at me as she held out the invoice.

I was inclined to tell her it was the bill, but kept my peace.

'This!' she repeated, indicating an item on the bill. 'And this. And this. Wong tells me this is your doing.'

I had no idea why she was cross but I admitted I ate salad cream.

'Eat it!' my mother replied. 'Wong tells me you put it on your bloody breakfast!'

Every morning, I ate breakfast alone, after my father had departed for work in HMS *Tamar* and whilst my mother was still preening herself for a hard day at the canasta table. Wong always provided a fried egg on crisp fried bread, a fried tomato and stiff rashers of brittle, grilled bacon. I ate the bacon first with my fingers then waded into the remainder which I smothered with salad cream. How I first discovered this curious amalgam of tastes I do not know, but I loved it. Indeed, I could go through a bottle in three days, especially if I asked Wong for salad cream instead of Marmite and lettuce sandwiches to take to school. My father being at the office, I was not punished for my abnormal gourmandizing but that avenue of pleasure was promptly closed.

Wong was paid $300 (approximately £19) a month plus
an allowance of $75 for food. He lived with Ah Shun and
Tuppence in the servants' quarters beyond the kitchen: a
closed-in balcony and laundry sink, two small bedrooms
equipped with cast-iron bunks and a shower room with a
squat-down toilet which my father referred to (in what he
claimed to be submariners' slang) as *the shit-shave-shower-
shampoo-and-shoeshine*. Wong and his family used our
kitchen to prepare their food but they ate it squatting on
the balcony until my mother found out. Thereafter, they
ate at the kitchen table.

My mother found having servants somewhat dis-
quieting and, if anything, ambiguous. She was a humanist
at heart who believed no man should lord it over another.
Yet here she was with two people who were there at her
beck and call. Indeed, there were to be many times when
my parents returned from a party in the early hours to
find Wong staggering into the lounge, bleary-eyed and
dopey with sleep, to see if they wanted a nightcap or a
sandwich. She suffixed every request with *please* and *thank
you* and made sure I did, too. It was impressed upon me
that I should never make unreasonable demands of Wong
or Ah Shun and I was never to say *Fide! Fide!* or *Chop!
Chop!* (Quick! Quick!) at him. (I did once, out of pique,
and he clipped my ear, whereby a mutual respect was
born.)

Although not much more than a mile from the
Fourseas, the environs of the flat were very different.
Close by was La Salle College, a major Roman Catholic
school primarily for Chinese. To the north-west was the
one-time garden suburb of Kowloon Tong, to the north
were the barren lower slopes of the nine Kowloon hills.
Indeed, the name Kowloon derived from the Cantonese

gau lung, meaning *nine dragons*. To the south was a residential area and the wooded grounds of the Kowloon hospital. Only the foothills offered the slightest opportunity for exploration and that was soon exhausted, my only find being that of a white plaster-of-paris death mask in a cave and a large chunk of mauve transparent volcanic rock. My mother and I hoped it was beryllium, a piece of which had been found in Hong Kong the month before, making its finder rich. She took it to the geology department of the University. It wasn't beryllium but silicate – glass.

Not a mile to the east, however, was the most romantic and allegedly dangerous place in the colony. It was called Kowloon Walled City.

The name was a misnomer. It was not and never had been a city. It covered not much more than 25,000 square yards and, although it had been surrounded by a crenulated wall, the defences had been demolished by British prisoners-of-war under Japanese command and used as hardcore for an airport runway extension and sea wall.

According to a history of Hong Kong owned by my mother, it had originally been established in the eighteenth century as a far-flung outpost of the Chinese empire; its subsequent history was convoluted and its sovereignty confused. After the British gained control of Hong Kong and, later, Kowloon at the end of the Opium and *Arrow* Wars in the early 1840s, the Chinese imperial government insisted on maintaining a local presence so the British turned a blind eye towards Kowloon Walled City. Behind its walls, a nominal Chinese garrison was maintained which primarily kept a watch on the foreign invaders and enforced Chinese law in the area not under colonial control. Pirates being a problem in the region, the mandarin stationed in the settlement was kept busy suppressing and executing them. When the New Territories were ceded to the British, Kowloon Walled City was to find itself twenty-five miles from the border with China, completely surrounded by British territory. The cessation treaty was also ambiguous. Kowloon Walled City was now, in effect, cut off and ruled and possessed by neither – or both – countries.

It remained a backwater for fifty years, visited at the turn of the twentieth century by Europeans in Hong Kong for vicarious excitement, a fragment of the 'real' China on their doorsteps. Ruled by a mandarin from his *yamen* in the centre, it was quaint and exotic. The salacious aspect of the place lay in the fact that British law did not necessarily apply there, depending upon the interpretation of the treaty. Few Hong Kong policemen patrolled it and no government official collected taxes. The power supply was illegally tapped from the main grid and the water supply from the main. Kowloon Walled City was in effect a minute city state all on its own, arguably the smallest ever to have existed.

When China fell to the Communists in 1949, many criminal refugees fled to Hong Kong, some of them gravitating to the walled city area where they quickly established fresh enterprises. When the buildings were full, they built more, many little better than substantial squatter shacks. A disastrous fire in 1951 destroyed half the city but gave the new arrivals the opportunity to clear and build: it was said they set the fire in the first place. Thereafter, Kowloon Walled City remained an enclave governed by no-one. It was to Hong Kong what the Casbah was to Algiers, with one exception: it was more or less closed to outsiders. Trippers avoided it. It was said that any European who entered it was never seen again unless floating out of it down the *nullah* that served as a sewer. If ever the police entered the area, they went in armed patrols of three.

We had not been in Boundary Street a day when my mother took me aside.

'Martin,' she started, signifying her seriousness, 'I know you like to roam and explore, and round here that's all right. But,' she continued, unfolding a map of Kowloon, 'you do *not* go even near here.'

She pointed to the map. Kowloon Walled City was left as a blank uneven-sided square.

'What is it?' I enquired.

'Ask no questions and be told no lies,' my mother replied evasively, 'and *don't* go to find out.'

To utter such a dictum to a street-wise eight-year-old was tantamount to buying him an entrance ticket.

The following afternoon, homework hurriedly completed, I had a quick glance at the map and headed east down Boundary Street. In ten minutes, I was on the outskirts of Kowloon Walled City.

Nothing indicated to me why this place should be forbidden. A number of new six-storey buildings were being erected, with several already occupied or nearing completion; and a lot of shanties and older two-storey buildings were leaning precariously. It looked like a squatter area but with permanent structures in the middle in ill repair. A *hutong* lay before me, winding into the buildings and shacks. There being, I reasoned, no way my mother was ever going to find out, I set off down the alleyway, easing my way past a man pushing a bicycle, the pannier laden with cardboard boxes. He paid me not the slightest attention.

Through the open doors I spied scenes of industrial domesticity. To one side would be a *kang* or metal-framed bed, piled with neatly folded bedding; to the other several people seated at a table sewing, assembling torches, placing coloured pencils in boxes or painting lacquer boxes. Behind other doors were businesses, pure and simple. In one a baker was placing trays of buns in a wood-fired oven; in another, two men were involved in making noodles, swinging sheets of thin dough in the air around a wooden rolling-pin, the interior of their shack ghost-white under a layer of flour dust.

Wherever I went, the air was redolent with the smells of wood smoke, joss-sticks, boiling rice and human excrement. The effluent from this community, I soon discovered, flowed down open gullies at the side of the *hutongs* to disappear through holes in the ground lined by stone slabs.

Arriving at one of the older stone buildings, I was about to peer in through an open door when a Chinese man rushed out and slammed it shut. Stripped to the waist, he bore a coloured tattoo of a dragon on his back. He glowered at me.

'W'at you wan'?' he asked.

'Nothing,' I said, fighting to stop myself sounding guilty, although of what I did not know. Then, hoping it might soften him a bit, I added, '*Ngo giu jo* Mah Tin.' I held my hand out. '*Nei giu mut ye meng?*'

He was much taken aback by my introducing myself – especially in Cantonese – and it was at least thirty pensive seconds before he took my hand and firmly shook it. During that time, he eyed me up and down, much as a butcher might a bull being led to slaughter.

'Mah Tin,' he said at last. '*Ngo giu jo* Ho. Why you come?'

'Just looking,' I answered, shrugging and adding in pidgin English, 'Come look-see.'

'You no look-see,' he answered sternly. 'No good look-see for *gweilo* boy.'

I smiled, nodded my understanding, said, '*Choi kin*,' (goodbye) and turned to go.

'You look-see,' he declared, changing his mind. He opened the door, indicating I follow him.

What until now had seemed a harmless saunter through just another warren of passageways immediately took on a sinister aspect. No-one knew I was here. What, I considered, if this old stone building with its substantial door was the headquarters of the evil Fu Manchu? I had recently read Sax Rohmer. If I stepped over the high lintel, I could vanish. For ever. On the other hand, not to accept Ho's invitation would result in a massive loss of face. I would never be able to come here again: and I had seen nothing yet. And so, I threw caution to the wind and followed him into the building.

The entire ground floor consisted of one vast room, heavy beams holding up the ceiling and second floor. It was furnished with upright rosewood chairs, the wood even darker with age, low tables and several ornately framed mirrors, the silvering missing in places. Half-way down the room stood a wooden screen, the top half pierced by intricate fretwork, the rest a painting depicting sheer-sided hills and lakes. I sensed I was being observed through it but, as I walked by the end, there was no-one there. The wooden floor was devoid of any covering. There was an air of much-faded gentility about the place.

To the rear was a staircase beneath which a door opened and an old hunched woman entered, walking with the aid of a stick. She took one look at me and grinned toothlessly, hobbled to my side and, inevitably, stroked my hair. This put me at ease. First, Fu Manchu was hardly likely to employ crones (unless, god forbid, this was his mother) and second, my golden hair was a passport to my security. No-one would risk harming such a harbinger of good fortune.

'You come.' Ho beckoned me up the stairs.

I followed him into a room along three sides of which were placed wooden *kangs*. Upon one of these lay a supine man asleep upon a woven bamboo mat, his head on a hard Chinese headrest, his legs drawn up, his hands twitching like a dog's paws in a dream of chasing rabbits.

'*Nga pin*,' Ho announced and beckoned me further towards the fourth wall, the whole length of which was shuttered. I refrained from asking him what *nga pin* was for fear of seeming ignorant. Again, the last thing I wanted to do was lose face with him. He unlatched one of the shutters and we stepped out on to the balcony, which sloped forwards alarmingly towards a crumbling balustrade.

From here, I was afforded a panoramic view of the walled city. The shacks were so tightly packed, it was well nigh impossible to see where the *hutongs* ran between them. Yet the real surprise was the few larger buildings tucked between them. One stood in a wide rectangular courtyard with a number of outbuildings close by; from another rose a faint cloud of bluish smoke which meant it had to be a temple. Three or four were in a row suggesting that, in olden days, they had stood upon a street. In the distance was Kowloon Bay, a cargo ship riding at a quarantine buoy. Over to my left was the bulk of Fei Ngo Shan, the most easterly of the Kowloon hills, the slopes sharp and clear in the late sun. To the south-west, indistinct in the haze, was Hong Kong Island.

Ho took me back inside. We passed the sleeping man, who was beginning to wake, and descended the stairs which creaked loudly. Once outside, Ho bade me farewell and went back into the house, closing the door. I set off along the way I had come, considering to myself that I had taken a terrible risk. Other than a shop, I had never accepted an invitation into a building. Reaching the edge of the squatter shacks, and stepping out on to a road with traffic going by, I resolved not to be so foolhardy again. Yet, where Kowloon Walled City was concerned, I knew I had to return to investigate the temple and the building in the courtyard.

When I returned to our apartment, I went into the kitchen where Wong was preparing supper and asked him what *nga pin* meant. He stopped stirring a pan for a moment, looked quizzically at me and replied, 'Opium.'

On his return to Hong Kong, my father had taken delivery of a Ford Consul saloon which he promptly had resprayed two-tone grey with white walled tyres: my mother, with her penchant for Chinese names, called it *Ch'ing Yan*, which translated as *Lover*. *Ch'ing Yan* opened up a wide horizon for all three of us. It also gave my father a pastime. Never a man for a hobby, the car became the centre of his leisure activities. Having never owned a car before, he mollycoddled it as much as he might have done a mistress. The interior was kept pristine: no food or drink might be consumed therein. He checked the oil and tyres at least weekly and spent hours polishing the bodywork, dusting the interior and hoovering the carpets and seats. No-one was allowed to help in this endeavour. He rejected all the approaches of the itinerant car washers-and-waxers who did the rounds of residential areas every Saturday afternoon. When he saw Wong knocking dead leaves off the bonnet with a feather duster, he hurtled downstairs to stop him: the ends of the feathers, he explained, might be scratching the paint.

The first Sunday after the delivery of the car, my father announced we were going for a drive around the New Territories. And so, after a hearty breakfast which Wong insisted on cooking although it was his day off, we departed.

My father had decided to take a circular route without deviation, digression or diversion. My mother had been hoping we might have a look at a few places on the way, but my father was adamant and my mother did not drive. I really did not care. For the first time, I was going to find out what lay the other side of the Kowloon hills.

We crossed them by way of a pass on the Tai Po road next to a deep blue reservoir and descended to Sha Tin, a small fishing village on the shores of a large inlet. The tide was out, leaving mudflats upon which sampans lay settled on their hulls. Across on the other shore, on the northern slopes of the Kowloon hills, was a rock outcrop that, if the imagination was stretched, looked in silhouette like a woman with a baby in a carrier on her back.

'Amah Rock,' my mother declared, reading from a notebook she was compiling in the hope that, one day, she might write a Hong Kong guide and history. She went on to relate a story about a fisherman lost at sea, his loyal wife who waited on the outcrop for his junk to return and the gods who changed her into stone so she could wait for ever. The story I had heard was that the stone was a childless baby amah who had stolen her mistress's baby and been frozen in stone by punishing gods, but I said nothing.

We drove along the shore until my mother's eye alighted on a small isolated building ahead between the road and the sea wall, surrounded by paper bark trees. It had an awning and a few car parking spaces, but little else.

'Pull in, Ken,' she said as imperiously as she dared. 'I fancy a coffee.'

'You've only just had breakfast, Joyce,' he replied peevishly, edging his pride and joy into a parking space. He checked there were no boughs likely to become detached from the tree overhead in the next hour and led us inside.

The Sha Tin Dairy Farm Restaurant (aka The Shatin Roadhouse) was a small American-style diner with con-siderable pretensions. The menu was designed to be mailed to friends and it referred to itself as *the magic kiosk by the side of the magic Tidal Cove*, which bore reference to the fact that the Sha Tin inlet had four tides a day. At the top of the menu, in small print, were the words *Please let us service your car while you eat*. ('Fat chance!' my father remarked on reading it.) We sat at a table overlooking the inlet. The mountains were just beginning to shimmer in the day's heat. On the other side of the inlet, a cluster of ancient houses stood between woods and the water's edge. A junk sailed sedately but slowly by, heading for the open sea. My father studied them all with his binoculars.

'The rice grown in Sha Tin was so good it was reserved

for the emperor alone,' my mother remarked, reading from her notes.

I studied the menu. All the main dishes – even salads – were served with rice or toast. My parents ordered a coffee each and I requested a Chocolate Soldier, a sickly sweet bottle of thick, cold cocoa made with cow and soya milk. All three were automatically accompanied by toast.

As my parents drank their coffee, I read the blurb on the menu which outlined the attractions of the roadhouse: *This is the only place you can watch and feel a roaring train while you eat . . . Occasionally you'll be thrilled by the shooting vampires smacking out of the Blue . . . Your junior folks may enjoy fishing, fording, boating, ferrying, crabbing, clamming or simply playing around in the shallow mangroves. This is the place you'll enjoy most! Please come again and save a trip to Miami or Geneva!* I gazed out at the mudflats and tried to envisage my car-proud father's response to a request to go crabbing in the mangroves (whatever they were: all I could see was an expanse of mud). I saw no vampires.

Leaving Sha Tin, the road more or less followed the coast and the railway, grass-covered hills rising on the left with heavily wooded valleys. The next town was another fishing community called Tai Po. My father, having lost time over the enforced coffee stop, drove straight through it. My mother attempted to take some photos from the moving car but had to give up.

Just beyond the town, the road divided. Left went through the Lam Tsuen valley to the market town of Yuen Long, right took a longer route to the same destination. My father signalled left. My mother wanted the scenic route. We drove three hundred yards towards the Lam Tsuen valley, my father swore a lot, reversed into a farm track, muddied one wheel arch, got out, wiped the mud off with a rag and a bottle of water provided for just such an emergency and took the other road. We scowlingly bypassed Fanling and Sheung Shui, not stopping save for petrol. Then we entered old China.

The land became a patchwork of rice paddies separated by low dykes, the rice beginning to sprout above the water, bright green and pristine. The villages and farmhouses were ancient and could have changed little in two centuries. Farmers walked slowly along the side of the road wearing wide-brimmed conical hats, their trousers rolled up to the knee, leading docile-looking buffaloes. Man and beast had mud caked on their legs. Hakka women with coolie poles over their shoulders carried heavy loads of fodder or bundles of *pak choi*. It was my favourite Chinese vegetable, delicious when steamed and served at most *dai pai dongs*. Dogs ambled along just off the tarmac, moving from the shade of one eucalyptus or paper bark tree to the next.

Every now and then, my mother demanded my father stop for her to take a photo. Inevitably, every time she requested a halt, it was twenty yards before we came to a standstill so my father had to back up. Before long he was seething. When my mother suggested turning into a side road into the countryside, he lost it completely.

'Joyce!' he said through gritted teeth. 'We've come to drive round the New Territories. Not into them. I am *not* driving into the blithering hills. For all I know, we could wind up in Communist China.'

'That's not likely,' I injudiciously piped up. 'If we take a road on the left we'll stay in Hong Kong. China's to the right. Anyway, you can't drive into China because there's a

border and a river to cross and the river's only got one
bridge for the train and the police and the army—'

'Shut up!' my father exploded.

Several hundred yards further on, his patience was
again tested by a duck farmer moving his gaggle of about
two hundred birds from one pond to another, driving
them ahead of him by means of two long, thin and very
flexible bamboo poles. The ducks and a few geese waddled
down the middle of the road. My father tentatively beeped
his horn. The duck farmer turned. My father signalled
curtly with his hand for the man to get a move on. At this,
he turned and walked towards the car. My father unwisely
wound his window down.

'*Mat yeh?*' the farmer said, somewhat belligerently.
This translated roughly as: What d'you want? The added
sub-text was: Damn your eyes, foreign devil.

My father, who spoke barely a word of Cantonese,
looked blank.

'*Mat yeh?*' the farmer repeated, more antagonistically.

My father, still with a vacant look on his face, then
suggested, 'Martin, you're always playing in the street.
What's he saying?'

'I don't know,' I lied.

At this juncture, the farmer shrugged and turned. The
ducks had meantime broken ranks and were all over the
road and grass verge. The farmer picked up his herding
poles. Taking his time, he rounded them up and continued
to make his steady way ahead of us. We edged forward in
a grinding first gear accompanied by my father's grinding
teeth.

At the next left junction, we turned up a narrow road
towards a steep hill, the road eventually petering out in a
grassy bank. We stopped and got out. My mother took

photos of the view, my father stood wondering how he was going to do a three-point turn. Whilst he pondered, my mother and I set off up a path.

In a short distance, we came to a semi-circular stone platform with a horseshoe-shaped wall about two feet high running round half its circumference. In the wall was a tiny stone door upon which some characters had been written in red paint. In front of the door were two rice bowls containing a sludge of dead leaves and rainwater and a stone weighing down a wad of faded Hell's Bank-notes.

'What is this?' I asked.

'It's a grave,' my mother answered. 'Behind that door is the coffin.'

I looked at it with a feeling of suppressed terror. I had visited my maternal grandfather's grave in a municipal cemetery in Portsmouth but had never really come to terms with his body lying six feet under an oblong of stone chippings. Here, there was a man reclining in death just behind a door.

Higher up the slope we came upon a narrow terrace cut into the hillside. It was overgrown with grass and held a row of very large urns with lids like inverted plates. The view was spectacular, a vista of wetlands over which soared flights of ducks and, beyond, the sea.

My mother busying herself with her camera, I decided to look in one of the urns. It seemed strange that they had been left there, in the middle of nowhere, on a bleak and windswept mountainside. I took hold of one of the lids and lifted it clear. Inside, neatly packed away so that it might all fit in, was a human skeleton, the skull on top. The bones were brown and looked as if they had been lightly varnished. I quickly replaced the lid.

'It's called a *kam taap*,' my mother said, not taking her eye from the viewfinder. 'I've been told that when a Chinese dies, they bury the body for seven years then they exhume it, clean the bones and put them in an ossuary – that's one of those urns.'

We walked down to the car. My father had turned it round and was buffing off scuff marks – caused by his reversing into a bush – on the rear bumper with a soft cloth.

'The view's wonderful,' my mother said sweetly as we joined him.

'You're a bloody nuisance, Joyce,' my father snarled.

We drove down to the main road and along it as fast as the surface and law would allow and my father's temper could contain. It was not until my mother saw a sign off to the right reading *Kadoorie Beach* that she spoke.

'Go down there, Ken,' she commanded in a voice that would brook no opposition.

My father did as he was asked and we drove down a narrow lane overhung by Chinese pine trees, the wispy, delicate variety one saw in classical paintings. The lane culminated in a small car park and a sandy beach gently lapped by the sea. Removing her shoes, my mother tripped off down to the water's edge. Beyond her, indistinct under the early-afternoon sky, was the island of Lan Tau, its peaks rising into a sub-tropical sky almost devoid of colour in the hot sun. A request that I might be allowed to join her was bluntly rebuffed by my father, so I sat in the car for fifteen minutes with my mouth shut.

When my mother returned to the car, my father said, 'Make sure there's no sand on your feet. I don't want to be hoovering the bloody carpets for weeks.'

'I do wish you'd shut up, Ken. It's only a bloody car,'

she answered and, without removing the sand from her soles or putting her shoes back on, she got in the front and slammed the door.

In a mile or so, we came upon another sign by the road. It pointed to The Dragon Inn. My father, unbidden, turned and parked. Inside the inn, a cross between an English country pub, a Chinese tea house and a French café, we were served a plate of hot buttered toast, which my mother and I now considered must be obligatory once one crossed the Kowloon hills. My mother ordered tea, I asked for a Coke and my father requested a San Miguel beer. Then he had another. At the third, my mother reminded him he was driving. He ordered a fourth to make his point. She commented that the car was brand new, the first he had ever owned, and would it not be a pity if it got dented.

'Already bloody ruined by that benighted bush,' my father grumbled, but he did not order a fifth beer.

The bill settled, we went to look at a tortoise the size of a half barrel that was said to have been hatched in the Ming dynasty. A notice stated rather obviously: *A Tortoise Several Hundred Years Old*; it occurred to me that it would have to be in a country where eggs could be a century old. The poor creature lived in a concrete-walled enclosure about four times its size, with a trough of stale water and a pile of bedraggled greens. At least it had a roof to protect it from the searing heat of the sun.

Disturbed by these conditions, I suggested to my mother that we either set up a tortoise protection society or come back that night and kidnap it. Her reply was that the car boot could not take the weight, with which I had sadly to concur. However, I was permitted to sit on it to have my photo taken.

At about five o'clock, we arrived back at Boundary Street. My mother strode directly into my parents' bedroom and locked the door. I heard her running herself a bath. My father spent an hour rubbing imaginary scratches off the rear panelling of the Ford Consul. I went to my room and kept a low profile.

Over the coming weeks, I paid repeated clandestine visits to Kowloon Walled City. I did not, however, become acquainted with many people. Whereas the stall-and-shopkeepers of Soares Avenue and Mong Kok were open and welcoming, those of the walled city were polite but reticent.

Whenever I arrived, Ho appeared before I had gone twenty yards, trotting towards me and smiling expansively. It was as if some unseen sentry had been watching out for me, relaying news of my impending arrival. For as long as I was in the enclave, he would accompany me, talking all the time, improving his English and my Cantonese. Sometimes, we took a bowl of soup together in a shack done out as an eating-place, with tables and chairs and an elderly waiter who limped. On many occasions, I offered to pay but Ho invariably pushed my money aside. On the other hand, he never paid either.

Apart from inviting me into the opium den and to drink tea or broth with him, Ho took me nowhere else. I had hoped he would show me the temple but any attempt to steer the conversation or our feet in its direction were futile.

After a while, Ho told me he was going 'long time

Macau-side' and introduced me to his *ho pang yau* (his good friend).

This man was in his mid-twenties, not tall but immensely handsome, lacking the prominent cheekbones, Adam's apple and slightly flared nostrils of the average Cantonese male. He could, I thought, easily have been a film star. Muscular in a trim way, his hands were small but very strong. To my surprise, he spoke good pidgin English.

'My name is Lau,' he introduced himself when we first met. 'I am Ho's friend.'

'I am Martin,' I replied.

'*Mah Tin*,' he repeated. 'In Cantonese, this mean *horse, electric*. You are electric horse.' He grinned at his interpretation and mimicked riding a lively steed. 'Like at Laichikok fun garden.' It was a reasonable translation of *fairground*.

We shook hands and drank tea to cement our new-found friendship.

'When you come Kowloon Walled City-side,' he went on, slurping at his bowl of tea, 'I be here for you. If I not here, you no come. You unner-stand? If you are good boy, I will show you this place.'

I agreed to these terms. After all, to have a personal guide to this maze of shanties and ancient buildings was more than I could have hoped for.

Our tea finished, I said goodbye to Ho and set off with Lau. He walked with a measured, easy pace. Everyone greeted him and stepped aside to let him pass in the narrow alleys. In his turn, he invariably made way for heavily laden coolies and young women. The former breathlessly grunted their thanks whilst the latter giggled.

'I will show you some thing,' Lau said as we made our

way past the building with the balustrade. 'From long time before. When China have emperor.'

We reached a place where the *hutong* widened. Lying beside the wall of a larger than average shanty were two massive cannons.

'This', Lau began, 'Chinese gun one time on city wall. Fight English like you.' He grinned. 'But no more fight. Now live no trouble, make money.'

Carrying on, we arrived at the temple and entered. At first, my eyes adjusting to the gloom, it looked no different from any other – dim lighting, incense smoke, the occasional wavering candle . . . Yet, as my eyes accepted the twilight, I saw that this one was grander than any I had previously seen. First, it had three larger-than-life-size effigies completely covered in gold except for the carving of their tightly curled, black painted hair: yet even that had a gold finial on top. All three were seated in front of intricately embroidered gold tapestries. The altar table was huge, made of black wood and finely carved with gold-painted designs of leaves, dragons and curlicues. Upon it were not only the customary offerings but also exquisitely painted porcelain vases and two gold-leaf-coated lanterns. To one side, an old man was carefully applying gold leaf to one of the idols with a damp sponge. Second, the temple was spotlessly clean: usually they were dusty places, the floor scattered with the ashes of Hell's Banknotes or the fine powder of burnt joss-sticks. Third, there was a sleeping dog chained to the wall on the left which got to its feet and snarled menacingly at me.

'You like?' Lau enquired.

'Like plenty,' I replied, took a joss-stick and, lighting it, bowed to the effigies with it held between my supplicating hands before sticking it in the sand of the incense bowl.

Lau watched me, bemused.

'You no . . .' he looked for the word in English and failed to find it '. . . *Gai duk toh*?' He made the sign of the Cross on the palm of his hand.

'Yes,' I answered. 'Church of England.'

'Why you . . . ?' He pointed to the altar and made a cursory bow.

'Respect,' I said, but Lau just smiled in his incomprehension.

We walked on. Suddenly, Lau stopped and said, 'You no like ovver *gweilo* boy.' For the first time, he touched my hair. 'Now I show you good place.'

Our destination was the balustraded building I had visited on my first excursion into the Walled City. We entered it, passed through the downstairs room, still devoid of occupants although I could hear the noise of snoring emanating from upstairs, went behind the screen, out through a door into what might once have been a flagstoned courtyard and down some steps to a semi-cellar about thirty feet square. At the bottom of the steps was an old wooden door secured by a large padlock. Lau produced the key and we entered.

There was a small table in the centre of the room, the walls of which were lined by benches similar to those used for gym lessons in the KJS school hall. Upon the walls hung various pennants and banners in red with serrated black borders and black writing upon them. Opposite the door was an altar bearing a small idol of a male god with a fierce-looking face, one candle alight before it.

'God Kwan Ti,' Lau explained. 'This my god.'

Yet it was something other than the banners and Kwan Ti that caught my eye. Hung between the banners were macabre, sadistically ferocious-looking weapons. One was a chain with a ball set with spikes at one end; another chain culminated in a spear-point blade. Balancing in a wooden rack were a number of metal six-pointed stars of varying diameters. From their shine, the points were clearly well sharpened.

'What is this place?' I enquired.

Lau made no attempt to explain but said, '*Gweilo* no come here. You *vew'y* lucky boy I show you.'

Taking the chain with the point on it, he gave it a quick flick. The blade flashed through the air, faster than the eye could follow, and embedded itself in the rear of the door. It took both Lau's hands to dislodge it. Once the blade was free and hanging back on the wall, he took down one of the smallest stars. With a brief twist of his wrist, it spun through the air and also lodged itself in the door timbers.

'More good gun,' Lau said. 'No boom boom.' He ushered me out. 'You no tell you see here,' he added as he locked the door. 'You tell, plenty trouble for me. Plenty more for you.' He made the sign of a knife slicing across his throat. 'You, me,' he said pointing from me to himself.

I nodded and we went back the way we had come. As we moved through the big room in the building, a boy of about my age descended the stairs carrying a tray upon which there was a small lamp, several minute bowls, a number of metal needles and the most bizarre pipe. My grandfather always smoked a simple-looking Dunhill with a wooden bowl; my father, on occasion, smoked a swan-necked Meerschaum. This was very different. A good fifteen inches long, the stem was made of bamboo, the mouthpiece of milky-coloured jade or soapstone. The bowl was a curious device for it had nowhere that I could see in which to put the tobacco: indeed, it appeared to be a virtually sealed container. All there was in it was a tiny hole in the top.

'*Nga pin?*' I asked tentatively.

Lau stared at me.

'How you know *nga pin?*'

'I know,' I shrugged, still not knowing exactly what it was.

He took me by the hand and led me up the stairs.

'No talk,' he whispered.

As my head rose above the first-floor level, I saw half a dozen men lying on the *kangs*. All but one were asleep on their sides, their hands tucked between their drawn-up legs or under their necks. One snored, another inter- mittently moaned softly, the only other sound was their breathing. The air had a strange and familiar perfume to it and it was at least a minute before I recognized it as the scent of the rickshaw coolies' pipes on my first night in Hong Kong.

The man who was awake had by his head one of the little lamps, the flame contained within a thick glass funnel. The boy moved past us, giving me a quick and puzzled glance. He went to the man and impaled a small bead of something on one of the needles, starting to revolve it in the lamp flame: then, very adroitly, he placed it over the tiny hole in the pipe bowl, passing it to the man who lay on his side and sucked evenly on the pipe. After doing this three times, the man lay down and closed his eyes. The boy removed the pipe and blew out the lamp.

'We go,' Lau murmured.

Once we were outside, I asked, 'What was that man doing?'

'He smoke opium,' Lau answered. 'Get dream, go good time-side.'

'Can I smoke *nga pin*?' I suggested.

'No,' Lau said emphatically. 'No good for *gweilo*. Only for Chinese people.'

As I went to leave the walled city, Lau escorted me. Passing a very big shack indeed, I glimpsed a large pig through the wide door. Its feet were tied together. A man in a pair of bloodied shorts stepped up to it, grabbed one ear and yanked it back. The pig squealed, an eerie, unearthly sound. The butcher ran a sharp knife under its neck and slit its throat, stepping smartly backwards. The pig fell on its side, thrashing about and gurgling obscenely. Blood sprayed from its neck.

Lau put his hand on my shoulder in an affable manner and said, 'You talk you see, maybe you like this.'

He pointed to the pig, its lifeblood soaking in the earth floor of the shack. And I knew he meant it.

The row of old buildings stood to the eastern end of the walled city. One day, as Lau and I were walking through the *hutongs*, the heavens opened. We ran for cover under one of the balconies. Standing on what must once have been the arcaded raised side of a street, I somehow sensed in a daydream the ghosts of history walking by: a mandarin in his fine brocades, a peacock feather in the jade finial of his hat, his retinue behind him; a Chinese soldier with an axe-bladed pikestaff; a British naval officer in a cocked hat accompanied by a platoon of marine ratings, bayonets drawn.

The rain fell in torrential sheets, curtains of water moving inexorably across the shacks.

'What you think?' Lau asked.

'I think long time before Kowloon Walled City,' I answered, his question snapping me back to the present. 'See people walk here.'

'You see ghost,' Lau replied matter-of-factly. 'Plenty ghost Kowloon Walled City-side.'

I accepted this without question. England had hardly any ghosts but China was steeped in them. Wherever one went, it seemed, there were ghosts, demons, devils, spirits and gods to ward them off.

'I show you *ve'y* old place,' Lau said. 'All same like China long time before.'

He turned, walked ten paces along under the balcony, from which rainwater was pouring down, and knocked on a narrow double door. Once again, my heart fluttered and thoughts of evil men with wicked intentions momentarily filled my mind, but I had now been into two buildings – the *nga pin* house and the half-underground house – and had come through each time unscathed.

'You come,' Lau beckoned.

I stepped over the characteristic high lintel to find myself in a small entrance hall. To one side, seated at a tiny desk, was an old woman. Lau greeted her and they spoke in quiet voices until Lau stepped aside to reveal my presence. The moment she saw me, the woman cackled asthmatically and entered into a conversation with Lau that was filled with much suppressed hilarity and sidelong glances at me.

Feeling I was being made the butt of their humour, and not quite knowing how to react, I looked down. It was then I saw the old woman's feet projecting out from under the desk. They were minute, encased in scuffed brocade slippers no bigger than a baby's knitted bootees. The toe end was squared off like the ballet dancing pumps girls wore at school.

'Lotus foot,' Lau said, following my line of sight. 'Long time before, China-side, men say tiny foot on lady ve'y . . .'

he paused, searching for a word '. . . booty full. Like lotus flower.'

I nodded sagely but could not see how, with the wildest imagination, a foot could resemble a flower.

After the obligatory caress of my golden hair by the old woman, Lau led me down a corridor of dark wooden panelling, passing a number of narrow doors split like those of a stable. At intervals, dim bulbs provided the minimum of light. Towards the end of the passage-way, Lau stopped at a door and knocked. The top half opened and a pretty Chinese woman looked out. She wore an imperial yellow silk cheongsam, her hair piled up and held in place by a soapstone pin. As they spoke in subdued voices, she did not take her eyes off me for an instant. Needless to say, she still reached out to touch my head.

There was the sound of a pulling bolt and the bottom half of the door also opened to reveal a panelled cubicle lit by a red lamp in front of a tiny shrine. The only furniture was a wide *kang* raised higher than normal from the floor and a Chinese-style chair. Upon the *kang* were a tangle of quilts and a Chinese paperback book on the cover of which were portrayed a man and a woman kissing. On a shelf below the shrine was a row of Chinese scent bottles.

'You go in,' Lau instructed. 'Sit down.'

I perched on the rim of the *kang*. The young woman sat next to me, talking to Lau through the door but all the while watching me. The air – and the young woman – smelt of orange blossom slightly tainted with sweat.

'You know this place?' Lau enquired at length.

'No know,' I admitted.

'This old place,' Lau continued. 'Maybe more one

hundred year. Long time before place for rich man come jig-a-jig. Fam'us place. Man come long way from Canton jig-a-jig here. Fam'us girl stay here long time before.' To lend meaning to his words, he put his thumb between his index and middle finger and wiggled it. The young woman giggled. I was lost as to the meaning.

'You lo know jig-a-jig?' Lau asked.

I shook my head.

'Lo ploblum,' he replied dismissively. 'Come! We go now.'

He said goodbye to the young woman. I added my own *choi kin*. She burst into a peal of giggles, put her hand demurely to her mouth to stifle them and closed the doors on us.

Whenever I visited Kowloon Walled City, Lau was always there, ready to guide me around, drink tea with me and talk. When, after a few months, the place started to lose its appeal and I stopped visiting, I never saw him again.

It was some years before I realized that he and Ho had been Triad members – Chinese *mafiosi* – infamous for their utter ruthlessness, whose secret fraternity ran the opium dens and brothels, and held Kowloon Walled City in its thrall. The semi-subterranean room had been their meeting place.

My growing penchant for reading gave me a new reason to seek permission to range farther afield than I had previously. Both my parents agreed that I should be permitted to go to Tsim Sha Tsui where, in the next street to Mr Chan's jewellery and curio company, there stood the Swindon Bookshop. The only stipulation placed upon this extension of my legitimate borders was that I did not, under any circumstance, take the Star Ferry to Hong Kong island.

Tsim Sha Tsui was a completely different world from Mong Kok. The latter was the world of *dai pai dongs* and whole roast pigs whilst the former was camera-toting, rubber-necking tourist country, banker and briefcased businessman territory.

I had been there on a number of occasions with my mother. Indeed, my first night in Hong Kong had been spent there, for the Grand Hotel was in the heart of the district. However, apart from Tkachenko's, Hing Loon and the bookshop, I hardly knew it and savoured discovering it on my own.

Using Hing Loon as an informal Coke-provisioning station, I wandered the streets. Here, the shopkeepers stayed behind closed doors. If they were jewellers, their doors were sometimes guarded by bearded, be-turbaned Sikhs in old British military uniforms and carrying blunderbusses or shotguns. The only vendors to appear on the pavement were Indian tailors vying for custom. The Chinese tailors viewed this flagrant touting with distaste. They were never so pushy and their workmanship was far superior.

Apart from the tailors' window displays of lengths of cloth and suits hanging off mannequins, every shop window was a glittering tableau of expensive watches, men's and women's jewellery, pens, cameras, lenses and binoculars.

I knew I could not just walk into one of these shops so I worked the obvious ploy, waiting until a tourist couple entered and tagging along camouflaged as their child. It worked time and again and I got to study – close up – such marvels as Audemars Piguet, Longines and Vacheron et Constantin gold watches, emeralds as green as still water and as big as peas, and Rolleiflex and Leica cameras with a shutter movement so silent you could not hear it. All of these I gazed at with the avidity of a magpie. At times, the palms of my hands actually itched with temptation and desire.

Yet the crimes of Tsim Sha Tsui were not conducted by me but by the wily shopkeepers and even more artful pickpockets.

One of the shopkeepers' scams was brilliant in its simplicity and succeeded because of the arrogance and gullibility of, particularly, American tourists. Be they civilians or sailors on shore leave all were open to it, from well-heeled world cruisers and senior United States Navy officers down to ratings and stewards off the liners. The first time I saw it happen was in a watch shop. I was lingering by the counter when I overheard a conversation that went something like this:

'OK, buddy, I'll take this one.' (*Tourist*)

'V'wy good choice. Suit you good.' (*Shopkeeper*)

'How much is it?'

'Fi'e hund'ed dollar.'

A few minutes of haggling followed, culminating in an agreed price of $450, the shopkeeper declaiming with a disarming smile, 'You too cleffer for me. Beat me down too much. Now my p'ofit only small.'

At this point, it must be appreciated that all the prices were shown in Hong Kong dollars and the price label on the item marked up by at least 100 per cent over the wholesale buy-in cost.

Then came the question bolstered by a belief in the universal power of the US greenback.

'Say, buddy, is that American or Hong Kong dollars?' *Hong Kong* was always spoken with a slight air of condescension.

The shopkeeper, after a brief pause as well timed as the best comic actor's, would always reply, 'Ame'ican dollars.'

Out would come the wallet of American Express traveller's cheques, the customer grinning broadly at his bargaining skill.

In 1953, when I first saw this trick pulled, the foreign exchange rate was approximately HK$6: US$1. Even my elementary school arithmetic, at which I was a resoundingly poor pupil, told me the customer had paid HK$2700, over five times the original, and already much inflated, asking price.

I could never feel any sympathy for these dupes. In my puerile opinion, they asked for it. Besides, I was a *gweilo* on the shopkeepers' side. With the victims of Tsim Sha Tsui's other tourist crime, who could be of any nationality, I felt considerable empathy but, whereas I could have exposed the exchange rate scam, I could do nothing about their plight.

The pickpockets of Tsim Sha Tsui must have been the slickest in the world. They mostly operated in pairs, keeping in the crowds. Once a worthwhile target had been spotted, they would move in, one bumping hard into the victim, knocking them slightly off balance. The other, with lightning speed, would slip their hand into bag or pocket, grab a wallet, purse or billfold and immediately pass it to the barger who would disappear in the crowd. This was a failsafe. If the victim found they had been pickpocketed, had a suspicion who had done it and accosted him, he could plead innocence. The proof – the wallet or purse – would already be three streets away and moving fast towards a fence who dealt in traveller's cheques.

Another form of theft was considerably less clandestine. A number of urchins would accost a target under the pretence of begging. Once the target's attention was distracted, one of the urchins would produce a pair of very sharp tailor's scissors, slide a blade under the victim's leather watch strap and cut it free, catching it and disappearing in the crowd. If the target was aware of what had happened, they could not give chase for the obstruction of the throng.

Only one class of person was completely pickpocket proof: the US Navy ratings who carried their wallets folded over the front of the very tight waistbands of their uniform trousers. They were in full view of any pick-pocket but not one could pull a wallet clear without the owner knowing.

Although these kinds of street theft must have ruined many a holiday, I could not bring myself to condemn them. The perpetrators were often boys even younger than myself, street urchins, the children of squatter shack dwellers and pavement sleepers. They were doing the best they could to stay alive and I could not help wondering whether some of their fathers had owned cars and horses in China and were now reduced to sweeping out offices or serving in restaurants. Or worse.

Despite their criminality, I felt at one with them. They were expatriates who had made their home here. So was I. There were even moments when I wondered how I might join them in their illegality, but I realized I would not have had the stomach for it. And that was the difference between a *gweilo* and a Chinese: we were bound by the rules that ruled the rulers and they were not.

One sweltering day, the humidity over 90 per cent, my mother and I went shopping, our mission to buy a wedding anniversary gift for my paternal grandparents.

Under normal circumstances, I would have strenuously attempted to avoid this outing. Traipsing in my mother's wake round shops containing little of interest to me, in streets I had explored and which were now fairly sterile to me, was not my idea of an ideal morning. However, I wanted to take part in the choice of a gift for Grampy.

With a military methodology, my mother went up and down the streets, traversing Tsim Sha Tsui in a mental grid, but she could find nothing suitable. It was either tourist tat or too fragile to post, or too expensive and therefore likely to cost my grandparents inordinately high customs duties. Finally, having exhausted most of Tsim Sha Tsui – and me – we had a Coke each at a pavement stall and headed up Nathan Road at a brisk pace. My shirt clung to my back: through my mother's sweat-soaked blouse I could see her bra strap and felt very embarrassed that it was so prominent. None of the Chinese women seemed to be even lightly perspiring.

My mother's intention was, if she could find nothing in an area catering mostly for European taste, she would have a go in that providing for the Chinese. Turning into Shanghai Street, we started to patrol the shops selling crockery. It was utilitarian stuff but one variety caught my mother's attention. Known as rice-patterned ware, neither of us could understand how it was mass-produced. Each dish, bowl or cup was made of white porcelain with a patterned blue border and base, between which the porcelain was speckled with what looked like rice grains fired in the matrix. If the bowl was held to the light, each grain appeared translucent.

'This is it,' my mother declared as she held up a large serving bowl to the light. 'Bugger the fragility! This is the one, don't you think?'

I agreed. My grandmother would regard it as a nice bowl to put on the dresser but my grandfather would see it for what it was – an exotic piece sent from a far-off land with all my love brimming out of it. It cost only a few dollars.

'It's a bit on the cheap side,' she commented as the shopkeeper wrapped the bowl in wood straw and newspaper.

'It's the thought that counts,' I remarked.

She smiled and sauntered round the shop, picking up a piece here and a piece there. I sat on a stool and sweated. The shopkeeper did not offer me a drink for he no longer had reason to keep us in the place. We had parted with our money and the cost of a Green Spot would simply erode his profit margin.

Finally, my mother returned to the counter, said, 'Sod it!' and ordered a six-setting complete dinner service of the same sort, asking for it all to be delivered to the Boundary Street address.

The shopkeeper beamed, shouted for an assistant, relieved my mother of $110 (about £6) and gave us each a chilled bottle of Watson's lemonade.

'I don't think', my mother said as we walked at a

leisurely speed towards Nathan Road, 'that we need to mention this to your father.'

'Why not?' I asked. 'How can you hide ninety plates and bowls and things?'

My mother took my hand and jauntily swung it back and forth as we walked on.

'I'm a wife,' she answered obtusely.

The arcaded pavement ahead was obstructed by a row of barrels being off-loaded from a green lorry with a canvas awning. As we entered the restricted space, we were ambushed by a young Chinese woman. She wore the clothes of a coolie – a stiff black cotton jacket and matching baggy trousers. She was barefoot, her hair awry and her face, as my mother would put it, in need of a kiss from Mr Flannel. In her arms she carried a baby about a month old. There was no way we could avoid her without turning heel.

'Missee! Missee!' she said as she approached us.

My mother opened her handbag, snapped the catch on her purse and took out a violet-coloured dollar bill. To my mother's surprise, the young woman refused it.

'No *kumshaw*, missee. No *kumshaw*!'

The woman held the baby out. It gurgled with infantile pleasure and kicked the air. Its legs were podgy. I could see it was a girl.

'You tek, missee, pleas'.'

My mother stopped dead in her tracks. The look on her face was one of sheer bemusement.

'Missee! You tek. You tek.'

She reached forward with the baby, trying to convince my mother to accept it in her arms.

'You tek, pleas'.'

The woman was pleading now. The pain in her soul

tainted each of the only four English words she knew, had learnt especially for just such a confrontation.

'Pleas', missee. Pleas', missee.'

I looked at my mother. Tears ran down her cheeks. She made no effort to wipe them and they dripped on to her already sweat-dampened blouse. She shook her head.

The Chinese woman made one last attempt, as if she was a stallholder pressing my mother to buy something she did not need.

'*M'ho*,' my mother murmured.

At that, the woman turned and disappeared down a narrow and fetid *hutong* from which blew the stench of open drains.

We walked on in silence until we reached a rickshaw rank. My mother hailed one and we travelled home together. Once in the apartment, my mother poured herself a gin and tonic and sat heavily in a chair.

'What did that woman want?' I enquired.

'She wanted to give me her baby.'

'Why?' I replied, taken aback at this information.

'Who knows,' said my mother with a sigh. 'Perhaps she can't afford to feed it. Perhaps the father told her to get rid of it. It was a girl . . .'

'So what?' I came back.

'In China, boy children are precious. They are even sometimes called little emperors. Girls are not.'

I could see no difference between a girl baby and a boy baby, other than the obvious anatomical one, and said so.

She took a big swig of her gin and tonic. 'To the Chinese, nothing is more important than keeping the family name going. So sons are important and daughters, who will marry and take another name, aren't.'

'But what will happen to the baby girl?' I half-wondered aloud.

My mother was silent for at least a minute before speaking.

'She will die. Either her parents will smother her or they'll take her into the Kowloon foothills and leave her to die of exposure.'

'But that's murder!' I exclaimed.

'Yes,' my mother agreed dully, 'and this is China.'

'Can't we go back again?' I began. 'I don't mind if . . .'

The appeal of an adopted Chinese sister was suddenly growing on me. And it was now of paramount importance to me that we did something.

'No,' my mother said, 'I'm afraid it doesn't work like that . . .'

She patted the cushion on the settee beside her. I sat down and she put her arm around me.

'It is terrible, but it has been going on for centuries in China. There's nothing we can do about it. You cannot change a culture overnight.'

'What about calling the police . . . ?' I suggested.

My mother sadly shook her head and said, 'She's long gone now.'

That night, lying in bed with the lights of Boundary Street barred by the venetian blinds on the ceiling, I wondered if the baby was already dead. I wanted to cry – and felt I should – but found I could not. I had already accepted the inevitable cruelty of life in the Orient. It was, I considered as I drifted wearily to sleep, no surprise China was so full of ghosts.

By early May 1953, Hong Kong was gripped by Coronation fever. A vast *pi lau*, a sort of Chinese triumphal arch, was erected across Nathan Road near the Alhambra cinema. Made entirely of bamboo poles lashed together by bamboo twine, it looked like the scaffolding on a building site, within which it was intended to construct a pagoda-cum-watchtower. By the week before the Coronation, it was festooned with gold and scarlet decorations, a row of lanterns, a picture of the new Queen and the letters *EIIR*. These also appeared on virtually every lamppost on every major thoroughfare. Shops displayed framed pictures of the Queen, sometimes next to ones of Chiang Kai-shek. It was a brave shopkeeper who displayed the Queen next to Chairman Mao. Even if he had Communist sympathies, which some had, discretion was deemed the better part of colonial valour and he joined in with the festivities.

On Coronation Day itself, there was a huge parade on Hong Kong-side. Keeping to Queen's Road, it wound its way through the city for six miles, the pavements jammed with tens of thousands of spectators. The queues for the Star Ferry on Kowloon-side stretched for well over a mile but we avoided these by crossing the harbour on a Royal Navy launch from which we were ushered into a dockyard office building overlooking Queen's Road and allotted seats at a window.

The parade was interminable. Soldiers, sailors, airmen, marching military bands, St John Ambulance volunteers, Boy Scouts, *kai fong* associations, nurses from the Bowen Road and Mount Kellett military hospitals, police and fire brigade marched by in dizzying, monotonous ranks, flags flying, pennants whipping the warm air. The tedium was only relieved by a drive past of tanks, howitzers, scout cars and other military paraphernalia. Several times, I tried to make my escape to explore the dockyard but had my collar felt by my father and was forced back into my seat.

It was just as well. After the pageant of imperial militarism, and a break of a quarter of an hour during which I managed to get my father to buy me a Coke, came the Chinese half of the parade.

At the head were two stilt-walkers and a classical marching orchestra – and it did not play 'When the Saints Go Marching In' but stirring melodies and lilting airs. Other Chinese bands followed, instilling in me that day a lifelong love of Chinese classical music. Between each of them were several flatbed trucks decked out as floats with tableaux being enacted on them by children dressed as characters out of Chinese mythology. They wore pancake make-up, as detailed and as stark as a Chinese opera singer's. My mother commented several times on how uncomfortable it must have been for them under the hot sun.

The highlight of the whole parade, however, were the lion and dragon dances.

Their approach could be guessed at by the increasing agitation of the crowds on the pavement opposite us. They began to grow restless, craning their necks and pointing. Finally, to the clashing of cymbals and striking of hand gongs, the lion appeared. It consisted of a brightly coloured stylized head on a bamboo frame, with fur-lined jaws and bulbous eyes. As big as a barrel, it was held aloft by a dancer who swung it to and fro, ducked it down and lunged forward with it, shook it from side to side and generally acted in a ferocious fashion. Behind him was the lion's body, a covering of less decorated cloth under which another dancer jostled and jived. The movements of the head were dictated by the cymbals and gongs. It was, for all intents and purposes, a sort of legendary Oriental pantomime horse.

Stilt-walkers and jugglers followed the lion, there was a gap and then the dragon arrived on the scene.

It was magnificent. Its head was at least nine feet high, excluding the horns on top. Its mouth – red-mawed and lined with white teeth – was big enough for me to have sat in. The mouth was operated by a man walking in front of the dragon with a pole connected to the dragon's lower lip, whilst the remainder of the head was held high by one man. As with the lion, he swung it to and fro, lowered it to the ground then looked at the sky, in time to the percussion instruments. Several yards in front of the dragon pranced a man with a paper fish almost as big as himself on a pole, with which he teased the beast. Behind the head was a one-hundred-yard-long reptilian body constructed of coloured cloth painted in scales and stretched over a series of bamboo hoops. Under this danced several dozen men, only their legs showing and giving the dragon's body the appearance of a multicoloured circus centipede. The body curled in on itself, twisting across the road and generally behaving in a serpentine fashion. The crowds applauded, the cymbals clashed, the gongs clanged and then, with two police wagons driving side by side, it was all suddenly over.

'What did you think of that?' my father asked as we lined up for the launch on the wall of the dockyard basin.

'Very impressive,' I replied noncommittally, having just heard someone else in the queue make the same remark.

'Just think,' my father went on, 'all over the Empire, these celebrations will be going on today. All for one young woman, our new Queen.'

For a moment, I thought he was going to cry. Whatever else he was, my father was definitely a monarchist.

7

LIVING ON CLOUDS

WE DROVE ON TO THE VEHICULAR FERRY AT YAU MA TEI, THE ramp was raised and the vessel headed out across the harbour. My mother and I stood at the front, a light spume blowing over us. My father remained with the car at the back of the deck, industriously wiping any hint of spray from the paintwork with a chamois leather.

'Where are we going?' I asked insistently and not for the first time.

'I've told you, I'm not telling you,' she retorted impishly.

Living in Kowloon, I rarely crossed the harbour to the island of Hong Kong. My parents frequently visited friends for dinner there, went to HMS *Tamar* for a mess night or to dine on a visiting warship – and, of course, my father crossed the harbour daily to go to his office in the dockyard – but I only accompanied them on select occasions, such as an Open Day on an aircraft carrier or submarine, or the annual Dockyard Fête, at one of which I won first prize in the .22 rifle shooting competition, with a score of 97/100. The first prize was a fully stocked blue-and-white woven rattan and plastic picnic hamper which my mother used for ten years before it finally unravelled. My success, over adults as well as children, had infuriated

GWEILO

my father who scored only seventy-something, yet who regarded himself as a top shot. In front of his colleagues and inferiors, he had lost considerable face: Commodore Blimp had been beaten by his boy. At home that night, my father had roundly derided the prize, although I noticed he removed the two bottles of wine it contained as well as the cashew nuts to which he was – as was I – more than partial. I never got to eat a single one of them. That, my mother told me, was my punishment for being a crack shot.

On Hong Kong-side, we drove off the ferry and a short distance through the city streets before skirting the Bank of China building and starting to ascend a steep wide road. Ahead was verdant mountainside with low blocks of apartments on the gentler slopes but, as the mountain rose more precipitously, houses half hidden in trees. My father had to change down to third gear and then to second for the first corner on a junction. The car remained in a low gear to negotiate two sinuous hairpin bends and a long straight to a four-way junction in a pass.

'Magazine Gap,' my mother said as my ears popped and, looking out the rear window, I caught a glimpse of the harbour and Kowloon beyond and well below.

The car continued to climb through luxuriant forest, plants with leaves as big as elephants' ears crowding each other out in the shade. Lianas and aerial roots hung down like ropes while butterflies flitted through the shadows and dappled light. Through gaps in the trees I caught snatches of open sea: at Magazine Gap we had crossed on to the south side of Hong Kong island.

Still we climbed. Edging the car into first gear, my father gunned the engine and we set off up an incline of at least 30 degrees called Mount Austin Road, moved round a

190

right-hand corner in second gear and turned up another steep road that looked as if it ran along a knife-edge ridge. At the end of this was a four-storey block of apartments. My father parked the car and we entered the building, climbing the wide stairs.

'Who lives here?' I asked my mother.

'We do,' she replied. 'From the day after tomorrow.'

On the top floor, my father produced a key and we entered Apartment 8, Mount Austin Mansions. Despite a few pieces of furniture, it echoed like a cathedral.

'Close your eyes,' my mother said as we went in.

I did so. She led me through the apartment. I heard another door open then the faint sound of birdsong, a cicada and the gentle shush of a mountain breeze.

'Open them.'

I was on the veranda. At my feet lay Hong Kong.

The view left me speechless. Down below was the central business district, the Bank of China and the Hongkong and Shanghai Bank next door little more than a child's building bricks. The harbour was a pool with small boats moving across it. Alongside HMS *Tamar* were two grey warships whilst, in mid-harbour, several others swung at anchor. Beyond lay the peninsula of Kowloon. A P&O liner was berthed in Tsim Sha Tsui, cargo vessels unloading at jetties further along the waterfront. The Yau Ma Tei typhoon shelter was a mere rectangle of water partly crammed with a brown wedge of junks and sampans. In the distance were the Kowloon hills and, further away still, a progression of hills disappearing towards China. Looking east was a sylvan ridge dotted with houses. Below them, beyond the eastern urban areas, were more hills and, far away, a scatter of islands.

The sun was now low and hidden behind a summit

surmounted by a copse of radio aerials: the riot of neon in the streets to the east and on Kowloon-side started to come alive in readiness for the approaching twilight. The last rays of the sun tinged the top of the Nine Dragons. In fifteen minutes, it was night, the lights of the colony shimmering in the heat. The walla-wallas and ferries were now trails of light upon blackened water, the warships decorated with white bulbs strung between their masts or lining their sides.

'So?' my mother asked.

'I don't know,' I replied.

'What do you mean, "I don't know"?' my father snapped. 'This is one of the most famous panoramas in the world and you are going to live on top of it. People would commit murder to live here. People sail halfway round the world to see this view for fifteen minutes and you're going to have it twenty-four hours—'

'Do stop harping on, Ken,' my mother muttered.

'Well, honestly . . .' my father replied, determined to have the last word. 'We give him the earth and—'

'We have not given him the earth,' my mother retorted. 'We have been allotted this as our quarters and he – and we – are bloody lucky. You had nothing to do with it.'

'I had nothing to do with it? My job – my rank – played no part in it?'

'You're a DNSO, Ken, not the First Sea Lord. You have a wife and son. That gives you X amount of housing points. This is an X-points quarter. It has been vacated. We were next in line for allocation. Now shut up!'

In truth, I was fully appreciative of the view. It was just that the enormity, the grandeur of it did not match my eight-year-old vocabulary. Fantastic or incredible or even stupendous seemed utterly devoid of the emotion I felt. It was, like the song, as if I really was sitting on top of the world.

As if that view were not enough, crossing through to the dining room, we looked south, out over the South China Sea. A fairly substantial island lay between Hong Kong and the horizon on which there were other low strips of land with pinpricks of light bunched in one spot on them.

'The island close to is called Lamma,' my mother said. 'Those in the distance are Communist Chinese.'

Yet I was not looking that far. On the sea around and beyond Lamma twinkled tiny lights. There were perhaps a hundred of them. They did not seem to move but were drifting on the tide.

'What're those lights?' I asked, but I realized the answer before being told.

'Fishing sampans,' my mother explained.

We headed back to Boundary Street. As the ferry edged across the harbour, I asked my mother to show me the building in which we had just been. Distinguished by the lights in its windows, it was perched on the very top of a secondary promontory to the east of the Peak, the mountain that stood guardian over the colony.

'What's it called?'

'The little summit is called Mount Austin and we have Apartment 8, Block A.'

'That's lucky,' I declared.

'What do you mean?' my father asked, folding his chamois leather into a wad.

'Eight's a lucky number,' I said. 'The Chinese think eight brings riches.'

'He does pick up some drivel,' my father remarked to my mother.

Yet she winked at me. She was by now well down the *hutong* to becoming a dedicated sinophile: unbeknownst to my father, she had even enrolled herself in Cantonese classes.

Life on the Peak had as much in common with that in Kowloon as a bowl of fish soup at a *dai pai dong* had to a traditional English fried breakfast, with or without salad cream. First, there were no shops except for a small Dairy Farm general store. Second, there were hardly any people about except around an observation point where tourists with cameras mingled with touts trying to sell them packs of photographs of what they were themselves about to photograph. Third, there were no eating places except the Peak Café, a low, red-roofed building that I had spotted as my father halted to change gear on our first visit. Finally, there were very few buildings and those that did exist were either the houses of the rich *taipans*, secure behind walls topped with barbed wire or broken glass, or apartment buildings.

From a busy urban existence, I was suddenly catapulted into a pacific rural one, with a gamut of new experiences to undergo and new lessons to be learnt.

The morning of the move, we arrived at Mount Austin shortly after two dark-blue Bedford lorries with RN painted in white upon the sides. Half a dozen Chinese ratings leapt out, lowered the tailgate and began to carry all our belongings up to Apartment 8. To complement the general-issue furniture provided by the Navy, my parents had purchased a low Chinese coffee table with bow legs, reminiscent of an English bull terrier's, a Chinese dining-room suite and a bar – an essential for my inabstinent father.

As soon as the unpacking commenced, it was diplomatically suggested that I might like to go outside and play. With whom or at what was not an issue. Hardly believing my good fortune, I left the building and set off down the curving ridge road. At the T-junction I turned right and started to ascend to the summit of the Peak.

The road was steep and passed a derelict lot where the foundations of a building were laid out in the ground with a few fragments of wall remaining. It was, in effect, a cleared bomb site: I had seen enough of those in Portsmouth to recognize it. Higher up, several rather fine houses stood to the right of the road with magnificent views of the city below. I walked on, my legs beginning to ache. A few hundred yards on there appeared at the side of the road a small stone building not much bigger than my grandfather's garden shed. The door was open and the sound of voices emanated from within. I knocked and looked in. Sitting at a desk was a policeman. Another sat to one side, his chair tilted back. In a corner, a kettle simmered on an electric ring. They nodded a greeting. I expected to be invited in for a bowl of tea. That would have been Mong Kok protocol. I wasn't.

Beside the police post were some stone steps. I descended them and found myself on a path that, after fifty yards, crossed a small tumbling stream. Tiny fish darted in the sandy-bottomed pools. It seemed amazing that, not three hundred feet from the top of a mountain, there was a flowing stream filled with fish. I stepped over the water by a small stone bridge and walked on. The path was narrow and clung to the not-quite-sheer side of the hill, keeping to more or less the same contour. It was obvious few people came this way, for the undergrowth met over the path and my legs were soon scratched and bleeding. Yet it was worth it. The views were breath-taking. Below me was a pale azure reservoir, Lamma Island across a narrow channel and the South China Sea beyond it. To the west, beyond the next, conical hill, were the distant islands of western Hong Kong and, beyond them, Lan Tau Island, the biggest in the territory. I did not realize quite how high I was until a kite, rising on a thermal, briefly hovered near me. It swivelled its head from side to side with avian wonderment at finding some-one so close on the normally deserted mountainside.

The following morning, I woke to find my room bathed in an eerie, soft light. Getting out of bed, I opened the curtains to discover we were in the clouds. Unlatching the metal-framed window, a warm and invisible damp-ness drifted in, touching my face as a ghost might. It occurred to me that perhaps I was allowing demons to enter so I closed it quickly.

At breakfast, my mother announced, 'You're going to go to the Peak School now. It's much too far to go to Kowloon Junior every day. We've an appointment with the headmistress at eleven o'clock.'

By the time we set off for the school, the sun had burnt off the clouds and we began our walk under a blazing sky. The air, however, was cool, with zephyrs tickling the tall, sparse grass and wild flowers on the bomb site.

'What building stood there?' I asked my mother as we passed it.

'I don't know,' she said, 'but you'll find ruins here and there on the Peak, of buildings destroyed by the Japanese in the war.'

The Peak School was about twenty minutes' walk away on Plunkett's Road, but to get there meant descending the very steep hill to the café. My mother, wearing a smart cotton print dress and high-heeled shoes, attempted the descent, stopped after a few yards, removed her shoes and continued barefoot. We arrived at the school hot and harried. The headmistress showed us into her office, a few formalities were undergone, I was taken to a classroom and obliged to stand in front of my future classmates, declare my name and then sit down at a desk next to another *gweilo* with pre-pubescent acne and breath that smelt as if he had breakfasted on hundred-year-old eggs. It did not bode well.

The pupils were predominantly British with a few Chinese, Americans and others of European extraction. Many of them seemed particularly distant and snooty. I preferred to keep myself to myself, get on with my work, read in break times and head for the door at the first chime of the bell. I ate my lunch on my own, rebuffed most approaches of friendship and worried my form teacher. As a consequence, when the school play was being cast, I was auditioned under duress and given a lead part, perhaps to bring me out of my shell. The play was *Toad of Toad Hall*. I was Mole.

The part was not too demanding. I learnt my lines with ease and only regretted being involved because it meant staying behind after school each day for over a month, rehearsing.

Only one memorable facet of my thespian adventure remains – the costume.

Each parent was asked to provide their child's outfit. My mother, not being adept with a needle and thread, asked Ah Shun if she could make it, but she admitted it was beyond her, too. My mother summoned her tailor.

Mr Chuk was a soft-spoken, elderly Chinese gentleman who came on occasion to the apartment to measure my mother. When this was done, the two of them would sit and drink bowls of jasmine tea whilst she went through his pattern books and material samples. He could make a midnight blue silk cocktail dress in five days, a lady's two-piece suit in seven. A mole costume was another matter.

I was taken into my parents' bedroom, stripped to my underpants and measured. My mother – no artist, she – then poured the tea and produced her drawing of a mole. The tailor studied it and shrugged.

'I no look-see dis an'm'l,' he said. 'Maybe dis no an'm'l China-side.'

'Maybe they've eaten them all,' my mother said to me as an aside.

She tried sketching it again. The result looked like a tailless, earless, eyeless rat with copious whiskers and exaggeratedly large front feet.

'He no can look-see?' the tailor enquired, noticing the sketch had no eyes.

'He no can look-see,' my mother confirmed. 'Live underground.'

'*Loh siu* liff unner groun'. Can see plentee good,' the tailor responded.

'This is not *loh siu*,' my mother said, exasperation creeping into her voice. 'It is not a rat. It is a mole.'

The tailor cupped his ear. 'He no can . . . ?'

'Yes,' my mother declared firmly. 'Can hear very good.' She was getting fed up with discussing the physical disabilities of a mole. 'You can make?'

'Can do,' came the optimistic reply.

It was deemed I did not require a fitting and so, two days before opening night, the tailor arrived at the apartment carrying a bundle containing a dark chocolate-brown, one-piece cross between a parachutist's jump-suit and a Glaswegian shipbuilder's boiler suit. I tried it on. It was as loose-fitting as a maternity smock and just as shapeless. My mother stifled a laugh, which was not a good sign.

The tailor had sewn whiskers (made of thin bamboo strips taken from a broom) on the top of the head. My face peered out through the mouth which was lined by white cloth teeth, serrated like a dragon's. What was more, the tailor had clearly taken pity on the mole's disabilities and given it two shiny glass eyes and a pair of cat-like ears. My mother paid the bill. On opening night, Rat (grey hairy costume, tail, beady eyes, bowler hat, waistcoat), Toad (grey-green painted mottled rubber attire made from a frogman's wet suit, a pair of cut-down plus fours and a deerstalker), Badger (tweed jacket and cut-down tartan golfing trousers with a realistic black-and-white papier mâché head) appeared on stage alongside a mutant creature of indeterminate species and origin which, not wearing any human clothing, was, presumably, naked. At curtain call, I received resounding applause and was asked to step forward for an extra bow. It was not, I was certain, due to my acting abilities.

Once a month, a cylindrical package arrived for me by sea mail. It was rolled up tightly, wrapped in brown paper and had twine tied round it and running through the middle. It had been mailed by my grandfather. When the string was cut, the rolled-up contents opened out to show the previous month's issues of the *Eagle*, *Dandy* and *Beano*. Tucked somewhere in them would always be a ten-shilling postal order. Unrolling the comics, I envisaged Grampy walking to the newsagent's once a week, an aroma of tobacco following him down the street like an invisible shadow, buying the comics, keeping them safe in the cupboard under the stairs that smelt of ale and stale bread, then once a month making his way to the Post Office. This was, to me, the height of love and I promptly wrote back by blue air mail lettergram to thank him and give him my news.

I held no information back from him, telling him of all my escapades, even into Kowloon Walled City, in the sure and certain knowledge he would not report them to my grandmother and, through her, to my father. She could not be trusted with a pod full of peas. Not once did he betray my confidence and he always replied, although my questions were not always answered. He did not tell me what *jig-a-jig* meant so I assumed he did not know.

My grandfather was not alone in sending parcels. The comics were certainly unobtainable in Hong Kong, but almost everything else was: in England, food, clothing, petrol and much more were in short supply and had been since the war. Some items were still on ration. An elderly maiden aunt called Olive assumed, despite many letters to the contrary, that we not only lived under rationing but also in pretty primitive conditions. Every two months for our first year in Hong Kong, a 'care' parcel arrived from her containing cotton handkerchiefs, soap, aspirin, adhesive and crêpe bandages, safety pins, Dettol, Reckitts' Blue laundry starch, thick woollen socks for my father, a lipstick for my mother and a Dinky toy car for me. She fell short of sending toilet rolls, presumably assuming we had plants with leaves large and soft enough for the job. (We had.) Eventually, my mother made up a parcel for Olive containing intricately embroidered napkin sets, silk handkerchiefs, brocade cushion covers, a cotton blouse, a tourist book of the sights of Hong Kong, a hand-painted lacquer dragon, a set of chopsticks (with instructions for use), a packet of jasmine tea (also with instructions) and a small jar of Tiger Balm ointment, the ubiquitous Chinese cure-all containing tiny quantities of opium and morphine which could fix, my mother claimed, anything from a wart to an unwanted pregnancy. Parcels from Olive ceased forthwith.

All expatriates referred to the country of their origin as 'home'. Even the old China Hands, those who had lived 'in-country' since the 1920s, did so. At first, my mother followed suit. However, by the winter of 1953, her outlook had subtly changed. She started to write to her mother that she wanted to remain in Hong Kong after my father's three-year-long tour of duty ended. In addition to learning Cantonese, she attended classes in Chinese history and culture, sought employment first on the local English-language radio station and then as a secondary school teacher of English and geography in a Chinese school, both without success. Her problem was that she lacked a formal higher education, yet she more than made up for it in intelligence and intellectual curiosity.

Of the old China Hands, I was to come to know two.

The first was a friend of my mother's, an English woman called Peggy who had married a Dutchman in the 1930s. When war broke out in 1939, her husband may have returned to Holland to fight for his homeland but he may have also stayed in Hong Kong and been killed when the Japanese invaded in 1941. Certainly, Peggy was rounded up and thrown into the civilian camp, the pre-war high-security prison at Stanley. I think they had no children: whenever I met her, she spoiled me rotten. As every colonial housewife did, she employed servants. In her case, she had a traditional *saw hei* amah.

This amah was one of those who had risked her life over and over again smuggling food and Chinese herbal medicines into the camp for her missee. Indubitably, her clandestine activities saved Peggy's life and probably those of several of her fellow prisoners-of-war. After the Japanese surrender, Peggy remained in Hong Kong and the amah returned to work for her but now they had a different relationship. Both of approximately the same age, they were no longer missee and amah but two spinsters living together and looking out for each other. Peggy obtained employment with the Hongkong and Shanghai Bank and, in time, rose through its ranks to a position of authority and responsibility. The amah kept home for both of them in a small flat on Robinson Road which they shared with at least two dozen rescued stray cats that Peggy loved with almost religious intensity. She and the amah were to die in their late seventies within days of each other.

The other China Hand, whom I came to both like and loathe, was Sammy Shields. As a man, I adored him, but he was also my dentist.

His surgery was in Star House, a two-storey building facing the Kowloon Star Ferry pier across the bus terminal. In actual fact, Sammy was not a qualified dentist. Before the war, he had been a dental technician, making and fitting dentures or braces. When he, too, was incarcerated in Stanley, it was found that he was the only person in the camp with any real dental know-how, so he became the camp dentist by default. After the war, with a large number of patients on his books – most of them ex-civilian prisoners-of-war – he set up in practice, his reputation growing, as it were, by word of mouth.

I visited his surgery with mixed feelings. The whine of his belt-driven drill could be heard in his tiny waiting room and was sure to send shivers of apprehension up the spine of the bravest man. His dentist's chair, the cantilevered arm of his drill and every other metal fitting were covered in cream enamel, chipped in places. It looked as if he had bought it second-hand, which was probably the case. It was certainly of pre-war vintage.

Sammy had a special technique with small boys such as myself, whose mothers he refused to allow into his chamber of tortures. Whenever my mother left the room, I felt suddenly terrified, but Sammy would soon put me at my ease . . .

'Right now, open wide. Ah! Let's see . . . a bit of plaque here . . . we'll chip that off in a tick . . . Good . . . wash out . . . Open wide again . . . a filling needed here, I'm afraid . . . just a little prick for the cocaine . . .' ('Aarrhh! Ah hurhs!') 'All done . . . wait for it to put your jaw to sleep . . . Did I ever tell you about my time as a guest of his Imperial Japanese Majesty?'

From then on, the sound of his drill and the abrupt jab of pain as he hit the nerve were mere momentary interruptions in a narrative of roasting rats on shovels over a fire of dried cow dung collected on Stanley beach, of boiling barnacles and steaming giant snails which had to be purged first in case they had been feeding on poisonous plants, of face-slappings and rifle buttings, of outbreaks of diphtheria, of men dying of disease or being shot on the beach, of removing fellow prisoners' molars without any anaesthetics, of the Americans' bombing of two prison buildings, killing the occupants.

'Bloody fools, Americans,' Sammy would appendix this story. 'What I'd give for one of those pilots sitting where you are now . . .'

I heard these stories every six months. They never lost their potency and never failed to take the edge off what I was undergoing. It was, I thought, nothing compared to what he must have endured for four years.

A fortnight before my ninth birthday, Wong asked me, 'What you likee you burfday cake, young master?'

'A cake,' I replied, puzzled by the enquiry, 'with nine candles.'

'What shape you likee?'

My consternation multiplied. As far as I was concerned, cakes were round and that was an end to it.

'Maybe you likee house?' he suggested, seeing my bewilderment. 'Likee tempul? Wong can do tempul good for you.'

Without really thinking about it, I answered, 'I'd like a battleship.'

Several days later, I went to the kitchen to find my way barred. The swing door had had a wooden wedge jammed under it.

'You lo can come kitchen-side now,' Wong declared with an authority I had not previously seen in him. 'You wantee somef'ing, makee bell.'

'I only want a Coke,' I said, conscious of my parents' orders that I did not ring the servants' bell for petty demands.

He took one out of the fridge, opened it and handed it to me through a crack in the door, adding, 'Two week, you lo go kitchen-side. You go, Wong v'wy ang'wee.'

I complained to my mother. Her reply was that I was to obey Wong.

On my birthday, which fell on the second day of the new academic year, I arrived home in eager anticipation as it had been decided that I should not receive my presents until teatime. I burst into the apartment to be confronted by my mother.

'Tea first, prezzies second,' she announced.

I should have guessed something was up. Most unusually, my father was home two hours before normal. I was led into the dining room where Wong had laid out tea – sandwiches, bread and butter, scones, the teapot . . . Yet the moment I saw the table all thought of gifts and food evaporated.

In the centre of the table was a two-and-a-half-foot-long model of a Royal Navy destroyer, exact in every detail. It was painted battleship grey with its identification letter and numbers on the hull. At the bow hung the Union Jack, at the stern the White Ensign. On the bridge were the Aldiss lamp and searchlights, the wheel and a brass compass and engine room telegraph. On deck, the guns pointed fore and aft, the anchor chain lay on the deck and there were rope loops on the Carley floats and lifeboats. Even the rigging existed, thin lines of what I assumed to be fuse wire running from deck to mast.

Models such as this were only to be found in maritime museums. I was speechless. Wong stood by my side.

'Dis you cake, young master. Happy burfday for you.' In the background, Ah Shun smiled, bemused by the whole affair.

'Cake?' I replied.

'You say you wantee warship cake. Wong do for you.'

I just hugged him.

The cake had taken Wong a fortnight. He had worked every spare moment he could afford, often late into the night. The hull and superstructure were a rich fruit cake chock-full of glacé cherries and sultanas and covered in hard royal icing, the lifeboats made of marzipan and icing, the main armament and gun turrets of solid icing. Most astonishing of all was the rigging, made of spun sugar. To keep the cake as it was assembled, it had been hidden in the windowless dry room off my parents' bedroom where clothes and shoes were kept to avoid them going mouldy in the humid tropical air. Despite this precaution, they still quickly grew a hazy fur of fungus, and the cake would have grown a microscopic lawn in hours, but Wong knew a trick. A small charcoal burner was kept alight in the room which absorbed any humidity that got in.

I did not want to cut into it. Neither did my mother. At the end of the table was a smaller ordinary cake with candles on it. We ate that instead but, the following day, we started on the destroyer. I forget what presents I received.

The destroyer was not Wong's only artistic culinary masterpiece. He could carve chrysanthemum blooms out of raw carrots and decorative leaves out of cucumbers. Mashed potato was always served in small volcano shapes with the tops slightly browned under the grill. Crown roast New Zealand lamb arrived on the table with the rib ends culminating in parsnip, not paper, decorations. For cocktail parties, Wong prepared what was known as *small chow*, but which my father preferred to refer to as finger fodder, possibly a naval term. Mushrooms stuffed with anchovies, cheese and soy sauce sticks, thinly sliced fresh pineapple and shrimps on toast with home-made mayonnaise and a scattering of sesame seeds – his repertoire and penchant for experimentation seemed inexhaustible.

At drinks parties, Wong being occupied in the kitchen, my father delegated me to help him wait on the guests. My responsibilities were to see that no-one's glass was empty and to serve the trays of *small chow*.

At first, I regarded this as an onerous chore but I came to look forward to it. My father taught me how to mix drinks, I was able to consume Wong's delicacies on the sly and I became privy to the world of adult conversation which, on occasion, I found fascinating. It was by such eavesdropping that I learnt the true story of HMS *Amethyst*, attacked by Chinese forces on the Yangtze River in 1949 and the Rape of Nanking by the Japanese in the winter of 1937. Such parties also had their lighter side. On Christmas Eve morning, 1953, I went into my parents' bathroom to get a new tube of toothpaste only to discover a Royal Navy Commander, resplendent in mess uniform with gold braid and medals, asleep on his back in the bath, gently snoring, his arms crossed over his chest with a tiger lily thrust between his fingers. I tip-toed out and never saw him again.

That same winter, my father returned home in the early hours from a mess night with the Royal Air Force at Kai Tak airport. He was well oiled and humming tunelessly. This was most unusual, for my father was typically morose and self-pitying when the worse for booze. His dinner suit was caked in congealed blood.

I stood by as my mother, simultaneously concerned and furious, stripped my father to his vest and Y-fronts, sat him in the bath and washed him down. He had a nasty gash on the inside of his arm but it was insufficient to account for the quantity of blood all over him, even matted in his hair. When he was clean, my mother pulled the plug, sent him into the spare room, covered him with a sheet and went back to her own bed. I withdrew to mine.

In the morning, my mother held a breakfast inquisition.

'What the hell were you doing last night, Ken? Your dinner jacket's ruined. So's your shirt. And you've lost two of the gold studs your father gave you.'

My father made no reply.

'That's not a rhetorical question, Ken.'

'Fan cricket,' my father admitted at length. He looked down at his arm, his wound covered by a large adhesive bandage.

What had happened was that, after the formal dinner, the RAF officers' mess members had decided on a game of fan cricket, mess vs. guests, which involved everyone present forming a circle around a ceiling fan. This was set at maximum speed and an empty beer can tossed into it. Wherever it flew out from the spinning propeller, it had to be caught. Of course, after the first toss, the metal was mangled into pieces as sharp as razor blades.

'You'd better visit the *Tamar* MO and have a tetanus shot,' my mother stated. 'God knows what bacteria were breeding on the can.'

My father got up to leave the table, his breakfast untouched.

'Sit down!' my mother commanded imperiously.

My father obeyed. I had never seen him so docile and compliant.

'What's more, your trousers are torn and the remnants of your jacket smell of petrol.'

'Better than perfume,' my father answered back, smiling sheepishly and hoping to bring some sense of levity to the breakfast table.

'What . . . !' said my mother, her jaw set and her eyes wide with rage.

My father confessed how the evening's jollity had ended. The mess piano had been carried outside and placed at the rear of a Hawker Hunter jet fighter parked on the apron. The engine was then fired up and the piano incinerated.

My mother listened to this in silence then commented, 'A fine example for Martin. Now eat your bloody breakfast.'

My father prodded his fried egg with his fork and made to stand up again.

'Wong gets up before six to see you have a breakfast,' my mother remarked, 'so kindly show him the respect he deserves and eat the bloody thing. And one more matter,' she continued, 'when the mess bill comes in, the cost doesn't come out of my housekeeping money.'

This was the second occasion during our years in Hong Kong when my father's drunken escapades had cost my mother dear. When stationed in Japan, one night he and a friend had gone into a saloon in Sasebo where there was an American naval rating shooting his mouth off about the Royal Navy, the Queen and the British in general. He made it abundantly clear that the Royal Navy was not worth the water it sailed on, the Queen was 'a nice piece of ass' and the British as a nation were spineless, gutless and worth less than their navy. My father and his friend agreed with him and kept his glass full until he was paralytic.

They then carried him out of the bar and down the street to a tattoo artist who tattooed his entire chest in full colour with the White Ensign, the Union Jack and *God Save the Queen*. My mother's house-keeping allowance was somewhat short that month.

As time went by, my father's increasing delight in and reliance upon the company of Johnnie Walker, Messrs Justerini and Brooks and his namesake (but no relation) Mr Booth – not to mention his friend, Mr Gordon – grew. When he arrived home from the office, his first visit was to the drinks cabinet, Wong running in from the kitchen with a jug of water, a container of ice and a cold bottle of tonic, covering all the angles with them. Sometimes, my father returned late having, as he put it, *just popped into the wardroom*. His favourite snifter was pink gin, popular in officers' messes on every warship afloat. It consisted of gin diluted with water, with a dash of Angostura bitters. My father took it without the water.

My father's drinking never got him truly, staggeringly, equilibriumly challenged, sad-song-singingly, punch-flingingly, bosom-friend-makingly drunk. Furthermore, he never suffered from a hangover. Consequently, my father never felt himself to be sozzled, as my mother termed it, trying to make light of the situation for her own sanity and self-respect. Worse still, he would never admit to being under the influence. No matter how much alcohol slid down his gullet, my father remained vertical, comparatively lucid and even able to drive without incident. The only obvious sign of intoxication other than his breath was his attitude towards my mother and me. He was psychologically abusive, skilfully criticizing or belittling us in front of our friends. His attacks were never short, sharp, soon-to-be-forgotten, even forgiven, episodes. They were

calculated, long-term personal projects bent on under-
mining his subject's spirit and, as his drinking increased,
these melded together into a continuous animosity which
drove people – my mother, myself, my parents' friends –
away in disgust. As a result, my father was tolerated rather
than liked and became a lonely, disenchanted and bitter
man.

He never praised but only criticized or admonished,
muttering through clenched teeth that my mother and I
did not come up to his standard – but then he never told
us where the benchmark lay. After one confrontation
with him, my mother declared to me that we had already
exceeded his standard and that that was the problem, but I
did not understand what she meant.

One Saturday lunchtime, not long after we moved to
the Peak, my father arrived home in a foul temper. Something had gone wrong at the office.

'What's the matter, Ken?' my mother enquired, coming
in from the kitchen.

'Don't you start!' he snapped as he mixed himself a
quadruple pink gin.

'I was only asking—'

'Well bloody well don't!'

My mother let this roll over her and said, 'Let's have
lunch. Philip and Ray'll be here at two.'

'I'm not going swimming,' my father replied. 'Bloody
waste of time.'

Normally, this would have upset my mother. She did
not drive and we were therefore reliant upon my father or
public transport to take us everywhere. But Philip and Ray
Bryant were close friends of my mother's and owned a
huge pre-war grey Jaguar saloon with massive headlights
and leather seats. I sensed Philip was critical of my father's

naval pretensions and despised his treatment of my mother. A handsome and jovial man, he was a Royal Navy Commander, Ray a vivacious and pretty woman with black hair and the refined movement of a ballet dancer. They had met in Egypt during the war.

'Well, we're going swimming,' my mother rejoined firmly. 'You can do what you like. You can sleep all bloody day for all I care.'

At this, my father grabbed a cushion off the settee and hurled it at the glass doors to the balcony. It was a hot day. They were open. The cushion spun through them without touching the sides and sailed, like a brocade extra-terrestrial craft, out into the air. It disappeared from view on its way down the steep mountainside towards the city below. My mother and I rushed downstairs and out on to the lawn that surrounded the building. Arriving at the retaining wall, we looked down. Hong Kong and the harbour, with Kowloon in the distance, lay at our feet. The cushion was lodged in some bushes about fifty yards down on a not quite sheer slope. A short distance beyond it, the angle of the hillside sharpened before dropping into a band of trees.

'You're right, Ken,' she said as we returned to the apartment, 'you're not coming. You're going down the bloody hillside and you're going to retrieve my bloody cushion.'

As we drove to the beach in Philip's Jaguar, my mother recounted what had come to pass. I asked what would happen if my father slipped.

'No need to worry,' Philip answered. 'Lugard Road'll break his fall.'

When we returned at dusk, the cushion was back on the settee, cleaned by Ah Shun. A filthy white shirt, shredded by thorns, lay on my mother's bed, a sort of trophy of war.

At home, when my father threw things, they were always items – books, the newspaper, cushions – that were sure not to make a dent in the wall or parquet flooring. In the office, it was a different matter. There, midway through berating a Chinese clerk or typist standing trembling before him, he would, to emphasize a point in his tirade, grab the black bakelite telephone and hurl it at the wall. It would smash to pieces. Women would burst into tears. The men would keep on quaking. If the telephone was not handy, he threw the office wall clock. In the end someone fitted a shorter cord to the telephone so that, when he flung it, it reached the extent of its flex and fell harmlessly on to the carpet. The Chinese staff called him *mok tau* (blockhead) and worse. They often used these names to his face but as he spoke no Cantonese, they were safe. I once heard a clerk call him *gai lun jai* (chicken penis boy): the clerk must have assumed that, as I was my father's son, I spoke no Cantonese either.

Having met one or two at school, I came to the conclusion that my father was a natural-born bully. On the other hand, I did grow up mixing a mean cocktail. Maybe that was one of his benchmarks of a good son.

Although we now lived on the Peak, across the harbour from and over a thousand feet above all my mother's Chinese friends, she remained in constant touch with them, meeting the room boys from the Fourseas on their days off, going to tea houses with them, sometimes spending an afternoon with them and their girlfriends or wives at the beach. At other times, she went on picnics with them. These frequently took place on school days but when they occurred at a weekend or in the school holidays, I was invited along.

My father took a dim view of these outings. My mother ignored his opinion completely until one Saturday when she announced she was going out with 'the boys and girls', as she put it, the following day.

'I see,' my father remarked shirtily. 'So I'm left here with Martin.'

'No!' I chirped up. 'I'm going, too.'

'If you ask me, Joyce,' my father went on, giving me a filthy look, 'you should stay home at the weekends. To go off midweek is one thing, but . . . All this gallivanting about will get you a reputation.'

'Gallivanting with the natives will get me a reputation, will it, Ken?'

'You know what I mean.'

'I'm sure I don't.'

'Well, you should. Tongues'll wag.'

'I don't care if they flap in the wind like flags,' my mother rejoined. 'And neither should you. If some old biddy with nothing better to do starts bad-mouthing me, it's up to you to defend my honour.'

'Drawn cutlasses at dawn?' my father replied ironically.

'Don't be ridiculous, Ken. Besides, what's the alternative? Spend the weekend watching you snore. Some live spark you are, Ken. About as bright as a NAAFI candle.'

For some reason I could never fathom, my mother assumed that candles purchased from the Navy Army and Air Force Institutes were always incapable of burning brightly and frequently used this metaphor.

'I work hard all week and—'

'So does everybody else, Ken, but they don't spend the weekend sleeping and snorting like a grampus.'

Half an hour later, we met up with Ching, Halfie and some of the other Fourseas staff at the Outlying Islands ferry pier in Central District. A black-and-white Hongkong Yaumatei Ferry company vessel pulled alongside and we boarded it with a throng of boisterous Chinese weekend picniceers, all bound for Cheung Chau and carrying rattan baskets or bags.

No sooner was the ferry underway than everyone produced an array of snacks – chicken's feet, pork spare ribs, *wah mui*, crystallized ginger, pomeloes, oranges and melon seeds. Vendors travelled the deck selling bottled drinks and sweetmeats. The bones, peel and shells were thrown over the side, as in any Hong Kong street, with scant regard for those below: the ferry had a bottom passenger deck.

After an hour, the ferry turned into the harbour of Cheung Chau, a dumb-bell-shaped island with an ancient village in the centre. Deepwater fishing junks rode at anchor, with sampans weaving between them like agile aquatic insects. A drift of joss-stick smoke indicated the location of a large temple.

As soon as the gangplank hit the jetty, a phalanx of passengers ran ashore to claim the best tables in a nearby restaurant. We followed but by-passed the eating place with its tanks of live fish and crabs destined for the table.

'What is the temple?' I asked Ah Tang, one of the room boys.

'Pak Tai,' he answered. 'Sea god temple. More old all Hong Kong.'

I wanted to visit it but it was not on our itinerary. Instead, we went south along the *praya*, passing fish vendors, sleeping cats and vociferous dogs, fishermen mending nets or baiting lines and houses with their windows shuttered against the fierce sunlight. At the periphery of the village, we struck out along a path running through a tunnel of trees and rocks.

'Where are we going?' I asked my mother.

'I haven't the slightest idea,' she replied. 'I'm just going with the general flow.'

The path was alive with tawny Rajah and delicate cream-and-black dragontail butterflies supping on fallen fruit. In the dry leaves, smooth skinks with black side stripes rustled and flashed out of sight. Birds sang and flitted through the branches of a sacred banyan tree upon which pictures of the gods had been pinned. Joss-sticks smouldered in the roots. Here and there were groves of yellow and green striped bamboo, many of the stems substantial enough to make a coolie's pole. All the while, the sea glinted away to my right through sparsely needled pine trees.

My mother was happy, walking with a jaunty step, swinging our picnic basket. Where the path widened, she took my hand.

'This is fun, isn't it?' she asked.

I agreed that it was but, after a short distance, posed a question that had long been bothering me.

'Why doesn't Dad come to places with us?'

She looked down at me.

'He's a stick-in-the-mud,' she responded. 'And he's got a chip on his shoulder.'

I asked what that meant.

'It's hard to explain. It's just – well, he thinks he's better than everyone else but they don't agree.'

'Was he always a stick-in-the-mud?' I enquired.

'No! We used to go for cycle rides in the country and go to the pictures or for walks on the Downs, and we'd have lunch in a little village pub at Cowplain . . .' She paused. I sensed she was sad but then she perked up. 'What the hell! It was all a long time ago.'

Up ahead, our companions were singing a Chinese song in time with their steps. My mother joined in.

The path descended a hillside towards the sea. We halted by a group of boulders. Within minutes, someone had a small primus alight and was boiling water for tea. A cloth was spread over a flat rock and weighted down with stones. With the others, my mother set about laying out our picnic.

I settled myself on a slab of pinkish granite, the sunlight dancing on the mica fragments as if on tinsel. To my left was a cove surrounded by low cliffs, gentle waves sucking at the rocks. My mother approached with Ah Tang.

'Martin, come and see this!'

We followed Ah Tang along a cliffside path and down towards the shore where there was a tumble of huge boulders.

'You come all same me,' he said beckoning to us.

We slithered down the boulders to find several of them had formed a sort of cave. He gestured us in. The entrance was narrow, the roof low and the floor sand.

Squatting on his haunches, Ah Tang said, 'This place for Cheung Po Tsai. He live here.'

'Who is Cheung Po Tsai?' I enquired.

'Long time before, more four hund'ed year, Cheung Po Tsai big time py-rat. Got many junk, many men work for him, all same py-rat. He also got *gweipor* wife. Catch her on one ship one time. She love Cheung Po Tsai, no wan' go back Inglun'-side. Stay here.'

My mother gazed out of the entrance to the sea.

'Just imagine,' she said, 'living here with a pirate chief, thousands of miles from home and knowing you could never return.'

The romantic in her was working double-speed.

When the picnic was over, some of the room boys' girlfriends started to dance. It was a Chinese dance that involved tiny steps, moving in a circle, singing a song and, with arms raised, making a twisting motion with the hand, as if one were screwing in a light bulb. My mother was invited to join in, being taught the words and motions. I watched as she danced with these young Chinese women. She did not look, I thought, very different from them, except that her hair was blond not black. She was, as she would have put it, as happy as a sand boy.

We walked slowly back to the ferry jetty, the lowering sun warm on our faces. The butterflies on the path made no effort to fly off at our approach: Ching said they were drunk.

'How can a butterfly get drunk?' I said.

'The juice', Ching explained, 'can make alcohol in the hot sun.'

As we sailed back to Hong Kong, my mother leant out of the ferry window, the warm wind ruffling her hair. The gleaming sun reflected gold off the sea and on to the ferry cabin ceiling. The Chinese day-trippers were mostly quiet now. A few played cards but most dozed or read a newspaper or magazine. Ching and Halfie faced each other over a set of *tin gau* tiles.

At the HYF pier in Central, we said our goodbyes and took a taxi home. My father was sitting with a gin and tonic listening to the BBC World News on the radio. I went out on to the veranda and looked down on the city. The first neon lights were coming on, bright as coloured stars in the shadow of the Peak.

'Have a good time?' my mother asked.

I nodded.

'It's days like this you never forget, no matter how old you get,' she advised me. 'It's what life's all about. Warm sun, friendship and music.'

She did a little twirl, miming fitting a light bulb in the sky and went inside.

What first prompted the thought in my mother's mind I have no idea, but a fortnight after my ninth birthday, she warned me not to make any arrangements for the following Saturday morning. When I asked why not, she was uncharacteristically equivocal.

'Just wait and see,' she said, 'and don't – I repeat, don't – mention it to your father.'

On the morning in question, my mother waited until my father departed for the office then took me to the top terminus of the Peak Tram, the famous funicular mountain tramway. We descended over a thousand feet to the bottom terminus, hurriedly made our way past the cathedral and by banks and shipping line offices, crossing Statue Square to the Star Ferry pier. All this way, my mother hardly spoke, ignoring my enquiries as to our destination.

Once over the harbour and off the ferry, our pace slowed to a normal walk.

'What was all that rush about?' I asked.

'I didn't want to bump into your father. He thinks I'm having coffee with Biddy Binns.'

'So what we're doing—' I began to suggest.

'Is a secret,' my mother interrupted, confirming my thoughts. 'You must never tell your father. It's not that what we're doing is wrong but, if he found out, I'd never hear the last of it. And neither would you.'

Finally, we arrived at a tenement building, the ground floor of which was occupied by a camera and binocular shop. To one side was a narrow doorway closed by a galvanized metal door. My mother opened it and we started to ascend a staircase that smelt of cats and boiled rice. At last, we arrived at a door with a number painted upon it and a picture of Kwan Ti pasted beneath a spyhole. On the wall to one side was a brass plate in Chinese characters such as one might find outside a doctor's surgery.

Immediately, my anxiety grew. I was in for some kind of treatment: but I was not ill. A boy I'd known at school had recently been circumcised and told all in graphic detail to his friends. Was this my fate? I felt my penis and testicles shrink with fear. Then it occurred to me: was my mother ill? A shiver went down my back. She looked healthy enough, yet . . . What if she died? A future of Dickensian proportions and misery spread ahead of me.

My mother knocked on the door. The spy-hole momentarily darkened before several bolts were drawn and we were confronted by a middle-aged Chinese woman wearing Western clothes.

'Good morning, Mrs Booth,' she greeted us in a slightly American accent. 'Please come in.'

She stepped aside and we entered a small and sparsely furnished tenement flat. Upon one wall were a number of mathematical charts and tables. In the window hung the almost obligatory bird cage containing a lone zebra finch. A door opened and an elderly Chinese man entered wearing a long, dark-blue brocade gown, the character *sow*, meaning long life, woven into an almost invisible pattern. His face was lined and the nail of his left index finger was at least two inches long. This, I knew, signified he was a man of learning who never involved himself with manual work.

'Good morning. I am Mr Zhou,' he introduced himself. He shook my mother's hand then looked at me. 'And this is the subject?'

I felt instantly more apprehensive and wondered if I was here to receive some maths tutoring: the charts suggested that this might be the case and, indeed, I hoped that it was, preferring even maths coaching to circumcision. But then my father would have approved of maths coaching. This visit was to be kept secret. I was in a quandary.

'May I introduce my son, Martin?' my mother said.

'Hello, Martin,' Mr Zhou said without a trace of an accent. 'Tell me, when is your birthday?'

'I've just had it,' I replied.

'This I know,' said Mr Zhou, pulling over a stool, 'but tell me the date.'

'The seventh of September 1944.'

'You were born in the Year of the Monkey. It is a good year for you.' He started now to speak more to my mother. 'A male born in this year is very intelligent and good at solving mysteries or problems. Like a monkey, he can be devious or cunning. Very big-headed, I think you say. Maybe arrogant. Those born under this animal are always moving, have a quick mind. Now,' he positioned his stool directly before me, 'relax yourself.'

For the next five minutes, Mr Zhou thoroughly felt my head, studied my palms and looked intently at my face. All the while, he muttered in an undertone, the lady taking notes. This done, he produced a highly polished tortoise shell from a drawer. It was complete except for the tortoise. He studied this, muttered some more then put it away.

Upon a writing desk, Mr Zhou set out a fan of cards with pictures on them. Taking down the bird cage, he stood it on the end of the desk and opened the door. The tenement window was open, the sounds of the street below and the warm, diesel-tinged air wafting in. The chances of the zebra finch doing a Joey were, I thought, pretty high.

Instead, the bird flew out of its cage, strutted along the cards, picked one out with its beak and flew straight back into the cage. Mr Zhou closed the door and gave the bird a small berry from a jar.

He studied the card and the lady's notes. We watched as he wrote a long document in black ink on coarse, buff-coloured Chinese paper. His brushstrokes were rapid. Every so often, he used another brush to draw a red circle. Finally, he waited for the ink to dry, folded the oblong sheet and slipped it in an envelope on which he wrote my name.

'In summary,' he announced as he handed it to me, 'you will be a clever man but sometimes very lazy. You will be a leader, a famous man in what you do. You will live to be sixty-four years old and you will be prosperous and have sons. You will have a good marriage. In your fifty-seventh year, you will have much illness but in the remainder of your life you will be healthy.'

With that, he stood up, shook my mother's hand, briefly

put his hand in mine and left the room, closing the door behind him. My mother paid the lady with a cheque.

'So now we know,' my mother remarked as we reached the street. 'You'll have a good life.'

She seemed relieved, as if prior to this she had had her doubts.

'Mr Zhou is highly respected,' she continued. 'He's considered the best fortune-teller in the colony. They say the Governor's wife goes to him.'

I did not comment, but I saw little difference between him and those I saw outside the Tin Hau temple in Yau Ma Tei, except that he spoke English and operated from a tenement flat.

We walked to Tkachenko's for a mid-morning coffee and Black Forest gateau.

'Remember,' my mother warned me, 'not a single, solitary word to your father.' I nodded my agreement. 'If he finds out,' she went on, 'I'll be branded a witch, given a broomstick and sent to Coventry.'

'Why would he send you there?' I asked.

'It's just an expression.'

I sipped my drink and said, 'Well, at least I'm not going to be a dustman.'

My mother looked at me for a moment then broke out laughing. I liked it when she laughed. It was not that often that she did.

Christmas Day 1953 dawned bright. The sky was cloudless and blue, the air chill. At nine o'clock, we embarked upon the Christmas-morning ritual of present giving.

GWEILO

In the lounge, we had a Christmas tree, of sorts. Imported from California, it was about three feet high and had started to lose its needles somewhere around Hawaii. By now it was a tinsel-hung, glass-ball-strewn, fairy-lights-lit skeleton of near twigs with an embarrassed-looking angel on top. We gathered before it, shortly to be joined by Wong and his family. Tuppence held back. The master's side of the house was unequivocally out of bounds to him and any excursion into it was bewildering. My mother took him by the hand and led him in. Whilst she appreciated the exclusion rule and agreed it was necessary, the egalitarian in her disapproved of it. Tuppence was seated on an armchair and showered with small presents which included clothing as well as Chinese sweets and toys. Wong and Ah Shun received their presents, coffee was served and then we got on with opening ours.

Lunch that day could have graced a monarch's table. The turkey, a gift from The Asia Provision Company, which presented all its customers with a hamper of gratitude every Christmas, was raised in Australia. Its skin, as highly polished and varnished as the table upon which it stood, looked like that on a whole Ho Man Tin pig. It was stuffed with cranberry, sage and thyme and the flesh fell apart like fish. The pudding was traditionally round and the size of a football, with a sprig of holly on top. We wondered where Wong had got it: holly was not indigenous to southern China. Then we found out. It was made of icing sugar. As for the pudding, it was so big we were still eating it fried in butter in the first week of January. The only thing that marred the meal was my father's half-hour fit of pique when he found out the thing had been set alight with his best armagnac.

Christmas afternoon was spent playing Dover Patrol

224

on the lounge carpet, listening to the Queen's Speech (which my father considered obligatory) and settling the surfeit of food. Late in the afternoon, I walked down to a block of 1920s apartments near the Peak Café to visit a friend. We messed around a bit and I set off for home just before dark. It was a cool South China winter's night. A stiff breeze blew by the café, rippling the creepers on its roof.

Reaching the tourist observation point, I stood alone, the updraft of wind from the harbour below making my eyes water. The lights of the city glistened in the cold air. A lone vehicular ferry made its way towards Yau Ma Tei. In the middle of the Kowloon peninsula, I imagined I could see the red, blue and green neon sign on the front of the Fourseas and immediately felt homesick for Soares Avenue and the *dai pai dongs* of Mong Kok: I doubted there was a single hundred-year-old egg anywhere on the Peak. Especially on Christmas night.

Feeling, as my mother would have put it, a little blue, I trudged on up the steep hill to Mount Austin, hauling myself along on the railing. My parents were playing canasta at the bull terrier coffee table when I arrived home. My mother had a gin and tonic at her side, my father a tumbler more than half full of neat whisky. I went into the kitchen and opened the fridge. Wong immediately appeared and poured me a glass of milk. Without asking, he then set to making turkey sandwiches. I took my milk into the lounge and settled down in an armchair to read the latest *Eagle* album, a Christmas present from Grampy, along with a five-pound postal order.

After a while, my father put a 78 record on the phonograph: the Original Dixieland Jazz Band playing 'Tiger Rag'. It was tentatively suggested that I might go to bed, but I pleaded turkey sandwiches and Christmas night and the subject was dropped.

At about half-past ten, my mother went out onto the veranda. This was a nightly ritual. She would stand there sometimes for fifteen minutes, just taking in the panorama. I was not to know it, and nor was my father, but she was beginning to scheme secretly how she might make Hong Kong her home for the rest of her life.

'Ken,' she called a few minutes later, her voice tight with urgency, 'get your binoculars.'

'What is it?' I enquired, joining my mother on the veranda.

'I don't know,' she replied, pointing across to the north-western end of Kowloon. 'What do you make of it?'

A dull ruddy blush glowed behind some low hills. My father arrived and put his binoculars to his eyes, turning the focusing ring.

'Oh, my God!' he murmured.

My mother snatched them from his face.

'Can I see?' I insisted. I had to ask several times before she would relinquish them.

I adjusted the focus. It seemed as if a whole hillside was ablaze. It was the Shek Kip Mei squatter area going up in flames. The fire was intense. Even from a distance of five miles, individual flames could clearly be seen licking into the air. The highest must have reached fifty feet. I thought of my experience at Ho Man Tin, of the young man with only the photo of his family to link him to his former life back in China, before the Communists destroyed it.

My mother turned into the lounge, calling for Wong.

'Yes, you wanchee, missee?' he asked, expecting an order for more sandwiches or a fresh bottle of tonic water.

'Look!' she exclaimed, pointing once more at Kowloon.

He stepped on to the veranda and looked at the distant fire through the binoculars. His face showed no emotion whatsoever. To the Chinese, this was fate and it was his good luck to live and work in a comparatively non-flammable building, and the squatters' ill luck not to.

'No good for plenty people, missee,' he said.

My mother set to work.

'Wong, get all the blankets out of the camphor wood chest. Martin, you—'

'What are you doing, Joyce?' my father asked.

'What do you think I'm doing?' she snapped back. 'Go and get the car.'

'Get the car . . . ?' my father repeated. 'It's after eleven, Joyce! On Christmas night—'

'I know! Get the bloody car, cloth ears!' It was a derogatory expression my father often used on her.

In thirty minutes, all the bedding in the house was tied into individual bundles of one blanket and two sheets. My school Hong Kong basket was full of turkey sandwiches and there were two cardboard boxes of tonic and soda water. This was all loaded into the car and we set off. My father was all for leaving me behind but my mother would not have it.

We drove down the Peak and on to the vehicular ferry. There were only two other private vehicles on board, both large American saloon cars filled with raucous party-goers returning home. The remainder of the deck was occupied by several fire engines and ambulances.

Once landed at Yau Ma Tei, it was only a matter of a mile or so to Shek Kip Mei but we were halted by a road block at Prince Edward Road and forced to turn right. My father drove a short way and parked in the forecourt of an apartment block. My mother got out, piled me high with blanket and sheet bundles and, with as many as she could carry herself, set off in the direction of the fire. I followed. My father was forgotten in her rush: maybe she thought he would rather guard and polish the car.

We had not gone three hundred yards when a British police officer stopped us. Beyond him, crowds were gathering in the streets.

'You can't go beyond here,' he ordered my mother.

'St John Ambulance,' she replied, adding unnecessarily, 'blankets. More coming.'

Her bluff worked. He let us through. The side streets were thronged with hordes of people sitting down. What was unnerving was that they were virtually silent, unlike most Chinese crowds which usually chattered like a flock of migrating starlings. My mother handed out bundles to the first families she came across. They took them, smiling at her. One man stood up, said, 'T'ankee you, missee,' and touched my hair. For his family, at least, things were not going to be so bad after all.

The air was contaminated with the foul smell of burning rubber and cloth. Ash blew past us like grey snow, some of the flakes still alight. A fire engine pumped water down a fat undulating hose from a street hydrant but it could not have had much effect. The sky was alight with sparks and flames, a thick column of smoke rising into the night sky then bending away on the wind. Spotlights played upon the havoc.

Next, we distributed the turkey sandwiches but carrying the boxes of bottles was beyond us so we returned home with them.

'Bloody long way to come to give away a dozen blankets and a picnic,' my father remarked irritably as we halted at the vehicular ferry pier.

'Shut up, Ken,' my mother said tartly and, curling up on the back seat, promptly fell asleep.

My father and I settled down to drink the tonic and wait at the car ramp for the next ferry departure, scheduled for two o'clock.

The following day, the full extent of the fire was broadcast on the radio. Ten thousand huts over an area of forty-five acres had been totally destroyed; sixty thousand people had been made homeless. The blaze, which had developed into a fire storm, had reached such high temperatures that aluminium cooking vessels had been completely burnt away. Incredibly, no-one was killed. This prompted the conjecture that the fire had been set deliberately to force the government into speeding up the squatter re-housing and rehabilitation programme. If this were the case, it worked. Within a year, the site of the Shek Kip Mei blaze was a brand-new refugee housing estate.

In weeks I had become more or less *au fait* with the geography of the Peak. The path I had taken that first day was called Governor's Walk. The near conical mountain was called *Sai Ko Shan* (or, in English, High West), *shan* meaning mountain. I attempted to climb it but it was too steep for me. At its base was a rifle range where I collected deformed .303 bullets, digging them out of the butts with my penknife.

To reach the rifle range, I had to take what must be one of the most spectacular walks on earth. It began – and ended – at the foot of Mount Austin Road and circumnavigated the Peak.

I would always set off clockwise, walking beneath over-hanging trees alive with butterflies and the birds that ate them, passing a waterfall and arriving at the place where the soldiers lay down to shoot across a valley at the butts. On one occasion, my walk was halted by a police barrier. A young woman had been murdered on the shooting platform, which I thereafter avoided for fear of ghosts.

After visiting the butts, my pocket full of spent ordnance, I carried on around the mountain. At first, the road wound its way by several houses, one of which was empty because no servants would work there. It was, according to Wong, haunted by the spirits of previous amahs who had been raped and murdered there by Japanese troops in 1942. A short distance further on, the road narrowed and became unsuitable for vehicles.

Holding more or less to the same contour, it continued around the mountain, sometimes as a viaduct, at others cut into the rock. Bit by bit, an incredible vista unfolded, first the western harbour approaches with merchant vessels awaiting a docking berth or discharging cargo into junks and flat barges called lighters. In the distance was Stone-cutters' Island, a military signals base. Further on, Kowloon came into sight, the peninsula crammed with buildings, ships lying along the jetties, ferries ploughing across to the island, walla-walla boats little more than aquatic insects. In another hundred yards, the central business district and the eastern suburbs came into view, the lower slopes of the hills dotted with houses and the red-brick block of the Bowen Road military hospital. Beyond Kowloon were the nine dragon hills.

Yet it was not the view that captivated me. I took that for granted. My bedroom window afforded me the same panorama. It was the sound. At first, I did not hear it but, gradually, it impinged itself upon me. It was a faint humming noise, as a wild bee hive might make. One weekend, walking the two roads with my mother, I asked her if she could hear it.

'Oh, yes,' she said, 'I can hear it. Do you know what it is?'

'It's the city,' I replied, surprised that she did not realize it.

'No,' she answered, 'it's the sound of a million people working hard.'

Halfway down the western flank of the Peak, on a promontory 1,100 feet above sea level and approached by a cracked and overgrown concrete track called Hatton Road, was a large gun emplacement known as Pinewood Battery. During the war, it had been equipped with two 3-inch anti-aircraft guns but had been destroyed on the morning of 15 December 1941, during the battle for Hong Kong. The gun platforms still existed, as did the subterranean block houses, the command post, ammunition bunkers and sleeping quarters. The concrete walls of the buildings were still decorated with their camouflage paint, whilst in the sleeping quarters, the metal-frame bunk beds remained standing, the remnants of palliasses draped upon them.

Pinewood was a special place for me. The ruins were a purpose-built adventure playground in which a few friends and I could enact the Japanese storming it and the British defending it, the latter always winning in strict contradiction of history. Yet it was when I went there alone that it was the most exciting. Just walking down to the battery made my spine creep and the hair on my neck rise. A man had died there during the four-hour-long bombardment of 15 December. Now, it was as if his ghost

GWEILO

still inhabited the place, rode the breezes coming up the mountain, sighed in the stunted pine trees and whispered in the azalea bushes.

I would sit on one of the emplacement walls and watch the ferries far below me, heading for Lan Tau or Lamma islands or the smaller outlying islands of Cheung Chau and Peng Chau. They carefully avoided Green Island directly in front of me where, as red warning notices on the shore stated, Hong Kong stored its explosives. Only fishing sampans risked passing through Sulphur Channel between Green and Hong Kong islands. The shoreline was strewn with treacherous rocks, the currents fast and unreliable.

Tiring of the view, I would then start hunting for wartime relics. Most of all, I wanted a British cap badge or uniform button. The battery had been manned by Indian Army troops when it fell and a Rajput regimental emblem would have been a find indeed. My wish list also included a Japanese shell from a Zero fighter – I was sure the place must have been strafed and knew that bullets hitting soft earth did not necessarily deform – machine-gun cartridge cases and, best of all, a shell case from one of the AA guns. What I actually found outdid the lot.

I was working through the low, dense scrub below the battery, about twenty yards out from the concrete skirt, when I came upon a piece of khaki material sticking up from the ground. Hoping it might be a fragment of discarded uniform with a button on it, I grabbed it and tugged. It was firmly embedded in the earth so I pulled harder. It would not shift. Kneeling, I set to work excavating it with my penknife. In less than a minute, I discovered the edge of a collar. Just beneath it was the smooth side of a skull, an eye socket filled with earth staring up at me.

232

Immediately, I knew what I had found and jumped backwards as if it had been a reared cobra, ready to strike. Scrambling through the undergrowth, I reached the battery, ran through it and headed up Hatton Road. It was a steep climb to Harlech Road. My legs ached as never before. I paused to gather my breath and wits and then ran on to the Peak Café where I asked someone to telephone the police for me.

An hour later, I was back at Pinewood with a dozen police officers and some coolies. They started to dig up the skeleton as I was asked questions by a British police officer who then took me home in a police car. My father was summoned from his office. I thought I was going to be for the high jump when he arrived, yet he was surprisingly mellow.

We were informed that the skeleton I had found was that of a Japanese soldier who had been shot in the back of the head. He had not, I was told, died in the war but afterwards, captured by local Chinese who had probably murdered him in retribution for what the Japanese had done to the local population.

'What's going to happen to him?' I asked. I toyed with the idea of asking if he had any badges on him but decided that was pushing my luck.

'His remains will be handed over to the Japanese authorities for return to Japan,' the police officer answered, 'where he can rest in peace.'

The next time I walked down Hatton Road, the hair on my neck did not prickle and I felt utterly alone.

This was not always the case during my Peak wanderings.

Whilst some of the mountain was covered in thick scrub, much of it was densely forested. Where there was a road, path or clearing, the fringes of the forest were heavily overgrown with plants seeking the sunlight but, under the canopy of the trees, the undergrowth was comparatively open. In this universe of dappled light existed creatures rarely seen.

The first wild animal I saw appeared fleetingly to me about a month after we moved to Mount Austin. It was early dusk and I was returning from the rifle range. A little way ahead of me, there was a rustle in the undergrowth and what I took to be a miniature deer stepped daintily out into full view. I froze.

Not much bigger than a large dog, it was reddish-brown in colour, had a short tail, two swept-back antlers and, to my astonishment, tusks. I was enchanted by it. The only other deer I had seen were in England, in the New Forest, where they seemed as tame as the feral ponies. This one was different. It was a truly wild animal that had chosen to show itself to me. Except for its disproportionately big ears, it too did not move: then it uttered a brief dog-like yelp and vanished.

'It must have been a muntjak,' my mother explained when I got home. 'They're also known as barking deer because their call is like a dog's yap. You were very lucky. Few people ever see one. They only come out at night.'

Discovering that such creatures existed, I started to explore the forests. Several evenings later, I saw a bushy-tailed, cat-sized animal appear quite suddenly out of a burrow. With a badger-like striped face, the rest of it was otherwise a nondescript brown. It stood at the burrow entrance, sniffed the air then, spinning round, vanished back down the way it had come. It did not reappear and I was later told it was a ferret badger.

I soon realized that entering the forest was pointless.

With the ground covered in dry leaves and twigs, walking silently would have been hard work for an experienced hunter, never mind me. The denizens of the forest could see, hear, smell and locate me long before I did them. Furthermore, most of them were nocturnal, and I could not stay out after dark.

At the bottom of the valley that dropped away to the south of Mount Austin was Pokfulam reservoir, the first ever built in Hong Kong to provide water for the embryonic city. As 1953 had been the driest year on record, by December and the school holidays the reservoir was very low indeed. This implied two things to me: first, that whatever lived in the valley would probably have to visit it to drink and, second, that whatever lived in the reservoir was now restricted to shallow water and therefore easily seen.

Supplied by Wong with a picnic lunch, I set off one Saturday morning and settled myself down on the cracked-mud periphery of the reservoir, as near as I dared to the water's edge and the soft mud. To my surprise, there were very few footprints pressed into the softer mud. I pondered this, found a stone and tossed it down to the water's edge. It struck the mud and disappeared with a sucking noise. The muntjak knew what I had not: the mud was quick. I shivered at the thought of what might have happened had I stepped another ten feet across the reservoir bottom. There was no-one about who would have heard my calls for help. I took up my picnic, left the mud and sat on the dam wall.

The water lay below me, as still and transparent as green bottle glass. I could make out every detail of the bottom. Schools of tiny fish occasionally darted by. A frog swam along. Suddenly, there was a large flurry of mud. It took a while to settle but I knew that something had put paid to the frog. As the water cleared, I noticed an oval outline in the mud about the size of a large meat-serving dish. Very slowly, it detached itself from the bottom and rose towards the surface, trailing mud that spiralled down from it. It was a grey-coloured turtle. From one end, a white and grey mottled head appeared, stretching out on a long neck which curved upwards towards me. It culminated in a prehensile nose that broke the surface for a moment before the head was retracted and the creature drifted back down to the mud. If I had not seen where it settled, I would never have known it was there.

Over the winter months, I also stumbled upon a pangolin feeding at an ants' nest in a wide crack in the concrete on Hatton Road, any number of giant African snails with shells the size of a whelk's, a dozing owl and, in a cave high up on the Peak, a colony of hibernating Japanese pipistrelle bats. Even the pangolin, normally nocturnal, paid me scant attention, feeding until I was almost upon it and even then just scurrying off.

Other encounters were not quite so benign.

The one warning my mother frequently issued was to beware of snakes. Hong Kong was home to over two dozen species of which at least four were venomous to man and potentially if not actually fatal. I kept an eye out for snakes but rarely saw one and, if I did, it was invariably heading away from me as fast as it might. Snakes in China appeared to know instinctively that there was a better than evens chance they might end up in a *wok*.

Walking to and from school, I daily passed along comically named Plunketts Road, at the side of which ran an open drain, or *nullah*, designed to shed heavy rainfall off the mountain as quickly as possible to prevent land-slides. One afternoon, taking the path beside it, I heard what sounded like a hissing water leak. As a main water line ran along the side of the *nullah* and the public was being exhorted to save water and report wastage, I exercised my civic duty and went to investigate. The *nullah* was about eighteen inches wide and two and a half feet deep, sloping downhill in a series of steps.

In it was a common rat snake. Approximately three feet long, it was dark brown for its entire length with no pattern. A fangless constrictor, I had seen them often enough in snake restaurants and had once watched as one crushed then swallowed a small bird on the Peak. This snake must have fallen into the smooth-sided *nullah* and could not get out. If it continued down the *nullah* it would reach a storm culvert and escape. If it headed uphill, it would arrive at several blocks of apartments and, I was certain, a place on the supper table in one of the servants' quarters. It was facing uphill.

A stick was needed to turn the snake. I found one of a sufficient length in the undergrowth, knelt down on the edge of the *nullah* and attempted to force the snake's head round to face the way to safety. I had given it a few prods when it reared up, spread its hood and spat at me.

This was no common rat snake. It was a cobra.

I recoiled, a smear of slimy venom on my shirt. Very carefully, so as not to touch it, I removed the garment and dropped it on the path. At this moment, two boys from my class arrived on the scene. We debated what to do. The primitive and illogical fear of snakes welled up in us. That cobras fed on rats and rats spread disease to humans was forgotten. This was the devil in serpent form, the creature that had tempted Adam – we had had Bible Studies in school – and seduced Eve, whatever that meant.

A decision was made. Like Stephen in the Bible, we would stone it to death.

Gathering as many large stones as we could find, we commenced hurling them at the snake. Some found their mark, most did not. All the while, the snake raised its head, the hood spread to show the black-and-white ghost-like pattern of a face on its surface.

We had been at this endeavour for five minutes or so when two coolies carrying poles over their shoulders came trotting down the hill. They looked over the edge of the *nullah*. The cobra seemed slightly wounded. One coolie dangled a coil of rope in front of the cobra's head. It struck at it then pressed its head to the *nullah* floor. The other coolie, signalling us to stand back, reached down into the *nullah*, grabbed the cobra by its tail, swung it up in the air and slammed it down on the concrete pathway. It was dead. They coiled it up, tied it with twine, hung it from one of their poles and set off down the hill. I walked home, ashamed that I had taken part in this assassination and vowing never to kill a snake again. Except in self defence.

My only other dangerous and somewhat farcical encounter occurred one evening on the Old Peak Road, a very steep footpath that wound down the mountain to the city below. Until the Second World War, it had been used extensively by sedan chairs and coolies but had fallen into disuse, the undergrowth on either side encroaching upon it, sometimes covering it completely. My reason for going down it was that someone had told me a Tokay gecko lived in the vicinity of the junction with Barker Road and was best seen at sunset when it appeared to go hunting.

The world's biggest gecko, at seven inches in length when fully grown, the Tokay gecko was spectacular, a light brown with red, white and black spots. Its call, a distinctive *tock-aye*, gave it its name. It was also very rare, mainly because it was a highly prized local entrée.

I had descended as far as Barker Road when I heard a noise behind me that sounded like someone rattling several half-empty boxes of matches. Turning, I found a fully grown porcupine coming at me in reverse, all its quills upright and a-quiver. I stood my ground, not thinking it would press home its advance. Yet it did, accelerating in my direction. I clapped my hands and shouted – to no avail. I fled. The porcupine, although not overhauling me, at least kept pace. The angle of ascent soon told on me. I slowed. The porcupine continued its attack. Moving backwards up a 1 in 3 slope seemed not to bother it. I found a new lease of fear and reached the level ground by the observation point. The porcupine stopped at the roadside and faced me. Now that I could see it clearly, it was huge, three feet long and bulky. Its nose was blunt, like a beaver's, its quills black and white. It shivered. The quills rattled. Then it was off, running clumsily down Harlech Road and into the twilight. It was only later that a Chinese friend of my mother's told me that porcupines could kill a leopard cat with their quills.

I was not only grateful to have avoided a leopard cat's fate but also glad no-one had witnessed the confrontation. The loss of face would have been mortifying.

There were only two ways to reach the top of the Peak, discounting walking up the Old Peak Road which would test the stamina of a marine. One was by car or bus, the other by the Peak Tram.

Built in 1888, this was the world's steepest funicular railway and it operated on the simplest of systems. A long and well-greased steel cable was wrapped around a massive drum in the engine house at the top. On each end was a tram car. As one travelled down the mountain, so the other rose up it. At the halfway point, the track divided in two so that the cars might pass each other. The only snag was that there were more stations in the lower half of the route than the upper. Consequently, when the lower car stopped at one of the stations, the upper car would halt in the middle of nowhere, surrounded by sub-tropical forest and birdsong.

The tram car was of unique design. Constructed of varnished wood on a steel frame and chassis, the uphill portion was an enclosed cabin. This was where Europeans or wealthy Chinese travelled. Other Chinese passengers, with the exception of baby amahs and their charges, were obliged to ride in the rear half which, although it was roofed, was otherwise open to the elements.

Whenever I could, I chose the rear portion. One just climbed on and sat down. There were no side walls, no restraining ropes, no safety bars. The only thing to hold on to was an armrest. Just before leaving the lower terminus on Garden Road, a tinny bell rang three times, there was a pause and the car edged forwards, running alongside a *nullah* and the Helena May Institute where, my mother frequently and convincingly but inaccurately remarked, Margot Fonteyn had taken her first ballet lesson. The single track then started to climb more steeply. To request it to stop, one pressed a labelled button; for boarding, one just put one's hand out to hail the brakeman.

All the while, the gradient increased. Above Bowen Road the angle of ascent was at least forty-five degrees. The May Road station, just below the halfway passing place, was at the steepest point. Here, when the car stopped, it yo-yo-ed alarmingly as the long steel cable flexed. Of necessity, it was elastic. This bouncing always set tourists chattering or American sailors chortling with alcohol-fuelled hilarity. Boarding or dismounting was difficult and one had to wait until the car stopped moving. Uphill from the May Road platform was a small signal box in which a man changed the points at the passing place. From here the tram car trundled steadily upwards, entering a cutting and turning a long bend in the middle of what was essentially sub-tropical jungle. This is where it would sometimes stop to accommodate the other car in a lower station. Huge butterflies would flit through the open rear, birds dance and jump in the tree branches. I once saw a small python sliding through the undergrowth, much to the frustration of my fellow amah and coolie passengers who could not disembark and catch it for the pot.

I grew blasé about the Peak Tram, for I took it as commonly as most people might a bus. The view, the harbour a backdrop at the top of the windows, the slopes of the Peak and the buildings apparently leaning back-wards at a bizarre angle, were everyday phenomena.

The comments made by the tourists and American sailors were as predictable as sunrise: 'Hey, you guys! You bin on the rides at Coney Island?' At a mid-jungle halt: 'OK! Y'all out 'n' push!' At the elastic stage: 'How many times you reckon this baby's snapped?' To the brakeman leaning on a dead man's handle, who spoke not a word of even pidgin English: 'Ya hold that baby real tight now, y'hear?' On any number of occasions, I was asked if I was the British Ambassador's son, to which I replied haughtily that Britain did not need a Hong Kong embassy because we owned the place.

The Peak Tram being one of Hong Kong's tourist attractions, it was also frequented by celebrities. I rode it with The Ink Spots, a famous black American jazz quartet; the film star Danny Kaye and the English actor Jon Pertwee who later became *Dr Who*. They never really impressed me: they were just people whose autographs my mother insisted I request. One day in 1954, however, was different. My mother met me after school at the Peak Tram terminus to take me down to the city. I forget why. As we waited for the next tram, a notice declared that Barker Road station was temporarily closed. When the car arrived, we boarded it, sitting in the open coolie section at my request, which was at the front of the car on its descent. My mother did not complain. It was a hot afternoon.

The tram set off. Barker Road station approached. It was thronged with people. A bright light switched on as we drew near. The car stopped in the station. Someone appeared briefly with a clapper board. Another called, 'Action!' A man in a light-coloured suit detached himself from the crowd, walked down the platform and entered the cabin. The tram set off. The powerful light switched off. My mother put her hand on mine. It was quivering.

'That's Clark Gable!' she whispered.

And it was. He was shooting a film called *Soldier of Fortune*.

She scrabbled in my school bag, took out an exercise

book, tore a page from it, fumbled in her handbag for a pen, then said the obvious.

'Martin, get his autograph.'

'You get his autograph.'

'I can't,' she fumed. 'I'm a grown up. You get it.'

'You tore a page out of my exercise book,' I complained. 'I'll get into trouble for that.'

'I'll square it with your teacher. Now get his autograph.'

'I don't want it.'

'He's one of the biggest film stars in the world.'

I remained unmoved. She grabbed my arm.

'Get his bloody autograph,' she threatened *sotto voce*, her lips tight. 'If you don't . . .'

'What if I do?' I parried. It seemed I might as well take advantage of the situation.

The Peak Tram reached May Road station and bounced on its cable for a minute. Clark Gable stood up, disembarked and walked off into a crowd of film people. The tram carried on down the mountain.

'Just for that,' my mother said peevishly, 'we're not going to Tkachenko's.' A thought then occurred to her. 'Maybe we'll be in the background as he got on.'

When it was released, we went to the cinema several times to see the film. We did not feature in it.

Apart from the vehicular ferry, and the walla-walla boats which were expensive, the only way to reach Hong Kong island from the mainland of Kowloon was by the Star Ferry, universally known as 'the ferry', which plied, every fifteen minutes for eighteen hours a day, across the mile-wide harbour from Tsim Sha Tsui to Central District, as the heart of Hong Kong's business world was called. As on the Peak Tram, the passengers were segregated, the wealthy and well-to-do – Chinese and European – travelling on the enclosed top deck, the rabble of coolies, amahs and others on the bottom – open to the elements – with their poles, boxes, bales and large, circular baskets of complaining chickens. To cross the harbour on the upper deck cost ten cents one way: the lower cost five.

I looked forward to taking the ferry. The craft would have to weave between warships at anchor, with Chinese women in rocking sampans painting the hulls or collecting the garbage. Cargo ships under a harbour pilot's control slid by like mobile cliffs of black metal, eager faces at open portholes. The ferry had to give way to sail and oar so it was common for it to slow to a crawl or change course mid-harbour to allow passage to an ocean-going junk in full sail heading for the open sea. On one occasion, the ferry on which I was riding had to stop for a massive junk flying the Communist Chinese flag and armed with two small cannon mounted on her stern. It really was a case of the eighteenth meeting the twentieth century.

Whilst the ferries themselves were perfectly safe, I had my doubts about the ferry piers. Constructed of a wooden deck on wooden piles, they creaked and swayed dizzily as a vessel came alongside. The piles screeched, the deck planking moaned like lost souls and everyone waiting to board swayed unsteadily. What was more toe-curling was the fact that there were gaps between the planks. Twice, I accidentally dropped my pocket money down them, only to see the coins hit the water below and sink without trace. Not that I would have accepted them back, for the harbour was notoriously dirty – the Kowloon sewers emptied into it – and, one day, pushing through a crowd of Chinese peering down through the cracks between the planks, I saw a dead coolie floating under the pier. He was face down, bare to the waist, his arms rising and falling with the rhythm of the wavelets. In the centre of his back, halfway down his spine, was a hole, washed clean of blood by the sea. I could see his vertebrae. Schools of small fish hovered around him. A small crab rode on his shoulder. According to the Radio Hong Kong news that evening, he had been murdered with a baling hook.

My mother and I frequently rode the bottom deck.

'Let's rough it,' she would say, approaching the coolie turnstile. 'See how the other half live.'

We boarded the ferry, the gangplank moving to and fro as the vessel rocked on the waves. There were few seats on the lower deck and, invariably, these were occupied by amahs who ran for them the minute they stepped on the deck. A running amah, dressed in her white jacket and black trousers, looked for all the world like an intoxicated penguin.

As the ferry set sail for the mile-long crossing, a mist of spume blew across the deck. Amahs carrying babies on their backs in cotton slings faced into the wind to protect their infants. Coolies removed the lengths of cloth they customarily wore like grubby cravats and rubbed their glistening muscles with them. My mother closed her eyes and let the spray cool her face. I, heedful of a bi-lingual notice on the bulkhead, watched out for pickpockets.

Another notice bluntly stated, *No Spitting*. The 'other half' had a habit of spitting to clear their throats of phlegm or catarrh. They also blew their noses by thumbing one nostril shut and then, leaning forward over the gutter, blowing hard. Consequently, it was commonplace to see gobs of pale green snot lying by the side of the road alongside cracked melon seed shells and chewed wedges of sugar cane. The concept of a handkerchief was alien to the Chinese. It seemed utterly ridiculous to them to blow one's nose then put the contents in one's pocket. Whilst spitting and hawking were disgusting habits, I had to agree with their logic and tried blowing my own nose in a similar fashion, yet I never mastered the knack. The snot came out all right but it dribbled as slime down to my lips and chin instead of flying free.

Once, I tried to get my father to see how the common man travelled on the ferry but he steadfastly refused. I asked why.

'If God had intended me to be a coolie,' he replied tersely, 'he'd've given me a bamboo pole.'

'But God doesn't give the coolies poles. They buy them.'

'It's a metaphor,' my father replied.

'What's a metaphor?' I answered.

'Do shut up, Martin,' was my father's response. 'Remember, it's better to keep your mouth closed and be thought a fool than open your mouth and prove it.'

I shut up, boarded the top deck and moved the seat back over so we were facing forwards. The seating was designed so that whichever way the ferry was going, one could face the direction of travel.

Several weeks later, I informed a guest at one of my parents' cocktail parties that a coolie's pole was called a metaphor. He kindly put me right and I vowed henceforth not to trust my father's sketchy knowledge of matters Oriental.

Although there was both the local and BBC World Service radio, and the cinema, I tended to make my own entertainment. My imagination was sharp and I had the whole of the Peak on which to ramble. As long as I kept clear of steep drops, rock faces and slippery surfaces, I was safe. No-one would molest me or accost me unless it was to pass the time of day. One of the constables who did duty in the police post took to engaging me in conversation. He was keen to learn English in order, I presumed, to get a red number flash on his shoulder, which indicated he was reasonably fluent in it. Everyone else I met would greet me, from the coolies carrying massive sacks suspended from their poles to the briefcase-toting *taipans* walking down in the damp morning mist to the Peak Tram.

One elderly European, always dressed in a grey suit with a gold watch chain, would be carried to the Peak Tram in a sedan chair, probably the last to be used in Hong Kong. It was a curious-looking contraption, a sort of mockery of an ecclesiastical throne made out of dark varnished rattan. If it was raining, the rattan was encased in a black custom-made canvas cover. The square roof, rather like those found on small shrines, was curled at the corners. Supported on two long bamboo poles, the chair was carried by two coolies. They had to walk in step to prevent their passenger rocking from side to side. At each step, the rattan creaked rhythmically, the occupant moving slightly up and down as the poles bent. Arriving at the Peak Tram terminus, the coolies knelt on the road, the rear coolie first, and lowered the poles. Their passenger stepped out and, without a word to the two men who had just transported him, walked off to catch the tram. He would, however, greet everyone else who was not Chinese, including me, with a gruff, almost begrudging, good morning. The Chinese he ignored as if they were made of vapour.

This I considered the height of ill manners and was of a mind to address the man on the subject, but he carried a gold-topped cane and I knew, from experience at home, what that could do to my buttocks or the backs of my thighs. And, on the other hand, the coolies seemed inured to his rudeness. Once, I followed them to see if I could have a ride and find out where they spent their day, but they disappeared through an imposing gate which was closed behind them. They were not for hire.

Public entertainment was limited, not through any law but because most people were too busy earning a living. Yet every Chinese New Year, temporary stages were erected on waste ground around Hong Kong for the presentation of Chinese operas.

The stages were marvels of Oriental ingenuity. Made of thousands of bamboo poles lashed together with strips of the same material, they could be a hundred feet wide, forty deep, fully roofed with canvas or *atap* panels and equipped with electric lights. The audience remained in the open, unprotected from the elements. Rather like the theatre in Shakespeare's day, the clientele talked, drank, ate (even cooked) during the performance, which could last six hours. The actors dressed in flamboyant classical Chinese costumes in primary colours and wore heavy, stylized make-up. They sang in very high-pitched voices, their movements exaggerated and carefully choreographed.

I enjoyed these spectacles, but not for too long. The falsetto singing prompted a headache in fifteen minutes and a migraine in thirty. What six hours would do beggared even my imagination. What I really enjoyed were the fights. Swords, pikestaffs and other weapons of bodily pain and torture were flashed and swung, the combatants whirling and ducking, thrusting and slicing while all the time the orchestra was going frantic, cymbals clashing as swords met, gongs booming when the main protagonists struck each other a mortal blow. It was controlled mayhem and I loved it.

Bedlam could also be experienced, admittedly for a shorter period, at my favourite entertainment venue, The China Fleet Club in Wanchai, an infamous area of tenements, cheap hotels, tattoo parlours, Triad gangsters, bars and bordellos. It was the land of Suzie Wong.

Close to the naval dockyard, The China Fleet Club was a social club established, as the title page of its programme proudly stated, *with funds contributed by the men of the lower deck – to whom this club belongs*. It was operated by Royal Navy sailors for their comrades and incorporated several bars, a restaurant, sleeping accommodation, a barber's shop, billiards room and a cinema. As the offspring of a parent attached to the armed forces, albeit as a civilian worker, I was permitted to go to the club cinema for Saturday matinées.

The main feature seldom interested me. What I went for were the cartoon preliminaries, and one in particular – *Tom and Jerry*. I was not alone. Sailors, many of them hung-over from a night on the Wanchai tiles, crammed into the seats, jostling, arm-punching and ribbing each other. As soon as the lights went down, the National Anthem was played. They all stood up. It ended. They sat down and the noise and kerfuffle began again. The screen came alive with the Pathé news. For this, the audience fell silent. Newsreels showed the colonial uprisings Britain was facing – Cyprus, Kenya, Malaya – soldiers fighting, struggling through jungle, advancing through rubber plantations or sun-baked rocky hills, dying. The screen went black. For a minute or two, the memory of the pictures of war kept the peace. Then someone would shout out.

'Where's Fred?'

Other voices would join in.

'Give us Fred!'

'We want Fred! We want Fred!'

Feet would start to stamp, hands clap and mouths hoot like owls or bay like wolves.

If the screen lit up with a Donald Duck or Woody the Woodpecker cartoon, all hell would break loose. The floor would vibrate as if an army were marching over it, the air thick with whistles and indignation. If, however, the cartoon was *Tom and Jerry*, the sailors would fall silent until the captions gave the name of the producer, then they all yelled 'Good old Fred!' in unison. The producer's name was Fred Quimby. Throughout the cartoon, guttural, masculine, lower-deck mess laughter greeted every twist in the tale.

About noon, after the matinée ended, I sometimes strolled through Wanchai, passing the bars with their bamboo bead curtains, young women standing in the doorways with bottles of Coke, smoking Lucky Strikes. Once or twice, I tried to enter one of these bars but was rebuffed by the girls at the door, never mind the barmen within. Either they were brusque and ordered me out, sometimes all but manhandling me to the door, or they accepted my presence, asking me if I *wanted jig-a-jig*, which sent everyone but myself into paroxysms of hilarity. I thought it all a bit of a liberty. I meant no harm, only wanted a drink and a bit of conversation but found myself either an outcast or the butt of incomprehensible humour. What was more, they all touched my hair. I gave them luck. Yet they would not so much as sell me a Green Spot. It was some years before I understood how the young women in the beaded curtain doorways of Wanchai made their living.

This aside, Wanchai did not appeal to me. The streets were sombre and lacked the vivacity of the rest of Hong Kong. Certainly, they were usually crowded, but there were few *dai pai dongs*, the streets were laid out in a severe, American-style grid pattern, the newer buildings square and characterless concrete blocks. There were no dried prawn or fish shops, no vendors of preserved eggs or rice, no little temples tucked away in back streets.

I mentioned to my mother that Wanchai seemed to lack soul.

'Maybe it's because it's on reclaimed land,' she remarked.

'Reclaimed land?'

'They knock a mountain down, pour it into the sea, let it settle and then build on it. Hong Kong hasn't got much land space, so they make more of it in this way.'

I could only wonder how they knocked down a mountain.

From the time my mother's mother was widowed in 1947, she had not left Portsmouth or, save to go to the shops, her tiny terraced house, and was living on a very meagre state pension. To give her a much needed holiday, my parents arranged for her to visit us, 'indulging' on an RFA vessel.

'Indulgence' was a quaint military arrangement dating back to the days when naval spouses accompanied their husbands aboard ship. By 1953, it meant that, if there was a spare cabin on a ship, it could be rented to a close relative of a serving officer for a nominal sum. The passenger had to take pot luck, however: departure and arrival dates were speculative. If the vessel was diverted *en route*, the passenger went with it. It was a potential military magical mystery tour.

My mother decided it would be best if my grandmother visited in the spring. She was sixty-four and it was considered that she would find the heat and humidity of the high summer debilitating. A request was put in to the Admiralty in London and my grandmother was found a berth upon the RFA *Bacchus*, a tiny, shallow-draft ship with a crew of about forty, which had been built as a sea water distilling vessel but was now used as a freighter carrying naval stores. My grandmother was listed on the ship's manifest as super-cargo.

The *Bacchus* arrived alongside HMS *Tamar* on the morning of 14 March 1954. My grandmother walked unsteadily down the gangplank, holding on to both side ropes. She looked a lot older and more frail than when I had seen her last. She was wearing a dark blue dress, a cardigan, an overcoat and heavy, flat shoes. Even her leather handbag looked cumbersome. All the elderly women I had met in Hong Kong – even my headmistress – dressed in light clothing, in bright colours, and walked with a spring in their step.

'Nanny's not sick, is she?' I enquired of my father as my mother ran to the foot of the gangplank, tripping like a little girl and embracing her mother.

'No,' replied my father, who intensely disliked his

mother-in-law. 'She's as fit as an old fiddle.' I detected a slight hint of wishful thinking.

'But she looks so old and ill,' I said.

'That's what England does to you,' he retorted bitterly.

For all his imperial, monarchist jingoism, my father loathed Britain – 'the lousy benighted weather . . . the bloody taxes . . . the blithering idiots running the unions . . . the bloody strikes . . . the blithering idiots running the government, the country . . .' – with a vengeance and yet he never felt really at home in Hong Kong.

Later that day, as my grandmother unpacked her suitcase, I related our brief conversation to my mother.

'Nanny's not ill,' she told me, 'but she's very tired. Living in England is not easy . . .' Her voice trailed off and she kissed me. 'Be nice to Nanny. She's had a rough time of it since Dan-Dan died.'

Staying for just under three weeks, my grandmother's time was filled with cocktail parties, Chinese banquets, shopping outings (which bedazzled her, coming from utilitarian Britain) and a drive round the New Territories, on which there was a near replay of my father's encounter with the duck farmer incident, this time involving a man with two huge sway-backed pigs, who refused to chivvy them on to the grass verge. I showed my grandmother the ancient Dragon Inn tortoise whilst the Dragon Inn monkey showed us a sizeable and bright pink erection which brought tears of mirth to my grandmother's eyes. My mother also took her in a rickshaw to Hing Loon where Mr Chan gave her a beer and she bought a string of pearls, to tea in the Pen (with sufficient funds this time), to Mr Chuk's establishment for new clothes, to the United Services Recreation Club for lunch, to the dockyard mess for dinner. It was a social whirl the likes of which my grandmother had never known.

One afternoon's excursion was to the Tiger Balm Gardens. These had been created in the 1930s by a Chinese multi-millionaire called Aw Boon Haw who had made his fortune from inventing and manufacturing Tiger Balm. What my grandmother had expected – as, indeed, had I – was a formal garden of flowerbeds, fountains, trees, lawns and notices keeping visitors off the grass. Instead, paths wound through rock grottoes, passing caves hacked out of the mountainside. Each cave housed a fantastical tableau featuring life-sized figures fashioned out of plaster or concrete and painted in garish colours. What made these tableaux even more bizarre was the fact that many of them depicted men being cast into Hell, their stomachs ripped open, their hands cut off, the stumps of their wrists scarlet with blood, as well as executions and scenes of the most vile torture imaginable. In one, a man was being consumed by a tiger, his face contorted with pain.

'Why do they want to portray such beastly happenings?' my grandmother mused.

My mother shrugged and said, 'I suppose they're a warning of what will happen if you stray from the straight and narrow. And the Chinese can be a very brutal people.'

'And you've chosen to live amongst these people?' my grandmother finally asked, passing a larger-than-life statue of a man with a dog's head and huge ears.

'Don't be silly, Mum,' my mother retorted. 'All mankind's like that. Think of the Germans and the concentration camps. Think of the Brandenburg PoW camp Dad was held in during the first war.'

'I don't choose to live in Germany,' my grandmother replied tersely.

Towering over the gardens, and an opulent mansion once the home of Aw Boon Haw, was an exquisite white pagoda. Seven storeys high, it was visible from virtually anywhere in the harbour.

'And look at that,' my grandmother continued. 'Such beauty next to such an abhorrence.'

'Maybe that's to emphasize how beautiful life can be if you don't sin,' my mother suggested.

My mother greatly enjoyed sharing her colonial life with her mother. It was not that she wanted to brag about her new existence, in which she felt so at ease, but that she wanted to share it with someone she loved. For my father, Hong Kong was just another place in which to work: he might just as well have been posted to a supplies office in Chatham as China.

I too revelled in showing my grandmother the Hong Kong I knew. Walking round Harlech and Lugard roads, I was quick to point out a butterfly, a blue-tailed skink, a giant snail. I took her to the rifle range and dug out a bullet for her. It had been my intention to take her to Pinewood Battery, but the walk was too much for her. I also took her on the Peak Tram, sitting in the open section. To my surprise, this frightened her. My parents drew the line at my taking her to eat out at a *dai pai dong*.

My grandmother's brief visit made me aware of how much I had changed. Sitting beside her on a bench along Harlech Road one afternoon, I recalled my life 'back home' in England, the cinder playground at Rose Valley School, the compost heap at the bottom of our garden which was my castle, the antiquated tractor that drew the gang mower on the nearby playing fields, the incessantly grey skies and that damp dog smell of drizzle-sodden pullovers. When a coolie trotted by and I returned his greeting in Cantonese, and my grandmother commented that I was now 'a proper little Chinese boy', I felt strangely proud. This was, I now understood, where I wanted to be. For me, 'back home' meant an apartment on the Peak with a world-famous view, not a semi-detached at the end of a cul-de-sac on the eastern fringes of London.

When the time came for my grandmother to depart, my mother was sad yet her mother was, I am sure, perplexed. She had arrived in Hong Kong to discover her daughter and grandson had in her eyes 'gone native' in all but clothing – and, even then, my mother occasionally wore a brocade cheongsam with modest side slits as a cocktail dress. It was light blue with pale green bamboo designs upon it, finches perching on the stems. I felt full of pride seeing her wear it. Most European women looked like a sack of sago pudding in a Chinese dress, with prominent bulges where there should most definitely not have been any, but my mother was petite, lithe and slim and fitted such clothing better than most *gweipor*.

I imagine that my grandmother realized, as the ship edged away from the dock, that she would rarely see her only child and grandchild again. Such was the lot of the colonial family whose existence was punctuated by partings. She knew that she was condemned to a lonely widowhood, looking out for the postman delivering a blue aerogramme or an envelope with exotic stamps upon it.

As the months went by, I came to learn a great deal more about the Peak, which for many years had been exclusively set aside as a European residential area. No Chinese was permitted to buy, rent or live there and the only Chinese allowed access were those who served the Europeans. By the time we lived there this law had been relaxed, but one clause, which forbade a Chinese from owning or operating a business on the Peak, was still in force.

There was, however, one exception to it. A Chinese lady owned and ran the café opposite the Peak Tram terminus.

A low, single-storey stone building with a tiled roof, originally erected in 1901 as a shelter for the sedan chair and rickshaw coolies, the Peak Café was an unpretentious place consisting of one large dining room under a roof criss-crossed with old wooden beams. The menu was un-assuming, offering toast (naturally), sandwiches and eggs and bacon as well as Chinese food, soft drinks, sundaes, beer and tea and coffee, ice-creams and popsicles. The latter could also be purchased from itinerant Dairy Farm ice-cream sellers riding silver-painted bicycles with cold boxes mounted over the front wheel. The popsicles were made in fruit flavours as well as milk, soya milk and red bean paste, which looked enticing but was an acquired taste which I never acquired.

Every day during term time, my mother gave me a dollar bill with which to buy a drink on my way back from school. The temperature was often in the eighties Fahrenheit, the heat bouncing off the mirage-liquid road surface, so I frequently forewent a Coke and had two ten-cent 'popsies' instead, thereby saving eighty cents a day. However, by artful manipulation of human character, I was frequently able to save the money completely.

Although the Korean War was all but over, Hong Kong was still experiencing a very large through-put of military personnel, especially Americans. Like all tourists, they would head up the Peak Tram to marvel at the view.

The Peak Café did a roaring trade when the US fleet was in. As soon as the sailors had taken in the panorama, they seemed programmed to need a beer and there was only one place to go. Yet before they could order a bottle of the local San Miguel beer, I would ambush them, leaning on the wall by the entrance to the café and panting with thirst. My face would be conveniently flushed from the heat and the walk from my school, my shirt sticking to my back. Within a few minutes, an American sailor would pause at my side and say something like, 'Hey, kid! How ya doin'?'

'Tuckered,' I would reply, using a word picked up in the Fourseas with which they would be familiar. I wiped my brow with my forearm.

'Sure is hot! Ya wanna Coke, kid?'

And I was in, seated at a table under a ceiling fan with a condensation-coated bottle of Coke, a waxed straw and the dollar bill still secure in my pocket. Our conversation ranged widely. They wanted to know where I came from, where I lived, what my father did for a job and had I any big sisters. These preliminaries over, they would embark upon their own life stories. I listened avidly. The sailors came from all over America, from every background. A black sailor told me how his grandfather had been a slave. A lieutenant – he pronounced it *lootenant* – from New York made me believe he was the son of a gangster. A Texan remembered the *corrida* and the *remuda*, and pined for the open range. Many may have told me tall stories, but I came to appreciate that a man may tell a stranger far more than he could his best friend.

This was not my only lesson in human nature. Ordinary sailors and non-commissioned officers were far more generous than commissioned officers who were usually only good for a drink – if that. Americans were by far the most generous. Next came the Australians, then Canadians and, finally, the British, who ignored me. No army squaddie ever offered me so much as a glass of water.

My sojourns at the Peak Café came to an abrupt end one day when the proprietor came out and shoo-ed me away.

'You no good boy,' she criticized me in very competent English. 'You like a beggar, always hanging round to get something from the sailors.' She shook her finger at me. 'But no more. You come here again, I tell your mother. I know where you live,' she threatened unnecessarily. The Peak community was not much more than a few thousand people and most of them used the Peak Tram on a very frequent basis. Accosting my mother would have been easy.

I apologized to her in Cantonese and thereafter took to buying a drink or a ten-cent popsy, if I needed one, from one of the bicycle vendors. She lost out on my custom yet I had saved over forty dollars in two terms.

My father's principal hobby, as my mother frequently declared with no small display of chagrin, was sleeping. He would return from the office at noon on Saturday and then, except for meals, the BBC World News and to replenish his glass of whisky or pink gin, he would essentially stay in bed until Monday morning. At first, my mother tried hard to get him to take an interest in life outside his work, but without success. On only a few occasions did he surrender to my mother's sense of adventure.

One of these was her desire to visit Sunshine Island, or Chow Kung Chau. To reach it, one had to take a ferry to Peng Chau then hire a *kai doh*, a sampan with a hunchbacked old woman and a long oar or a superannuated walla-walla past its best. Audacious my mother may have been but to risk life and limb drifting without a walkie-talkie in the open sea, towards a Communist Chinese-held shore, was another matter.

However, one winter Sunday, a naval launch was requisitioned by a party of my father's dockyard colleagues to visit Sunshine Island and have a picnic. Or so I was informed ...

A hilly island about three-quarters of a mile long by a third wide, Sunshine Island had been settled by a few farmers, fishermen and, in the nineteenth century, pirates, but abandoned since 1941. It was now home to two European families, one headed by an eccentric, the other by a China Hand driven by God to help his fellow man.

I was reluctant to go but my mother persuaded me with embroidered tales of the pirates. My father was enticed along by the prospect of being on a boat, which brought out the sailor in him.

At the appointed time, we stepped on to the launch in the dockyard basin and cast off. The harbour was fairly calm but we had to cross open sea which was choppy. One or two of our party of fifteen started to look green about the gills but managed to retain the coffee and biscuits that were served as we rounded Green Island.

My mother, dressed in an old shirt of my father's, a large pullover and a pair of jeans, enjoyed the crossing, as did my father, who, wearing a pair of neatly creased trousers with a cravat at his throat, persuaded the Chinese coxswain to relinquish the wheel to him once we were out of the harbour. The coxswain, assuming a naval *gweilo* would be familiar with the manoeuvring of a launch, agreed but soon regretted it when he noticed my father was heading straight for the wrong island. Not having the courage to admonish him, the coxswain mentioned it to Alec Borrie, a thin, tall, friendly man who was not only the trip's organizer but also my father's divisional superior – his Old Man.

'I think we need to go a few degrees to port, Ken,' he said quietly. 'You're on a heading for Peng Chau.'

My father looked extremely sheepish and altered course. A few minutes later, he surrendered the wheel once more to the coxswain and busied himself with his binoculars.

I noticed on these occasions that my father was often left out of the conversation and he seldom sought to join in. Sometimes, I felt sorry for him and wanted to go over and talk to him but, at the last moment, I would decide against it, knowing that I would be put down, dismissed or derided.

An hour out, we swung in to a small beach on the leeward side of a windswept, treeless island. The coxswain ran the bow of the launch up on the shore and a crew member sent out a gangplank. Boxes were unloaded and placed at the top of the beach. We all then went ashore and the launch reversed away. I felt marooned.

Carrying our boxes, we set off along a hint of a footpath across the island, coming first to an *atap*, a wood and straw hut. This was the home of Jack Shepherd, aka Jonathan Sly, of whom I had read in the newspaper. Formerly one of the managers of the Kowloon YMCA, he now lived with his wife in this hovel, making a meagre living writing

short stories for the local press. As we drew near, he
appeared at the door. Skinny, with short hair and a trim
beard, he was barefoot and wearing an ordinary shirt with
a dark blue Chinese padded silk jacket. Wrapped around
his waist was a multi-hued Malay *sarong*. This was a man
who had really 'gone native'. Compared to him, I thought,
the Queen of Kowloon was verging on normality. He
greeted us in a gruff, monosyllabic voice and closed the
door.

My father looked disparagingly at the figure as it disappeared.

'He's certainly letting the side down,' he remarked to
no-one in particular. 'Thank God he's doing it out of
sight.'

'Frankly,' piped up one of the women who had overheard him, 'I think individuality is a trait to be encouraged.'

My father was about to remonstrate but my mother got
him first.

'You do realize, don't you, Ken,' she said, looking pointedly at his feet, 'that you've got on one of your best pairs of
shoes? I hope you've got some others with you,' she added,
knowing full well he had not.

'Standards,' he responded, glancing at what the rest of
us were wearing. 'I'm not wearing pumps or clodhoppers.
Or jeans trousers, come to that,' he added: there had been
an argument over those before we left the apartment.

'On your own head be it, Ken.' My mother shrugged.

My father, determined to have the last word, said, 'This
isn't the Western Front, Joyce.'

'I don't think our brave Tommies in either war wore
denim jeans,' my mother retorted, grabbing the last word
for herself.

My father silenced, we walked on, descending into

the valley between the two hills where more *atap* huts stood amid some newly tilled plots. This, my mother informed me, was the home and dream-child of a remarkable Christian activist called Gus Borgeest.

Like so many in Hong Kong, Borgeest, his Chinese wife and their small daughter had arrived in 1951 as penniless refugees, in their case from Hangzhou. A Quaker, he was a humanist, which is what had endeared him to my mother who was not religiously inclined at all. At first, Borgeest had worked for the Hong Kong government social services department and came to appreciate first-hand the plight of the thousands of squatters and streetsleepers. It dawned on him that many had been farmers in China who had lost their land and livelihoods to communization. In them, he reasoned, was a workforce that merely required a chance to rise up above poverty and contribute to society.

Agricultural land being at a premium in Hong Kong, Borgeest turned his attention to the outlying islands. Chow Kung Chau provided what he required. He took out a lease upon it from the government at an annual rent of $180, less than the average servant's monthly wage, moving there and renaming it Sunshine Island. By the time we walked into the valley, the embryonic community consisted of the Borgeests, two Chinese associates and several families of impoverished Chinese farmers.

We were all introduced to Borgeest and given a short talk on his aims and ambitions. This over, we were taken on a quick tour of the centre of the island, interrupted by such expressions as 'Here will be the piggery' or 'This is the site of the fish ponds'. All I could see was a bleak, rock-strewn, grassy hillside with, here and there, plots marked out with white-painted stakes.

Pondering on the contents of the picnic, not to mention evidence of the pirates' occupation, my day-dreaming was interrupted when two of the launch crew strode over the crest of the hill carrying shining new hoes, spades, forks and other implements of manual labour.

They put them down and returned to the launch. Mr Borrie assumed charge and briskly divided us into work parties. It was then I realized my mother had brought me to the island under false pretences. I spent the remainder of the day helping to dig a ditch, carting the soil away in a bucket. The only relief from this toil was a sparse supply of sandwiches and a bottle of lukewarm Coke. We left the island at five o'clock. My back ached, my arms and legs were sore, I had a blister on my palm the size of a ten-cent coin and another to match on my heel, which had burst.

'The strain of honest toil,' my mother remarked, rubbing the base of her spine as we waited for my father, who was limping, to bring the car. He had spent the afternoon in charge of a wheelbarrow. 'Doesn't it make you feel good?'

'No,' I replied pointedly. It was not just that my every muscle ached. I had been duped by talk of piracy into becoming a forced labourer. 'And I didn't see any trace of pirates.'

'But think of the good you've done. You've helped those far less fortunate than yourself to start rebuilding their lives.'

Put that way, I felt smugly self-righteous.

'You have to realize this,' my mother continued. 'We do not own Hong Kong. It's a crown colony. We merely administer it. A hundred and something years ago, we stole this land from the Chinese. Because of that, we owe an obligation to the people who live here. And think.

Many of them have fled here from Communism. They are refugees. We must help them. In a tiny way, that's what you've done today. And,' she went on, 'even if you don't agree with me, at least we've ruined a pair of your father's best shoes.'

She put her arm round me and gave me a hug. It hurt.

I began to range further afield than the Peak. My mother's life was filled with Cantonese classes and her usual daily social whirl. My father, of course, was engaged in his office, often not returning until well into the evening.

Having been rebuffed from Wanchai, I decided to head in the opposite direction and see what Western District had to offer.

The oldest part of the city, it clung to the lower slopes of the Peak beneath an almost sheer rock face that glistened with water in all but the hottest and driest of summers. Many of the streets were narrow, built for coolie rather than car traffic, whilst many of those that ran north to south up the mountainside consisted of steps. Those vehicular roads that ran parallel to them were very steep indeed with sharp corners that tested many a clutch and burnt out not a few. The ladder streets, as the stepped thoroughfares were called, tested the calf muscles. Along all the streets, the buildings were ancient, some a century old, with ornate balconies from which projected the ubiquitous bamboo poles of dripping, freshly laundered clothes or from which hung tresses of plants. Some were almost entirely hidden by garishly painted shop signs hanging out over the pavement.

My first visit to the area was prompted by my wish to see a famous temple which stood on the curiously named Hollywood Road. Claiming to be the son of a guest, I acquired a tourist-guide map from the concierge of a hotel and made my way along Queen's Road West. At first, the buildings were modern office blocks and stores but, gradually, as if by some strange natural metamorphosis, they changed into narrow nineteenth-century buildings.

Dodging coolies slogging up the ladder streets with full loads hanging from their poles, I reached the temple. It was roofed in green-glazed tiles with a decorated ridge of warriors, gods, dragons and demons. I stepped into the forecourt to be surrounded by a gaggle of wizened crones, with arms outstretched for *kumshaw*. My claim that I had no money – indeed, I only had my Peak Tram fare and enough for a drink – cut no ice with them. I was a *gweilo*. *Gweilos* were rich. They closed ranks. A few hands tugged at my shirt. Then one of them tentatively touched my hair, much as one might risk a quick stroke of a dog the temperament of which one was not quite sure. Seeing I did not react, they all started touching my head, giggling and cackling and wheezing amongst themselves.

I gave them a minute to build up their stock of good fortune, which, by their appearance, was pretty reduced, then, extricating myself from their company, entered the temple through two massive red-painted wooden doors.

Inside, it was sumptuous, rich scarlet banners hanging down with thick, black, dramatic characters upon them. The altar was pristine and the deities most impressive. On the right, just inside the door, sat an old man selling joss-sticks and candles: on the left were a table of *lai see* packets and some shelves of dusty books. The air was heavy with incense smoke. Apart from its grandeur, however, it was no different from any other temple I had visited.

I was about to leave when a voice asked, 'Do you like it?'

Turning, I came face to face with an elderly Chinese man wearing a long black robe to his ankles and a skull cap with a red button on the top. He sported a wispy beard and, in one hand, he held a closed fan. He resembled a character from a biography of Confucius. I just stared at him, dumbstruck, sure that he was either an apparition or a wizard.

'Can you not speak?' he went on. He spoke slowly, pronouncing each word exactly, as if imitating a teacher.

'Yes,' I stammered, 'and I like the temple very much.'

'But do you understand it?'

I shook my head and answered, 'No, sir. Not really.'

'So I will teach you.'

He led me up to the altar, joss-stick ash falling from one of the spiral coils hanging from the roof beams. This he brushed off with his fan which he then flicked open, quivering it in front of his face like the half wing of a huge black butterfly.

'This temple', he enunciated slowly, 'is called the Man Mo temple. Man means literature and Mo means war. As you can see, there are two gods. Man Cheung, the god of literature, wears a green robe and Kwan Yu, who is also called Kwan Ti, wears a red robe. He is the god of war.'

I gazed up at their faces. They were powerful but impassive.

'Kwan Yu', the man went on, 'was a real man. He lived two thousand years ago in the time of the Han dynasty when he was a general in the emperor's army. Now he is the saint of brotherhoods, especially policemen and gangsters.'

That cops and robbers worshipped the same god seemed obtuse in the extreme but I made no comment. China was, I had learnt well, a land of extremes and contradictions.

'Who is Man Cheung the saint of?' I asked.

'He is the god of civil servants,' the old man answered.

I bit my cheek to stop myself laughing. The thought that my father had a god looking specifically over him and his kind was too much to bear.

The elderly man then showed me the side altar to Pao Kung, the black-faced god of justice, and, to the right, that of Shing Wong, the god of the city. Elsewhere were several heavy sedan chairs used in religious processions, a huge bronze temple bell shaped like an inverted tulip and a massive drum.

'Now I must pay my respects,' the old man announced.

He walked unsteadily to the altar and bowed to the god of literature. I left the temple, wondering who he might be. He looked like one of the letter writers at the Tin Hau temple in Yau Ma Tei yet there was somehow something more to him. He seemed to have the bearing of a learned man, rather than one who merely took down coolies' dictation. Who – or what – he really was I would never know. Perhaps he was a phantom after all.

Now that I had achieved my aim of finding the temple, I dropped the map in a drain grid. From here on, I was to wander without direction, discovering what I could. It was like being an explorer.

For two hours, I sauntered through the streets where Hong Kong had first begun, at least as far as the *gweilo* population was concerned. Many of the early buildings remained standing, in a dilapidated sort of way, their plaster cracked by the sun and eroded by typhoons.

From the narrow balconies projected the ubiquitous bamboo poles of laundry, small bamboo cages of song birds and, here or there, a larger cage containing a cockerel. Dogs slept out of the way under the arcades, cats slinking cautiously past them to investigate the latest fish bone thrown from an upstairs window. Some of the buildings had sprouted bushes from cracks in the walls. Bougainvillaea or jasmine trailed down from pots on balconies. All this was part and parcel of any Chinese street scene. What made this place different were the shops and businesses.

Whereas Mong Kok had its pavement *dai pai dongs*, Tai Ping Shan (as the Chinese called the area) had little cafés and restaurants inside the shop spaces under the buildings. They mostly sold noodles, *won ton*, soups and *dim sum*, the ingredients of some of which I could not identify, despite having attended and graduated from the Yau Ma Tei School of Street-Eating.

The ladder streets contained stalls balanced on the steps or constructed on platforms. These precarious entrepreneurial adventures sold buttons, thread and zips, cut keys or sharpened knives, repaired *wok* handles and swapped or sold secondhand domestic appliances. One stall sold ancient Imperial Chinese dynastic bronze coins with square holes in the middle. Dating back in some cases several centuries, people bought them to ensure fiscal good fortune. The coins cost only a few cents each and, if one had a spare dollar or three, one could buy a hundred coins tied with red twine into the shape of a short sword, the better for fighting off ill luck and malevolent spirits.

I passed a door guarded by a be-turbaned Sikh armed

with a shotgun. Behind him, the shop window was filled with gold, brilliantly illuminated by spotlights. It was all 24k fine gold – as near to pure as one could get it, soft, pliable and unsuitable for jewellery. Its colour was brash and it was not sold in blocks of bullion. Most of it had been fashioned into something – a crouching tiger, a fat Buddha, a Ming warrior or mandarin, a writhing dragon. I even saw intricate, solid gold sampans, junks, cars, pagodas, pandas and phoenixes. I knew the metal was sold by weight with only a nominal charge being added on for the exquisite workmanship. It seemed a waste of effort to me to fashion the metal into something when I knew the Chinese regarded it as merely an investment to be sold when times got tough. And, presumably, melted down. When I mentioned this to my mother, however, she gave me the explanation. To put a gold block on show in your house was in poor taste and arrogant, but to put on display a beautiful object not only indicated the owner's refinement but, at the same time, his wealth.

A short distance further on I came across a coffin-maker's workshop, open to the street. A carpenter was at work as I walked by, shaping the side of a coffin from a wide plank, curls of reddish wood peeling off from the blade. Another man was rounding off the clover-leaf end of a coffin, rubbing it with sandpaper. In the gloomy rear of the premises, completed coffins stood on racks. As I watched, the carpenter spied me and suddenly ran at me with a chisel. I fled to shouts of rage behind me. A wood off-cut bounced on the road at my side. Once in the next street, I stopped to get my breath back and to glance round the corner to check I was not being followed. He was nowhere in sight.

This episode of sudden, wild rage was not only

terrifying but also incomprehensible. I had blond hair. I was lucky. I brought good fortune. Apart from the skull-faced gardener at the Fourseas, who was in any case verging on the certifiable, I had never before seen the legendary sudden wrath to which the Chinese were prone. Later, I asked Wong if this had happened because it was considered bad luck for the dead to have their coffins peered at by a *gweilo*.

'No,' Wong replied. 'This man jus' no like you. Maybe he Communist.'

To gain my composure, I walked down the street to a tea shop. Entering it was akin to stepping back a hundred years. The walls were panelled, the sides lined with cubicles divided from each other by latticed screens, the fretwork cut in patterns of the characters for prosperity and longevity, and containing a dark wood table and benches. The brass tea urns steamed at the rear of the shop, next to a shrine and an elderly man sitting at a table with a cash box, an abacus and a book of receipts. I appeared to be the only customer.

A waiter approached me and jutted his chin at me.

'*Yum cha*,' I replied.

He looked at me for a moment then signalled me to sit in one of the cubicles. A minute later, he brought me a pot of gunpowder tea and a tea bowl. I filled the bowl and took a sip.

'*Ho sik!*' I exclaimed, adding in English, 'Very good!'

The waiter made no response whatsoever but walked away.

Although at first I was the only customer, over the next half hour, the place began to fill with elderly men, every one of them carrying a small bird cage containing a finch. They were tiny birds, some striped black, white and red, some yellow, some green, some a nondescript fawn. As they sat down, the men hung the cages from hooks suspended from beams in the ceiling directly over their seats. Tea was served. More arrived until every seat was occupied except the three in my cubicle.

Sipping their tea, the men conversed avidly amongst themselves. Overhead, the birds twittered and sang at each other. There were, it dawned on me, two different sets of conversation going on, human below and avian above. The tea house was like a social club for both species.

The waiter came over to me, signalling that I should leave. He was not antagonistic, but four men had entered with bird cages and wanted my cubicle. I nodded and asked for the bill. He shook his head and waved his hand from side to side, dismissing payment. I placed a fifty-cent coin under the teapot and left. I had not gone ten yards when the waiter came running down the street after me waving it.

'*Tipsee*,' I said. '*Kumshaw.*'

He looked at me and smiled broadly. It was then I saw his silence was because he had no tongue. I made an effort to ignore his infirmity. He made a throaty sort of laugh, pocketed the coin and stroked my hair. I wished, as his hand touched my head, that somehow I would not bring him wealth but return to him the power of speech. When I got home, I told Wong about him.

'Japanese cut plentee tongue wartime,' he said stoically.

As I walked along the street, a faint and unidentifiable herbal smell reached me. The further on I walked, the stronger it became until, finally, I arrived at the source. It was a shop unlike any ordinary Chinese store, with a shop-front window and a glass door bearing vermilion Chinese characters. A neon sign of a six-foot-high snake coiling itself around a bamboo stake hung outside over the street.

The window display was most curious. It included bowls of seeds, what appeared to be bits of dry twig, desiccated bark, dried leaves, dehydrated roots, shrivelled fungi and flowers. Behind them were a dozen or so large ground-glass stoppered bottles containing preserved frogs, lizards, snakes and other less easily recognized pieces of flesh. Other reptiles lay on trays in front, dried out and stretched on frames of bamboo splints. Beside them were trays of what looked like black dried turds.

Going in, I found there was only one other customer, a woman with a florid birthmark on her neck the size of my outstretched hand. Behind the counter a man was busy writing on sheets of plain paper and opening drawers in a cabinet that reached to the ceiling and ran the length of the shop. From each he took a pinch or a handful of the contents, putting them into the sheets of paper. Every so often, he studied an old book. This done, he skilfully folded each sheet into a small, self-sealing parcel and placed it in the woman's rattan basket. When she had paid and left, the man turned his attention to me.

'Wha' you wan'?' he asked in pidgin English.

'What dis shop?' I replied.

'Dis Chilese med'sin shop,' he replied. 'Can do for *gweilo*, too. You sick by 'n' by, you come. I see you lo more sick.' He looked me up and down. 'You lo sick now?' he enquired optimistically.

'I lo sick.'

'You wan' see med'sin? Lo all same like *gweilo* med'sin.'

Never one to turn down an opportunity, I said I did and he showed me round the shop. In addition to a vast array of dried plant and fungal material, there were velvet-covered deers' antlers, tiny birds' nests, powdered pearls like grey talc shot through with stardust, the ghostly pale exoskeletons of sea-horses, dried bears' spleens (the 'turds' in the window), an assortment of dried insects, a mummified tiger's penis ('. . . make you good wif you lady fr'en' . . .') and his *pièce de résistance*, a rhino's horn. When I asked for what these were cures, he reeled off a list of ailments, most of which I was ignorant of and hoped to so remain. When he was unable to give the English name, he mimed the symptoms, reminding me of the grotesque tableaux in the Tiger Balm Gardens.

Before I could leave, he mixed up a packet of dried plant matter for me.

'Good gen'ral med'sin for you. Like tonic. You put water, boiloo wung hour. Drink wung cup wung day. Make you st'ong.' He flexed his biceps and felt them. 'Lo ill for maybe t'ee mumf.'

When I got home, I gave the packet to my mother who was in the kitchen making a light supper, it being Wong's day off. She tipped the contents into a saucepan and boiled it for an hour. The apartment filled with such a noxious odour it woke my father, asleep in the bedroom. It also brought a shine to the interior of the saucepan not seen since it was new.

My mother and I let it cool then poured a cup. It tasted execrable. We left the remainder for Wong. When he returned, he was most grateful for it. As far as he was concerned, this was only a few drops short of being the elixir of life, its cost prohibitive on his wages.

The main mercantile district of Hong Kong, the city of Victoria, referred to by everyone as Central District – or just Central – held little interest for me. Most of the buildings were the offices of banks, shipping lines, lawyers, insurance companies and import/export firms. The Hongkong and Shanghai Bank towered over the parked cars in what was known as Statue Square. To one side were the law courts, a classical colonnaded building with a dome on top. It could have been transported there from any European city. Yet, for all that, the old China still impinged itself upon the mid-twentieth century.

In rush hour, the chances of a rickshaw jam were greater than one composed of vehicles, for many office workers and businessmen coming from Kowloon took rickshaws from the ferry pier to their offices. Of those who chose to walk, many paused at the shoe-shine 'boys'.

I could not understand why grown men were referred to as boys. The Fourseas had had room boys: only the bellboy, Halfie, had actually been a boy. Wong was our house boy; my father employed a Chinese office boy who was at least twice his age.

The shoe-shine boys bucked the trend. Half of them were indeed boys, some of them my age, who squatted on the pavement under the shade of an arcade, a box before them. If a customer halted, tins of polish, brushes and cloths would appear from within the box. Deft fingers rolled up trouser legs and, within minutes, the shoes would appear pristine, scuff marks and dust removed.

On one occasion, my father having withheld my pocket money for some misdemeanour, I toyed with making a shoe-shine box of my own, stocking it with polish and brushes from the kitchen and setting up my pitch. At fifty cents a polish – the going rate – I could earn a week's pocket money thrice over in a morning. I mentioned my plan to my mother.

'You want to do what!' For a moment she looked at me, then burst out laughing.

'It's not funny,' I defended myself. 'I've got to earn some pocket money.'

'Can you imagine your father coming along the street . . . ?' She grinned broadly at the prospect. 'Now that would be "going native" in no small measure. A definite plunge in standards. You'd be in the paper! Photo and all!' She extrapolated further. '*Gweilo Boy Sets New Trend. The Shoe-shine Entrepreneur. Son Sets Up Shoe-shine Box: Father Commits Hari-kiri.*'

'So, can I do it?' I asked, sensing the wind blowing my way and wondering what *hari-kiri* was.

'No,' my mother said. 'It's not because you'd cause a scandal. That would be hilarious. It's that, if you were to set up in business, you would be taking earnings from the other shoe-shine boys and they need all they can get.'

As usual, my mother's common sense prevailed and I put the idea out of my head. She surreptitiously reinstated my weekly allowance.

The shoe-shine boys shared the pavements with a small coterie of beggars. One was a tall, thin man who was totally blind, his face always turned up to the sky, his hand holding a begging cup and a length of bamboo painted as white as his sightless eyes. He was invariably accompanied by a child whose role was not to induce sympathy in passers-by but to act as a guide dog might, seeing him across the road or on to a tram. Another beggar was a woman whose body and limbs were twisted by deformity into a grotesque embryonic crouch. She got about on a small wooden platform to which had been affixed the wheels of an old baby's pram. For her, in her miserable condition, beggary must have been particularly demeaning, for every day she sold newspapers by Blake Pier, cradling her limited stock of copies of the *China Mail* and *Wah Kiu Yat Po* in her arms like the baby she would never have.

Perhaps the most obvious intrusion of ancient Cathay into modern Hong Kong were the coolies. Throughout the day, swarthy Hakka women from the rural hinterland dressed in black, often wearing dust caps made out of folded newspaper, appeared down the street with bamboo poles over their shoulders from which were suspended anything from baskets of building rubble and bundles of waste paper to discarded wooden filing cabinets and office chairs. If it could be re-used, re-cycled or re-sold, it was.

These women were not restricted to carting débris. I once came to a hillside being blasted with dynamite and watched as the charges were laid by women, the detonator wire run out by women and the warning given by a woman with a gong. When the dust settled, it was women who carried away the dislodged rocks and earth. Not one man seemed to be involved.

Only one place in Central held me in awe and I visited it over and over again, like a rubber-necking tourist. It was the main banking hall of the Hongkong and Shanghai Bank headquarters. I had gone there first with my mother. Reluctantly.

On either side of the entrance was a life-size bronze lion. The left-hand one was growling.

'They're called Stephen and Stitt,' my mother said as we waited to cross the road.

'Which is which?'

'Stephen's growling,' was her reply.

'What's a stitt?'

'They're named after two bank managers, Mr Stephen and Mr Stitt.'

On reaching the lions, I was struck by their size, yet this was not all. They had bullet holes in them from the war and Stephen had a lump of shrapnel embedded in him. Both were covered in a dark brown patina except that Stitt's front paw shone like gold. I soon saw why. People walking by touched it. For luck.

'This', my mother announced as we entered the bank and turned to climb a flight of stairs, 'is actually the back door. The front door, and the address, are on the other side.'

This seemed nonsensical and I said so.

'It's to do with the laws of necromancy,' my mother replied. 'The main door has to face the hills, away from the harbour, to keep the sea dragon out and to stop the money flowing out into the ocean.'

Explained thus, it made perfect sense to me.

The banking hall was vast. The sound of voices was muffled by its immensity. Huge, square, dark brown marble pillars held up the ceiling – and what a ceiling it was: barrel vaulted and covered in a gargantuan mosaic. In the centre was an elaborate golden starburst set against an azure backdrop, around the sides was a multicoloured frieze of figures engaged in all manner of Oriental and Occidental craftwork and industry. The ceiling never failed to stun me. I would often take a detour through the bank on my way from the Peak Tram to the Star Ferry just to pass under the reflected glow of the mosaic.

Once, accompanying my father to the bank, I announced my determination to be an artist.

'What on earth prompted that ridiculous idea?' he

exclaimed, busying himself at the counter with his cheque book.

'That did,' I said, staring mosaicwards.

He did not look up.

'Well, put that notion out of your head. No-one gets rich by being an artist.'

'There's more to being rich than having a lot of money,' I answered.

The teller accepted his cheque. He turned to face me.

'No, there isn't,' he said succinctly, 'and anyone who says there is is a bloody fool.'

'Mum told me there is,' I said.

'Yes, well your mother doesn't have to earn it,' he rejoined.

When he had collected his money and put it in his wallet, I said, 'Look up at the ceiling, Dad.'

He did so, briefly.

'Very impressive,' he remarked offhandedly.

Once outside, as we walked to the car parked in Statue Square, I mused, 'I bet the artist was paid a lot of money to make that ceiling.'

'Probably drank it all and never did another thing in the rest of his life.'

That, I considered, was ripe coming from an experienced pink gin downer but refrained from saying as much. I was fast learning the art of knowing when, as my father put it, to keep my trap shut.

Not long after the forced-labour day on Chow Kung Chau, another trip was arranged by launch to the adjacent island of Hei Ling Chau. It was sparsely populated and consequently the location of a leper colony – and it was this we were to visit.

My mother heard of the trip from a newsletter sent out to naval wives and immediately announced we were going. My father was reluctant in the extreme. He and disease were not close relations, he declared, and he was damned if he was going to spend his Sunday leisure time wandering around staring at those who were.

'What's a leper colony?' I asked.

'It's where they lock away the poor buggers who've caught leprosy,' my father replied, hoping this would deter me from joining my mother.

I asked what leprosy was.

'Leprosy', my mother answered, giving my father a look that precluded his interrupting, 'is a disease caused by bacteria. There are two kinds – dry leprosy and wet leprosy. If you have the dry sort, your nerves die off bit by bit and you become paralysed. Or, because they have no nerves in them, parts of your body wither and drop off. Most common is you lose your nose and fingers and toes, but you can have a whole arm drop off. If you have wet leprosy, your entire body is covered in running sores and ulcers. That kind is dangerously contagious, meaning you can get it just by touching someone with it, but the dry is very hard to catch indeed—'

'And your mother wants to take you to meet some people who've got it,' my father butted in, no longer able to contain himself. 'Really, Joyce, sometimes you take the bloody biscuit. Anyway, you're not going. I shall simply refuse to allow it. I'm not having our son exposed—'

'Don't talk such bloody bosh. We'll be perfectly safe.

You think the people who run the leprosarium will put visitors at risk?'

'Why do you think they lock all the poor bastards away on a ruddy island?'

'They don't lock them away. They look after them and cure them.'

'And once they're cured, they just become beggars,' my father retorted. 'You can't do much with only one arm and half a leg. Better to let them die.'

My mother pursed her lips and replied, 'Sometimes, Ken, I wonder what I saw in you.'

A fortnight later, on a Sunday of bright sun and high scudding clouds, we were all three of us cutting through a choppy sea aboard a naval launch heading for Hei Ling Chau. On arrival at a short jetty, we were met by a Chinese man who helped us to disembark under an archway of gold and scarlet bunting. A dozen other private launches rode at anchor.

'Welcome to our fête!' the Chinese man said as we stepped on to dry land.

'How do you spell that?' my father muttered. '*F a t e* or *f ê t e*. I really do not see why they don't just have a bloody flag day like anybody else. This really is bloody madness, Joyce.'

Ahead of us were some low buildings surrounded by stalls. Everything was decorated with strips and banners of gold and scarlet crêpe paper, catching the sunlight as they rippled in the breeze. Several hundred people milled about, trying their luck at a coconut shy, a roll-a-ten-cent-coin table and other attractions such as might have been found at any church bazaar anywhere in rural Britain. The only difference was that some of the helpers were British Army privates and naval ratings and there was a

.22 rifle range set up for those who fancied their hand as a dab shot.

'Well,' my mother replied, 'it seems to be a pretty bloody widespread madness.'

We joined the crowd, tried the lucky dip, bought some raffle tickets and visited the tombola stall. My father hung back, smoking his pipe, his teeth clenched in anger on the stem. I wondered if he smoked to enjoy the tobacco or to fumigate the air around him. After a short time, we saw him strolling off southwards.

'Wouldn't it be funny,' my mother mused, 'if he missed the boat back? Marooned on a desert island with a colony of lepers and that bloody pipe . . .'

It was then I saw my first leper. He was sitting behind a trestle table upon which were arranged a number of home-made wooden objects such as bookends, desktop pen holders and paperweights shaped like the outline of the island, its name burnt into the surface with a hot poker. From the front of the table hung a sign in English and Chinese stating *Woodworks made by inmats. Please by. Garuntee very clean*.

As my mother had predicted, the leper had no nose, only a ragged hole surrounded by flaps of skin. He had also lost several fingers and an ear. Apart from this, he looked quite normal and healthy, certainly in better shape than many of the beggars I saw on the streets. I searched my pockets. I had ten dollars left from a postal order sent by Nanny for my birthday.

Walking up to the stall, I studied the wares on offer. They were simple items but very well made. The leper smiled at me but did not speak, his upper lip curling like a snarling dog's, his lower hanging loose. I picked up a pair of bookends.

'We get our wood from a timber yard,' a voice said over my shoulder. 'They're left-overs. Mahogany, teak, sandal-wood.'

I turned. A European man stood behind me dressed in slacks and an open-neck cotton shirt. He only differed from the rest of the Sunday crowd in that a stethoscope hung round his neck to denote his office.

'Having fun?' he enquired.

'Yes, sir,' I answered then, seizing the moment, asked him a question that had been bothering me for days. 'Is it true you only cure the lepers so they can become beggars?'

'Who on earth told you that nonsense?' he exclaimed, quite clearly taken aback. 'We don't just cure their illness, we cure their souls, too. We train them to do jobs. This man here's going to be a carpenter. Once he has a job, which we'll find for him, he'll get his dignity and his life back.' He smiled down at me. 'You don't want to believe everything you hear, sonny Jim.'

I pointed to the bookends and asked, '*Gai doh cheen?*'

The leper sort-of chortled and raised five assorted digits.

'*Ng mun?*' I questioned, to be sure of the price.

He nodded, his eyes bright at the thought of a sale. I gave him five dollar notes and he handed me the book-ends, bound together by several rubber bands. As I parted with the money, our hands met, his skin blotched, warped and stretched by leprosy, mine smooth with health.

'*Dor jei,*' I thanked him. He chortled again and I saw he had only half a tongue.

As I was about to go, he reached out with one hand, nodding enthusiastically at me, his eyes pleading for some-thing. His index and middle finger were missing. Going round the back of his stall, I stood next to him. Fleetingly, so that I hardly felt it, he touched my hair.

On the return launch trip, I took my mother aside, out of my father's earshot. 'I let a leper touch my hair,' I admitted, hurriedly adding, 'but he was a dry one.'

I expected a scolding, or at least an admonishing, but neither materialized.

'Well then,' my mother replied with a smile, 'let's hope to God it brings the poor man luck, shall we?'

When we got home, however, I accidentally mentioned my encounter with the leper to my father. He went apoplectic.

'You did what?' he bellowed. 'Joyce! Do you know what this stupid little sod has done?'

'Lots of things, I expect,' my mother urbanely replied.

'He allowed a bloody leper to stroke his hair. It's bad enough in the bloody street with the entire bloody population of China, but in a benighted leper colony . . .' His face was red with anger, going towards puce. He put down his pink gin. 'Go into your bedroom and stay there.'

I did as I was told. There were raised voices in the sitting room followed by a slammed door. My father entered my room carrying a red leather slipper.

'Bend over the side of the bed.'

'Why? I haven't done anything wrong.'

I was amazed at my defiance. Always in the past, I had meekly succumbed to a beating, accepting it much as a miscreant dog might a kick or a rolled-up newspaper. Yet now, I thought, I would not. I had not been disobedient or insolent, the usual crimes levelled at me, not always without reason. A paddling now would be an injustice. My father clenched his teeth.

'Bend over, damn you—'

'No.'

He swung the slipper at my buttocks. I side-stepped.

'And they don't cure them to be beggars. You were wrong. They find them proper jobs so they get their dignity back.'

I had no idea what dignity was but it had to be a good thing.

'What?' my father exploded.

'The leper doctor told me.'

'I'll give you bloody dignity, you little sod!'

My father's left hand struck quicker than a cobra. Grabbing me by the back of the neck, he forced me to bend over, then, with all his might, he hit me four times in quick succession on the buttocks. I did not cry: I would not give him the satisfaction.

'Now get into bloody bed.' He was grinding his teeth with rage.

It was from that moment that I hated my father, truly abhorred him with a loathing that deepened as time went by and was to sour the rest of both our lives.

8

IDA, SU YIN, THE LIGHT OF TIN HAU AND THE WRATH OF YEN LO

MY MOTHER AND I HAD PLANNED TO GO SWIMMING AT Repulse Bay on the afternoon of Sunday, 27 August 1954. My father reluctantly said that he would drive us there, returning home to indulge in his usual weekend pastime of pink gin and sleeping. As Wong set the table for an early lunch, my father stood legs apart on the veranda as if on the rolling deck of his own battleship, surveying the harbour through his binoculars.

'Lunch 'edy, missee, master,' Wong announced.

My father stepped into the lounge and announced, 'Beach is off, Joyce. Number One signal's up.'

By this, he meant that he had looked at the Hong Kong Observatory on Kowloon through his binoculars and seen a storm warning on the signal mast.

My mother, not to be done out of an afternoon's swimming, replied, 'Are you sure? It's a lovely day and One is only a stand-by . . .'

'Tropical storms can gather very quickly,' my father opined.

'Surely not between now and five o'clock,' my mother came back. 'I don't think we need to be concerned.'

To win the argument, my father telephoned HMS *Tamar*. The meteorological officer on duty confirmed it: they expected to raise the Number Five some time in the early evening. We sat down for lunch.

'What do the signals actually mean?' I asked.

My father, ever the knowledgeable maritime obfuscator, replied, 'Number One is a standby signal, Number Five to Eight predicts winds up to sixty miles per hour and designates the direction they will come from, Number Nine is winds up to gale or storm force and Number Ten hurricane force, over sixty with gusts up to a hundred and thirty.'

'What's this one going to be?'

'*Tamar* says a near hit, so Nine, possibly Ten.'

My mother called Wong and gave him the news. He immediately went out on to the veranda and brought in my mother's potted plants. After lunch, we prepared for what was coming, removing ornaments from window sills, parking the car well under the adjacent block of apartments, putting old towels along window sills and external door lintels. In her bedroom, my mother stored away all her make-up jars, hairbrushes, ring stand and my father's cufflink tray. Wong, meantime, emptied the bathroom shelves and placed the contents – and the glass shelves – in the dry room. In my bedroom, I removed my ornaments from the window sill – a pile of High West bullets, my carved wooden camel and a detailed model of a junk – placing them in my cupboard with my books.

I had experienced several severe tropical storms and one typhoon before, but we had been living in the Fourseas or Boundary Street at the time and only suffered a few leaking windows. Now we were positioned on the fourth floor of a block of apartments erected on the very pinnacle

of a summit secondary only to the Peak. With no protection on all sides, we were perched at about fifteen
hundred feet above sea level.

'What's this typhoon called?' I enquired.

Every typhoon was allotted a girl's name, for a reason I
could not fathom but which Philip Bryant had confided
was because all females were like typhoons: impulsive,
destructive, exciting, dangerous, single-minded, determined and immovable.

This one was called Ida. We had a spinster relative of
the same name, but she was a mousy, quiet woman who
lived in a rural shire town, spent her life baking scones and
lovingly scolding an old cat. Perhaps we were not in for a
bad typhoon after all.

I was wrong.

By the time I went to bed, the sky was covered with
dense cloud, the lights of the city reflecting off it. I read
my comics, recently arrived, and went to sleep to be woken
just after dawn by the booming gusts of wind. Each time
one hit the building, the air within seemed to contract. I
could feel the pressure on my ears. It was like living inside
a bass drum.

I switched on my bedside light and crossed to the
window. The cloud base had dropped to not much above
the roof of our building. I could still see the city below in a
monochromatic dawn light but under a metallic sky that
seemed to glower with rage and rob the view of colour.
Kowloon was invisible. Intermittently, squalls of heavy
rain blew by. They did not strike the window full on but
sprayed off the corner of the stonework as if it were
the bow of a ship. A substantial tree branch blew by –
vertically.

Yet what was most frightening, although at first I did

not recognize its significance, was my reflection in the window. When a gust hit the glass, it distorted like a circus Hall of Mirrors, the distortion lasting only seconds.

'Martin, get away from the window!' It was my mother in her nightie and dressing gown. 'Now!'

'Why? I was only looking—'

'The glass is bending. If we get a really hard knock, it'll implode and you'll be cut to shreds. Go to the front door.'

Suddenly, I felt vulnerable. This, I imagined, was what it must have been like in the war, never knowing if a bomb was going to hit your house. In the entrance hall to the apartment were piled suitcases filled with everything moveable and of value.

'Are we going away?' I asked.

'Don't be so bloody stupid!' my father retorted.

He was fully dressed and ready for action. By his side was Wong, armed with a mop, his weapon at the barricade in the battle against the typhoon.

'Use your bloody brain,' my father continued. 'How the hell do you think we'll get down the bloody drive?'

I had to admit he had a point. The curving driveway up to the building was completely exposed. We were marooned.

Over the morning, the wind increased. It howled, fizzed, whined, whistled and hummed. Water seeped in through the galvanized steel Crittal window frames which were allegedly typhoon proof, keeping Wong busy soaking it up with his mop to prevent the parquet floor from getting sodden and warping. My mother helped him, emptying the bucket and wringing out the old towels. All Hong Kong business was suspended, the ferries were in the typhoon shelters and radio messages warned every-one to stay inside. Scaffolding was blowing down, live electricity cables were lying in urban roads, shop signs were falling like ninepins, there were a number of landslides blocking major roads and flooding was reported in the New Territories. Social events – the Hong Kong Cricket Club whist night, Such-and-such a company's annual dinner at the Pen – were postponed by radio announcements.

Nevertheless, my father still thought he should be at work. The Royal Navy, he insisted, counted on people like him to keep things going. That there was not a single warship in the harbour, all of them having put to sea to ride out the storm, was neither here nor there. It was Monday: he should be at work. Consequently, he spent two hours on the telephone trying to organize supplies for a destroyer that had sailed to safety in international waters. Then the line went dead. He slammed the receiver down and cracked it.

'Intelligent,' my mother remarked bluntly. 'We're stranded on a mountain top in a typhoon and you break the bloody phone.'

'The perishing line's down,' he replied sourly. 'Fat lot of bloody use the phone is.'

'Yes,' my mother agreed, 'but they'll soon fix the line. It'll take days to get a replacement phone.'

'I'm military, an essential user,' my father said. 'They'll bring us a new one PDQ.'

The telephone line was operational by late the following morning. The telephone, which my mother fixed with Elastoplast strips, worked. A new telephone arrived four weeks later, when my mother remarked caustically it was a good job China had not invaded since Ida.

The Number Nine signal was raised at half-past eleven. By now, the wind was terrifying. Each gust curved the windows. The building creaked like a galleon under sail. According to the radio, the sustained wind speed was reaching sixty-five miles per hour with gusts at 130. The rain turned squally, lashing the windows. The veranda became an inch-deep pool. In the servants' quarters, rain sprayed through the lattice brickwork as if the building were forging ahead through a heavy sea.

Suddenly, over the space of fifteen minutes, the wind died to less than a summer zephyr and the rain let up.

'Eye of the storm,' my father announced. 'You come with me.'

He and I left the building and made our way down the drive. Leaves and branches were littered everywhere. At the bottom, we turned left and went beneath the next block of apartments. There, at the back, was my father's car, bespattered with leaves that were adhering to the entire surface. It might have been custom decorated by a miscreant sylvan elf or a wallpaper designer with a naturalistic bent.

'Get those leaves off the paintwork,' my father ordered. 'They'll discolour it.'

I started at the trunk. It seemed an utterly pointless exercise. I knew all tropical cyclones – we had done the topic in geography – were circular and that, in the middle, was the eye, a place of calm around which the storm revolved. Once that passed by, the winds would blow again, but from the opposite quarter. The leaves we removed would soon be replaced.

'Not the bloody windows, cloth ears!' my father said, breaking into my thoughts. 'The glass won't discolour, will it? We haven't got all bloody day.'

Indeed, the wind was already beginning to pick up again so we made our way back up the drive. It took my breath away. I could feel the gusts tugging at my lungs as it had the window glass. By the time we reached our apartment block my father – as he was keen to prove – could physically lean on the wind. Behind him, struggling up the drive, was one of our neighbours who had taken advantage of the eye to walk his wife's dachshund. The dog was being lifted as much as four inches off the concrete, a bemused look on its face. But for its lead, it could have blown away.

In the early evening, the Number Eight signal was raised and remained in force through the night. By noon the following day, the typhoon was gone, leaving behind squally showers and a gunmetal sky, and the clear-up began. My father revisited his car. It was, as before, heavily bestrewn with leaves. Worse, another car in the parking space had been blown against the rear of my father's, denting the bumper and nicking the paintwork.

'Bloody hell!' my father fumed. 'Why can't other benighted drivers . . . ? That one over there tied his car to the bloody pillars. Why couldn't this cloth-eared individual . . . ?'

I set about removing the leaves but the bonnet and front of the car were devoid of them. A downpipe had broken free and sprayed rainwater continuously over the car for hours. My father unlocked the door, got in and attempted to start the engine. The starter motor turned over asthmatically but nothing else happened. My father opened the bonnet. The engine was sodden, a deep puddle beneath it covered in a rainbow film of oil.

'Buggeration!' my father exclaimed and slammed the bonnet down. A piece of trim fell off.

We had got off comparatively unscathed. An apartment at the top of the adjacent building had lost a window, setting off a chain reaction with three or four others. The wind sucked out anything lighter and smaller than a coffee table, splintering them to pieces as they struck the window frames.

The wind having died down a good deal, I walked up the road to the police post. The bushes in some places had been stripped of leaves as if attacked by locusts. All the hibiscus bushes had lost their blooms, which lay in the road like sodden purple scraps of tissue paper. And yet the birds were singing and, when the sun came out between the squalls, the tarmac was alive with all manner of butterflies drying their wings in the warmth. I wondered where they had weathered the storm.

My mother and I went to the Peak School for an interview with the headmistress. I had been playing hookey from games lessons and she wanted to know why. So did my mother. Education was important to her because her own had been so minimal. I had my argument ready and expressed anathema for the concept of team sports because they destroyed one's individuality. This left both women momentarily flabbergasted. I was told to join in more, in lessons, in sports, in the social extra-curricular life of the school. I could hardly reply I preferred a *dai pai dong* to country dancing.

On the walk back, my mother was silent. Several times, she started to speak then thought the better of it. I guessed she felt torn. On the one hand, she had to back the school. On the other, she would rather have had an independently minded sinophile than a soccer player for a son.

We entered the apartment to find Ah Shun sitting on the settee, a duster in her hand and Tuppence disconsolately perched by her side. This was, to put it mildly, unusual. If servants ever did sit down on the furniture, they were sure to be swift in getting to their feet as soon as the key rattled in the lock.

'Are you all right, Ah Shun?' my mother enquired with a concerned look on her face.

'Lo, missee,' Ah Shun replied. It was about as far as her knowledge of English went.

'Go and get Wong,' my mother ordered me.

'Wong go,' Ah Shun said.

'Wong go? Go where?'

It was no use speaking Cantonese to Ah Shun. She only spoke Shanghainese.

'Go, missee.'

Wong was not in the kitchen or the servants' quarter. I reported his absence, admitting selfishly to myself that this diversion could not have come at a handier time.

'Oh, my God!' my mother exclaimed, jumping to conclusions. 'He's left her.'

A frantic phone call to my father drew a blank. Predictably, he could not get away. Looking out of the window, I could see an aircraft carrier riding at a buoy off *Tamar*. He would try and return early that evening.

My mother sat next to Ah Shun and put her arm round her. A short time later, we heard a movement in the kitchen. My mother rushed out to find Wong depositing the shopping bags on the floor.

'Thank God!' she said. 'Wong, Ah Shun is sick.'

'Lo sick, missee,' he answered calmly.

'Wong, she can barely get up. She's tired. I'm going to call the doctor.'

'Lo call, missee. Ah Shun no sick. Ah Shun got baby come.'

My mother stared at him for a long moment. I looked at Ah Shun. By now, I knew a fair amount about the birds, the bees and babies. She certainly did not look fat but then the uniform she wore was hardly close fitting.

'When?' my mother asked.

'Lo long time,' Wong replied. 'Maybe wung week.'

'One week!' my mother exclaimed. 'Wong, you cannot let Ah Shun carry on cleaning, doing the laundry.'

'Lo p'oblum, missee. Ah Shun can do.'

'Ah Shun cannot do!' my mother replied.

'Must do,' Wong said. 'Dis her job. Mus' work for money.'

'Never mind the money!' my mother replied. 'You help Ah Shun to her bed. I'll call a doctor and then put the shopping away. You find another amah to help you.'

It didn't occur to my mother until later that, in China, Ah Shun had probably delivered herself of her other children. I was told to ring my father and tell him what was happening.

'Ah Shun's having a baby,' I stated bluntly.

'Jolly good!' my father replied offhandedly.

'Now,' I added, feeling he had missed the point.

'Now? You mean this very bloody moment?'

'Soon. The doctor's coming.'

'Oh, bloody hell! Can't your mother cope? I've got HMS—'

'Can you cope?' I called out.

'Is that what he said?'

I nodded. She stomped over to the telephone table.

'Give me the phone. Ken? Yes, I can cope. Marriage to you is all about bloody coping. It's also supposed to be about sharing bloody problems.' She held the receiver three inches above the cradle and let it drop. 'I hope that's given him a bloody headache.'

An hour later, a naval midwife in attendance, Ah Shun's waters broke. I was told to stay in my room and amuse Tuppence. He had never, at least not to my knowledge, been in my room and we played with my toy soldiers and military Dinky toys.

Ah Shun gave birth to a little girl whom they named Su Yin. My mother was appointed 'godmother' and relished the role. Not only was she proud to be asked, but here was another link to China.

My father, who never broke any law, by-law, rule or regulation that might even vaguely apply to him, read his tenancy agreement and informed the naval quartering officer of the event. A month or so later, a letter came to the effect that the servants' quarters did not cater for four, that babies were not allowed in quarters as their crying might *discommode other residents*, that fire regulations were being breached and that, in general, the Royal Navy did not approve. It was tactfully but firmly stated that either the servants be dismissed or the amah be let go, or the infant be sent to live with relatives.

My mother went incandescent with rage.

'Sack my servants! Put them out on the streets! With a new-born baby! Remember, Ken, they've already got children lodging elsewhere.'

'Wong shouldn't be so fecund,' my father answered.

'What does fecund mean?' I enquired.

'You keep your bloody nose out of this.'

'They're not going, Ken.'

'I mean, don't the Chinese take precautions?'

'Against what?' I asked.

My mother went into the bedroom and slammed the door. The key turned in the lock. My father poured himself a pink gin. I decided it politic to keep my mouth shut.

An hour later, my mother reappeared, poured herself a gin and tonic, sat down and announced, 'Ken, get me an interview with the Commodore.'

'Under no circumstance whatever,' he answered.

'Either I have an interview or I have a ticket for myself and Martin on the next P&O liner to come into port.'

I knew this was a bluff – my mother would pull her own teeth out rather than leave Hong Kong before she had to – but my father begrudgingly said he would see what he could do. The outcome was that it was not a naval matter but a civilian one to do with fire regulations and suchlike.

'In that case,' my mother declared, 'I'm going to see the Governor.'

'That, Joyce, I certainly will not allow.'

'Allow?' my mother responded, her eyes narrowing. 'I'm not asking your bloody permission. I'm telling you what I'm going to do. Out of bloody courtesy.'

An exchange of letters with Government House followed, culminating in my mother being granted an audience with His Excellency, Sir Alexander Grantham KCMG. She demanded I accompany her partly, I suspect, because she was scared witless now that her persistence had paid off and I was acting as a sort of hip flask of Dutch courage, or perhaps she wanted me along to demonstrate that she was also a mother who would not be parted from her offspring.

My father refused even to drive us to the meeting – perhaps he was afraid his car licence plate might be noted down as belonging to a subversive – so we went to Government House by taxi. We were met by the Governor's ADC under the portico to the front door.

'His Excellency is fully acquainted with the situation,' he said as he guided us in to a large lobby. 'I'm afraid he can only give you ten minutes.'

The Governor appeared, shook my mother's hand, then mine. He asked my name.

'Martin, sir,' I admitted.

'Good name. Strong name,' he replied. 'Do you know who I am?'

'His Excellency the Governor, sir,' I answered.

He smiled and led us into a room furnished like an English country house, indicating we all sit down. A steward came in with a tray of Chinese tea.

'Would you like an orange juice, Martin?' the Governor asked.

'I would prefer tea, sir,' I answered.

'It's Chinese tea,' the Governor warned me.

'That's all right, sir,' I replied. 'I drink lots of tea at the *dai pai dongs*.'

His Excellency raised an eyebrow, smiled and said, 'Do you, indeed? A real little China Hand. Do you like Hong Kong?'

'Yes, sir. Very much.'

'I'm afraid,' he apologized, 'this tea might not be up to the standard of a *dai pai dong*.'

The tea was poured into cups, not bowls, and my mother and the Governor then got down to business. I minded my own, sipped the tea and studied the paintings hanging in the room. In less than the ten allotted minutes, the matter was settled. So long as the landlord did not object and the fire escapes were acceptable, servants' families would no longer be arbitrarily split up.

The matter would take some months to go through Legislative Council. In the meantime, as far as he was concerned, Wong, Ah Shun, Tuppence and Su Yin were to remain where they were pending a change in the law. We shook hands again and my mother and I were shown to the porch where a government car had been hailed for us.

That evening, when my father returned from work, my mother waited until he had a drink in hand then told him of the meeting.

'So the landlord has to agree,' he commented. 'That's the Navy.'

'I'm sure they will,' my mother responded sweetly.

'I wouldn't count on it,' my father forewarned her.

'I'm not,' she said mildly. 'I'm counting on you. You let me down and I will go to the Commodore, with or without your bloody say-so.'

And, now, my father knew, she would.

Several months later, the law was changed and the Wong family's tenure was secure. My mother felt she had struck a blow for Chinese rights – which she had. My father admitted defeat. And, as I heard my mother say to a friend, 'We'll still have Wong's marvellous sponges.'

One Sunday, my parents and I were invited to lunch on Stonecutters' Island in the western half of Hong Kong harbour. A colleague of my father's, a Mr Newton, lived there with his wife and son, Andrew, whom I liked. Even better was the fact that, near their house, there was a large anti-aircraft gun left over from the war. It was still operable, the gearing well greased. We could rotate it on its base and elevate or lower the barrel. It was the ultimate boys' plaything.

To reach Stonecutters', which was a closed military site on account of the signals station on it, one had to take the naval launch from HMS *Tamar* to the island. Once there, we walked to the Newtons' bungalow along narrow paths, the undergrowth encroaching over the wartime concrete. It was said that unique species of rare snakes lived on the island, escapees from a Japanese wartime laboratory that had sought to use their venom in biological weapons. All I ever saw there was a dead, red-necked keel-back water snake on the shingle beach, being voraciously picked over by dark blue and red rock crabs.

There had been a landslip on Garden Road caused by recent rain, so my father had to take a longer route to HMS *Tamar* via Happy Valley then through Wanchai. In Hennessy Road, a coolie on a tricycle suddenly appeared from a side street, pedalling hard. My father, used to demon-dodging pedestrians, slammed on his brakes. The road was wet. The car skidded and hit the front of the tricycle, the coolie jumping clear at the moment of impact.

One of the two front wheels of the tricycle was buckled but the vehicle had otherwise suffered no discernible damage. The coolie, however, was livid. He waved his hands in the air, appealed for justice to the inevitable crowd of onlookers (which was swelling by the minute) and harangued my father who, not understanding a word but capturing the general gist of the diatribe, just stood staring at the infinitesimal dent in the Ford's chrome bumper.

Finally, my father drew himself up and roared at the shouting coolie, 'Who do you think you're screaming at?'

The coolie fell silent.

'It was your own bloody fault,' my father bellowed. 'You didn't look, you blithering idiot. You just came swanning out with not a care in the world. Now look what you've done ...'

He pointed to the bumper. The coolie took a cursory look, waved his hand in the general direction of his tricycle and let off a stream of invective in a high-pitched squeal. This, I knew, was bad. When an angry Chinese voice rose an octave, there was soon going to be physical action. My father knew as much about street fighting Hong Kong-style as he did Cantonese. Or astrophysics. It was plain before it started who would win a punch-up.

My mother got out of the car, as did I. She was about to muster all her command of Cantonese to defuse the situation but, at that moment, a police paddy-wagon appeared, the crowd melting away. A Chinese sergeant told off the coolie for the dangerous driving of a tricycle. The coolie argued for money to cover the repair to his wheel but the policeman denied his appeal and sent him on his way. A European police inspector then had a brief word with my father and it was all over.

'He could've made that bloody coolie pay for the damage to the bumper,' my father complained as we set off again. 'It'll need re-chroming.'

'The cost of repairing a barely visible dent might equal a week's coolie wage,' my mother pointed out. 'You could've offered to pay to straighten his wheel. He could be out of work until it's fixed. That would have been the gentlemanly thing to—'

'What?' my father retorted. 'It wasn't my bloody fault. He ... and you side with ...' He was left spluttering for words.

The outcome of this minor traffic accident was that my father became an unnecessarily over-cautious driver. He would, for example, be driving along a wide road in the New Territories, in the high heat of midday, with nobody and nothing moving on it – no buffaloes, pigs, hens, farmers, duck-herds, ducks or dogs. We would pass, say, a country temple set well back from the road. Seated on a stool by the door would be an old crone smoking a thin silver pipe.

A hundred yards further on, my father would ask, not taking his eyes from the road ahead, 'Was that old woman back there OK, Joyce?' The sub-text was, Did I hit her?

For the first few occasions, my mother or I would be truthful and reply that we had not seen the old woman. At this, my father would do a U-turn and go back to ensure she was still smoking her pipe – or, as my mother put it out of my father's earshot, to have another go at missing her. Thereafter, my mother and I learnt to say automatically, 'Yes, Ken/Daddy, he/she/it's OK.' It was the only way to arrive at our destination on time, with our sanity intact.

Typhoons were not the only natural force with which Hong Kong had to contend. Heavy rain invariably caused landslides, avalanches of rock and soil sliding down the hillside taking trees, bushes, boulders, squatter shacks and even substantial buildings with it. People were frequently buried alive or crushed to death. Hundreds were made homeless. Roads were blocked, sometimes for several days.

Despite the prevalence of typhoons and tropical storms,

droughts were not uncommon either. The reservoir levels would plunge, brush fires spring up and smoulder for days, a terrible threat to the squatter areas. The wind, when it blew, was hot and dry, the only humidity in it picked off the sea. In such times of water shortage, restrictions were enforced, the mains water only being switched on for a few hours a day – or even every other day. When the taps were running, every receptacle in the house would be filled – baths, basins, saucepans, woks, empty bottles. It was common colonial practice to retain Gordon's gin bottles for, being flat on one side, they were ideal drinking-water containers which fitted in the fridge on their sides. In a drought, up to two dozen stood on the kitchen floor, filled to the brim and awaiting their turn to be chilled.

With the baths being used for water storage, and showers redundant, many people went to the beach in the evening to wash. It became an everyday sight to see bathers lathering their hair or soaping every inch of flesh not covered by a swimming costume. Sweetmeat vendors caught on to the exodus from the city, and soon the beaches were lined with purveyors of everything from sweet pickled turnip and sugar cane to Dairy Farm popsies. There would be almost a party atmosphere at the bigger beaches, especially at Repulse Bay where the Chinese occupied the strand whilst the Europeans, once they had bathed, dressed in smart casual clothes and decamped to the bar of the famous Repulse Bay Hotel.

My parents chose to drive further afield, to a wide sandy beach at the eastern extremity of Hong Kong island called Shek O. To one side, a tiny fishing (and once notorious pirate) village stood on a promontory. The bay, facing straight out into the South China Sea, was frequently visited by deep-water-dwelling sharks, and although they very rarely came close into shore, a lifeguard seated on a tall bamboo lookout tower kept watch for them.

At weekends, Shek O beach was crowded, all the beach tents rented by half-past nine, but on mid-week and 'personal hygiene' evenings (also known as sweat 'n' swim nights), the beach was usually all but deserted. The bus service ceased at dusk so only those with cars could reach it.

Shek O was my mother's favourite beach. The water in the bay was usually calm, there was no undertow and the sea floor shelved gently. By her own admission, my mother was a recreational swimmer, 'pootling about like a mermaid on holiday', as she put it, but despite his naval pretensions, my father hardly ever went in the water. Indeed, he could not really swim. His excuse for not swimming was that someone had to guard the tent containing our clothes, watches and so on, yet this was unnecessary. There were no thieves.

Late one afternoon, we drove to Shek O armed with swimming costumes, towels, shampoo and soap. Offices tended to close early on sweat 'n' swim days to allow staff to see to their maritime ablutions before it got dark. By the time we arrived, the beach was occupied by no more than a dozen parties, mostly Europeans. We rented a tent, bought a pannier of fresh water and, wading in up to our waists, my mother and I washed ourselves. Small fish, undeterred by the lather and unused to legs that were not thrashing about, nibbled at our shins and feet. Feeling clean – if salty – we then returned to the tent and sat in deckchairs while my father washed.

By now, it was dusk. The tent boy brought round two oil lanterns and placed them on the sand in front of the tent. The air was warm, the sea black and the world seemingly at peace. From the direction of the café beneath a huge awning of tangled vines on the beach before the village, came the distant clatter of mahjong tiles, the only sound other than the lap of waters. The only lights were our oil lamps, those of the café and perhaps the lanterns on a sampan fishing south of the islet.

'It's time we were going, Joyce,' my father suggested, studying the luminous hands on his gold Cyma.

'Not quite yet, Ken. It's a wonderful evening.'

'It's already night. I don't like driving on the twisting roads—'

'It's hardly the Khyber Pass under snow,' my mother interrupted. 'No highwaymen or wily Pathans. No black ice.'

At this point, my mother stood up from her deckchair, tugged the hem of her swimming costume down round her buttocks and announced, 'I'm going to have another quick dip before we go.'

'Don't be ridiculous, Joyce,' my father said. 'No-one swims in the dark. It's dangerous.'

'Rubbish!' she retorted.

'And I think it's against the law.'

'So call a policeman.'

'You'd never see an attacking shark,' my father continued. 'Or a jellyfish. What if . . . ?'

'I'd never see an attacking shark in broad daylight. In any case,' my mother came back at him, 'they don't stalk you, you know. As for a jellyfish, I'd feel the stings long before it drifted my way.'

It was truly dark by now. My mother set off for the water's edge. My father, abandoning his sentry post, followed her. I sat on a deckchair to watch.

'Joyce! Do not go in the water.'

My mother walked on, her tanned back glowing in the light of the lamps.

'Joyce! I'm telling you not to go in the water.'

There was no moon. The sky was a carpet of stars. Far out to sea were the lights of a cargo ship hove to until morning.

'Joyce! I forbid you to go in the water.'

'Forbid all you want, Ken,' she replied merrily over her shoulder and stepped into the sea.

My father returned to the tent, sat down next to me and said, 'Do you know, the stings from a jellyfish can give you a heart seizure.'

He got up, moved the lanterns behind us and, standing by a guy rope, squinted into the sea.

'I can't see her,' he murmured. 'If the tide's going out . . .'

To my surprise, he appeared to be genuinely concerned.

Then a voice called out urgently, 'Martin! Come here!'

'I forbid you to go,' my father said.

I got out of my deckchair.

'If you go down there, you'll get no pocket money for a month.'

I headed for the water's edge, my father keeping pace just behind me. My mother was the one who doled out my pocket money now and obeying her could hardly be construed as disobedience. It was, although I did not know how to express it, a conflict of interests. My mother's won.

'If you go into the water, I'll write to Grampy and tell him not to send any more *Eagles*.'

That I knew, as the water lapped at my ankles, was a bluff. My father enjoyed reading them too.

'Walk slowly,' my mother called. She was standing up

to her waist in the sea, not ten yards from the beach. 'You too, Ken,' she added.

'I think two corpses at Shek O are enough to make the headlines in the *South China Morning Post*,' my father replied sourly and, somewhat nonplussed by his family's rebellion, returned disconsolately to the tent.

I stood next to my mother.

'Watch!' she said.

She splashed the water. Suddenly, all around her radiated with a ghostly, pale green light.

'You do it!'

I brought my hands down on the sea. A fire of pale light spread out from my hands, dancing on the surface. The splashes on my body glimmered briefly.

I was entranced. Every movement I made produced an eruption of luminosity. China, I considered, was a land of spirits and spectres and this was incontrovertible proof.

'It's called phosphorescence,' my mother said. 'Isn't it marvellous?'

'Is it made by ghosts?' I enquired, feeling my toes dig into the sand. Whenever I felt uneasy, especially approaching dog shit on the pavement, they curled.

'No,' she answered, 'it's made by millions of microscopic organisms called plankton. When the air touches them, a chemical called phosphorus in their body glows. Look!' She pointed to some breaking wavelets approaching us. They were not white but an unearthly pale green, as if touched by death.

'Maybe,' I suggested, 'it's the light of Tin Hau come to save her brothers.'

'Maybe,' my mother replied, adding ironically, 'she's protecting us from sharks and jellyfish.'

I did not question how my mother had come to acquire

such information. I accepted it as I did all she said, for she was knowledgeable in the world whereas my father was only conversant with the ways of military chandlery.

We splashed around for a few more minutes then waded in to rejoin my father. He sat in the deckchair, smoking his pipe and staring out to sea as we took turns in the tent to dress.

'That was one of the bloody stupidest things I've ever known you to do, Joyce. And that's from a pretty bloody comprehensive catalogue of benighted stupidities. As for taking Martin with you . . .'

'Tell me, Ken,' my mother asked as we reached the car, 'have you ever, in your entire bloody life, done anything out of the norm, on the spur of the moment, because you suddenly felt the urge?'

My father did not answer. He got in the car, started the engine and waited for us to get in. We drove the length of Hong Kong island in silence. Back at the apartment, my mother turned on the radio while my father headed for the drinks cabinet. Ten minutes later, my mother came into my room to tuck me up although, in the hot weather, this involved nothing more than making sure the cotton sheet I slept under was pulled up. She had heard an old colonial wives' tale that, if the stomach was not covered at night, one could be dead by morning. Of what, it was never stated. Assured that my belly was protected from the diseases of darkness, she leant over and kissed me.

'Goodnight, Martin. That was fun, wasn't it?'

'Yes,' I confirmed. 'It was.'

'Don't ever tell,' she whispered, 'but if it weren't for you, I'd leave him . . .'

I did not at the time understand what she was talking about and closed my eyes.

'Goodnight, Joyce,' I said: I had taken on occasion to addressing my parents by their given names, although my father insisted I called him *sir* when we were in company.

She touched my head then. Perhaps for luck.

Close to Pinewood Battery there was a narrow road that ran down the north side of High West. It led nowhere, just petering out on the hillside, and it was extremely steep. Consequently, few people ever went down it and the wildlife that inhabited the undergrowth was undisturbed. I sometimes went that way in the late afternoon, the sun warm off the rocks, the sky hazy and tired to the west. Skinks rustled in the leaf litter or scurried ahead of me, their azure tails swinging from side to side to counteract their movement. Butterflies sunned themselves on the cracked concrete of the road bed or fluttered over the lantana florets. Balmy breezes blew up from the docks and narrow streets of Sai Ying Pun, carrying the sounds and smells of the city. Every now and then, the bellow of a cow in the Kennedy Town abattoir might lift up to me, to be abruptly cut short. All around me, unseen in the cover, birds caroused as they mapped out their territories for the night.

One particular afternoon, I went that way straight from school, hiding my Hong Kong basket full of games kit and homework under a bush a few yards from a boulder with the inscription: *25th. Battn Middlesex Regt. "Tyndareus" Feb. 6th 1917*. It was in memory of soldiers who had died when their troopship, bound for Hong Kong, struck a German mine off South Africa.

Setting off down the road, I had no specific purpose in mind. It had been a bad day at school. I had scored poorly in a maths test, been awarded fifty lines for sucking a *wah mui* in class ('It helps me concentrate, Miss') and been given a severe ticking off for putting the wire seal on my statutory mid-morning third of a pint of milk ration back in the empty bottle.

A little way beyond the *Tyndareus* memorial, I suddenly felt strangely ill at ease. It was not the maths test result nor was it the fact that I would have to own up to getting lines. The feeling was far more primeval, coming from the pit of my soul, from that part of the brain that has no apparent function. I looked back in case I was being followed, yet there was no-one – and no thing – in sight. I could see over a hundred yards in both directions.

Then, from the undergrowth, a small rodent appeared on the concrete not five paces ahead of me. It stopped, stared at me and then ran directly towards me, skittering between my legs and on down the road. In a few seconds, it was followed by two others which behaved in exactly the same way. I reasoned they were running from a snake and stood quite still. Yet no snake showed itself so, after a few minutes, I went back up the hill, collected my school basket and set off towards the Peak Tram terminus.

I had gone barely two hundred yards when a muntjak bounded out of the trees and down a steep bank. It stood in the middle of the road then, with one leap, was gone downhill in the direction of the reservoir. I could mark its progress through the forest by the noise it made. To see the creature in albeit by now fading daylight was rare enough. For it to make such a shindig as it fled was quite extraordinary. These were animals which could walk silently over a three-inch-deep layer of fresh cornflakes.

About fifty yards further on, the road narrowed, the trees growing over to form a tunnel that was always alive with birds. Used to people walking beneath their roosts, the dusk chorus was strident and melodic as I drew near.

Yet I was a short way into this sylvan subway when, all of a sudden, all the birds fell silent simultaneously. It was as if the current to them had been switched off. It was eerie and I felt apprehensive again, once more looking over my shoulder. There was no-one there. I quickened my pace and was soon at the junction by the Peak Café, heading as fast as I could up the steep road home.

When I recounted the experience to my mother, she replied that there had probably been a snake in the trees. I was not satisfied. When birds saw snakes they did not fall silent, they took to the wing.

After supper, my parents listened to the BBC World Service. I went to my room, wrote out my lines and hid them inside a textbook. Around nine o'clock, my father came in demanding to see my maths test paper. I reluctantly handed it to him. His face set as he saw the grade.

'Is there any point in us paying for you at the Peak School?' he asked in a sullen tone. 'It seems to me you must pass half your day gazing out the bloody window.'

'I don't understand maths,' I replied.

'If you don't pay attention, it's no bloody wonder.' He tore the test paper up and dropped the pieces on my bed. 'Pull your bloody socks up or, next September, you'll find yourself boarding at Hilsea College.'

As soon as he made the threat, I knew I was safe. He could not afford the fees at Hilsea College. Furthermore, my mother would never allow it. He was all bluster and I had seen through him.

'When's the next test?'

'Next month,' I admitted.

'Well, you'd better do a bloody sight better in that one or you know what . . .'

I knew what. This threat was not bluster. I would be paddled by the flat of my mother's hairbrush or one of my father's slippers.

I got into bed, pulled up the sheet to cover my stomach, switched off the bedside lamp and turned over to face the wall. I could not understand elementary algebra or fathom the difference between the discriminant and the coefficient and was sure I never would. And why substitute letters for numbers? It seemed particularly obtuse to me and I could see no purpose to it at all.

The door opened quietly. I knew it was my mother and feigned sleep. She left and I wallowed in my self-pity and fear of the next inevitable paddling. After a while, I drifted off into a troubled sleep.

Some time in the early hours, I woke. The room was in a faint half-light cast through the slats of the venetian blinds by the glow of the city below my window. Everything looked unreal and colourless. Even the bright cover of the *Eagle* annual on my table seemed leached of hue.

Quite suddenly, I heard a deep boom. It was not loud, more like a single peal of thunder far out to sea. I gave it little thought: summer lightning over the distant islands sometimes created a resonant, far off thunderclap.

Then, the sound fading, the venetian blinds started to ripple as if an unseen hand was running over them. The *Eagle* annual began to move across the table. At the same time, my bed edged away from the wall. The air filled with a strange vibrating hum. My model junk slid along the bookshelf. The books were starting to fall.

Instantly, I conjured up mental visions of the ghosts that

inhabited China, the evil gods, the cruel war-lords of heaven and hell to whom I had burnt no joss-sticks or paper money.

Screaming, I leapt from my bed and grabbed the junk before it could fall and break, putting it on the bed. I was fully awake now yet I was certain this was a dream.

My bedroom door slammed back. I jumped, the next scream frozen in my mouth. My mother rushed in, snatched me off my feet and ran with me to the front door of the apartment. My father was holding it open. Behind him, the occupants of the apartment across the landing were hurrying for the stairs.

Then it stopped. All was silent. My mother put me down. I pulled my pyjama trousers up. They had slipped halfway down my thighs and there was a girl my age living in the opposite apartment who was in my class at school.

Wearing assorted night attire, we joined the residents of the other seven apartments on the drive outside. The servants stood in a group near by talking urgently amongst themselves.

'Well, that was interesting,' my father commented with as much insouciance as he could muster.

'What happened?' I asked my mother.

'It was an earth tremor,' she replied. 'A small earthquake. It's all over now. There may be what they call after-shocks for a few days, but we'll probably not even feel them.'

It occurred to me that the strange behaviour of the muntjak, the birds and the rodents might have been a premonition. Could the animals have been aware it was coming? Yet, although convinced this was so, I held my peace. My father, I knew, would ridicule the assumption.

It was not logical, just another example of the bloody boy's vivid imagination.

We returned to our apartment to be met by Wong carrying a tray of tea, biscuits and a glass of milk.

'No p'oblum, master, missee, young master. Happen all time China-side,' he greeted us with a placatory smile.

My father took a cup of tea and started lecturing us about the earth's crust, the western Pacific earthquake zone, volcanoes and continental drift. It meant as much to me as quadratic equations. I went out into the kitchen to refill my glass of milk. Wong was sweeping up the shattered remains of some rice bowls which had slid off the draining board.

'What you think make this trouble?' I asked him.

'Yen Lo,' he said significantly and without any hesitation. 'He ang'wee. No like what man do. Tomowwwow, Ah Shun go tempul-side. Maybe burn some money. Make him happy one more time.'

I preferred Wong's supernatural reasoning to my father's logic. Yen Lo was the chief god of the underworld.

9

HIKING TO BUDDHA, SWIMMING WITH COLONEL NOMA

ANOTHER OUTING ORGANIZED BY MR BORRIE PROMISED, FROM the outline sent to my mother, to be a two-phase forced march. My father was once again reluctant to go but, as Mr Borrie was his Old Man, he was more or less faced with a three-line whip. Consequently, one winter's Saturday afternoon at thirteen hundred hours sharp, we and a party of about two dozen set off in a naval launch for the fishing village of Tung Chung on the northern coast of Lan Tau. I was the only child present. The outing guidelines had precluded those under sixteen because a good deal of walking would be involved, but my mother said I was probably fitter than half the adults and won the argument. This inevitably annoyed my father.

'It states quite clearly in the rules, Joyce—'

'Bugger the rules!' my mother retorted.

'Well, if the boy lags behind,' my father declared, 'you'll be the one to stay with him. If the two of you get lost in the mountains, be it on your own head.'

'I'll take that risk,' my mother retorted. 'It's hardly the Himalayas. We're not likely to get caught out by a blizzard.'

Progress had passed the village of Tung Chung by. The low buildings, most well over a century old, looked out across a valley of rice paddies, banyan, paper bark and lychee trees. Behind every house or farmstead was a stand of huge yellow, green-striped bamboos, some of the stems as thick as my thigh. These, I discovered, had been deliberately planted in times past to attract snakes. When I first heard it, this information astounded me. I asked if the snakes were there to be caught for the pot, but was told that the occupants of the houses were farmers who stored their rice in the settlement. And rats ate rice. And snakes ate rats.

Stepping from our naval launch on to a rickety wooden pier, we congregated on dry land to be addressed by Mr Borrie.

'Now, have you all your maps and directions?' he asked. 'After we leave the paddyfields, there are only two places where you might get lost. One is at the nunnery, the other as you reach the pass. Be sure to consult your maps at these points. Needless to say, do not enter the nunnery.'

'What's a nunnery?' I whispered to my mother.

'Another word for a convent.'

'Why can't we enter it?' I wanted to know. Such adamant exclusion had aroused my curiosity.

'The nuns don't like men entering their houses.'

'I'm not a man,' I argued. 'I'm a boy. Neither are you. Can't we go in?'

My father, overhearing this conversation, said, 'Don't ask so many damn questions. You can't go in and that's an end to it.'

As he spoke, he fought with the straps of a military knapsack. Unaccustomed to anything larger or more complicated than an attaché case, my father was finding it hard knowing which strap went where. My mother, who had already slipped hers on, watched impassively.

'Well don't just stand there, Joyce,' he muttered under his breath. 'Help me get this benighted thing on.'

'Didn't they show you how in the war?' she replied genially.

'I wasn't in the bloody Army.'

'Nor the bloody Navy,' she responded and set about untangling him.

'Where exactly are we going?' I asked my mother as my father tried to ease his shoulders and settle his pack.

'Ngong Ping,' my mother answered.

'What's at Ngong Ping?'

'Wait and see.'

'Where is it?'

She pointed two thousand feet or more up the mountainside and said, 'See that little dip to the left of that ridge? It's a mile the other side of that.'

We crossed a tidal creek on an uneven timber footbridge and went through the little village of Ma Wan Chung. The houses were ancient, their roofs covered with black glazed tiles. Dogs barked half-heartedly at us and chickens scattered under our feet. A large sway-backed pig lay in a patch of dust in front of a small temple, suckling a copious litter of squealing piglets. Out of the village, we set off along a wide, well-beaten track surrounded by fallow paddyfields. In another half a mile, we arrived in front of a small, derelict, grey-stone fortress covered in creepers. One of our party, armed with a *kukri*, sliced a path through to the battlements on which stood six cannon dating to the early nineteenth century. A short lecture by the *kukri* wielder informed us that the fortress was erected about 1830 in the Q'ing dynasty. It was not actually a fort *per se* but a *yamen* and centre for the administration of a number of other forts in the area. My mother whispered to me that, had my father been Chinese and alive then, he might have been posted here as a civil servant to supply war junks. At this notion, we broke out into giggles which my father attempted unsuccessfully to stifle with narrowed eyes.

We walked indian file across more paddyfields, keeping to the paths that ran along the tops of the narrow dykes dividing the fields. On either side, rice stubble projected from hardened mud into which the hoof- and footprints of buffalo and humans had been impressed. Coming to the end of the valley, the path started to rise into the mountains, rough rocks making the going hard.

I left my parents and moved to the head of the line where Mr Borrie was making good progress.

'Hello, young Booth,' he addressed me. 'Full of beans?'

'Yes, sir.'

'Being held up by the old fogeys?'

I was not quite sure how to respond but he saved me the effort.

'Go on ahead,' he invited. 'Scout out the way. But,' he paused for effect, 'when the path branches at a Y-shaped junction, the right-hand path consisting of steps, you stop and wait for the rest of us. You savvy?'

I savvied and set off up the mountain. The path grew steeper but I swung my arms, measured my breathing and was soon several hundred yards ahead of the party. It was not long before I came to the Y junction. A small rill tumbled down the mountainside and I wet my face in it but did not drink. One never knew if the water had already served a multitude of purposes in a settlement at a higher altitude. I crossed the path and sat on the steps to let the rest of the party catch up. Behind me stood a small group of buildings from which, when the breeze temporarily shifted direction, I could smell joss-sticks.

There came a soft shuffling sound from over my shoulder. I turned to find myself being observed by two Buddhist nuns. They wore grey, long-sleeved, ankle-length habits and their heads were shaven, so it was quite impossible to judge their ages. Around their necks hung simple necklaces of wooden beads. Not sure what to do, and heedful of Mr Borrie's warning, I stood up and stepped back on to the path. They watched me go, impassive looks upon their faces. I sensed that perhaps they were young and wanted to talk to me, this strange, small *gweilo* from the other world of which they occasionally heard talk but had not seen for many years, nor perhaps ever would again.

The remainder of the party arrived and I rejoined my parents to find my father in a mood.

'What do you think you were doing, you blithering little idiot?' my father demanded to know.

'Let him be, Ken,' my mother remonstrated.

'That's rich, coming from someone who took him swimming at night with the tide going out.'

'He's come to no harm.'

My father ignored these entreaties and directed his full attention to me. Keeping his voice, which was breathless from the climb, low he said, 'Where were you? Your mother and I were worried stiff.'

'No, I wasn't,' my mother chimed in. 'If Martin can find his way through the streets of Kowloon, he can sure as eggs is eggs find his way on a mountainside with only one path on it.'

'And if he had fallen?' my father replied.

'He has the run of the Peak, Ken, for God's sake,' my mother said with a hint of exasperation. 'I think he's intelligent enough to know a sheer drop when he sees one. Besides, do you notice any precipices, Ken? Cliffs? The worst he can do is slip on the path and slide down on his bum.'

She looked at me pointedly then at the rear of my father's trousers. They were covered in dust and I regretted having gone ahead. My father sliding downhill on his arse must have been a sight to behold.

'I had permission. I was asked to scout ahead as far as the nunnery.'

'By whom?' my father answered, in the tone of voice that suggested he was convinced I was lying.

'Ken—'

'No, Joyce, I'm getting to the bottom of this . . .'

At that moment, Mr Borrie called back from the head of the line, 'Hello, Ken, Joyce. Well, young Booth, ready for some more scouting?'

My father gave me a thunderous look. I had not been lying. My mother gave me a smile and a sly wink.

The path grew steeper as it approached the high flanks of Lan Tau Peak. I started to get breathless, my head spinning with the exertion, and was about to pause for a rest when the path levelled out and I could see, some way ahead, a ceremonial archway, or *pi lau*. Curiosity overcame exhaustion.

The *pi lau* was made of stone and stood silhouetted against the sky. The Chinese characters engraved over its span had once been painted red but the mountain wind had all but wiped them clean. From the *pi lau*, the path followed the contours of a hill to a plateau of neatly tended vegetable fields. I was surprised to find any agriculture going on at such an altitude but what really amazed me were the number of pagoda-like structures that dotted the landscape. They too were made of stone, about twelve feet high, painted white and resembling several iced dough-nuts placed one on top of the other, getting consecutively smaller as the structure got higher. On the top was a finial painted imperial Chinese yellow.

'What are they, sir?' I asked Mr Borrie who had caught up with me.

The remainder of the party was strung out behind him. The rearguard, which consisted of my father, had only just reached the *pi lau*.

'I believe they're either the graves of abbots,' Mr Borrie replied, 'or receptacles for holy scriptures. This is Ngong Ping, our destination. You've done very well getting up the mountain. Put the rest of us to shame.' He glanced back. My father was leaning against the *pi lau*. 'Your poor old dad's a bit out of shape.'

'What's an abbot?' I enquired.

'The head of a monastery,' came the reply.

'But why do they bring them all the way up here to bury them?'

'Step forth, young Booth,' Mr Borrie answered, 'and all shall be revealed.'

We walked on together. The path widened. Ahead, surrounded by low trees, was a group of stone buildings.

'Here we are,' Mr Borrie announced. 'This is the Po Lin monastery. *Po Lin* means Precious Lotus, so that should tell you what religion is worshipped here.'

It did and I replied, 'Buddhism, sir.'

'Well done!' he congratulated me. 'Now, as the others arrive, you tell them to wait here.'

Mr Borrie hurried on to the monastery. I felt adult and

important with my responsibility. In fifteen minutes, he returned and led us along a path through carefully tended vegetable plots, past an area of tea bushes and into the monastery complex, the buildings tucked under a low ridge. It was by now late afternoon. The sun was already down below the montane horizon and the temperature dropping fast.

Gathered together by a circular moon gate, we were introduced to a monk whom we were told was the guest master. Like the nuns I had seen, he wore a grey-coloured robe and his head was shaven. He welcomed us in broken English, informed us of the monastic timetable, invited us to join the monks in prayer around dawn and reminded us that this was a tranquil place so we were not to 'make big noise'. Our party was then divided into two groups by gender. The women were allotted a dormitory some way off, the men another in a two-storey building immediately behind the temple.

I was placed with the men. The room in which we were to sleep was on the second floor, had a low ceiling with beams that were nothing more than tree trunks supporting the roof. The beds were plain wooden *kangs* surrounded by screens, each one covered by a woven mat and a thin cotton quilt with a hard Chinese traditional pillow. Lighting was provided by three guttering oil lanterns which cast a timeless orange glow on the dark wood. It reminded me of the opium den in Kowloon Walled City.

My father, having struggled to escape the clutches of his knapsack, unpacked it. He had brought a dressing gown, flannel pyjamas and the slippers that doubled as instruments of summary justice back home. These neatly laid out on his *kang*, he took out his red leather wash bag and a towel, placing them beside his clothing. When he was done, his possessions looked like a naval rating's bunk in a lower-deck mess awaiting a daily kit inspection. No-one else bothered to unpack.

'Here's your stuff,' my father said, producing a wash bag from the knapsack. He rummaged further. 'I can find your towel . . .' he said at length, handing it to me '. . . but I'm damned if I can find your pyjamas. Your mother seems to have forgotten them.'

A sonorous bell, almost as deep as a bass drum, boomed in a nearby building. I went outside to discover Mr Borrie standing by the moon gate.

'Excuse me, sir,' I asked, breaking into his thoughts, 'but why are we allowed to stay here when we aren't monks?'

'Good question, young Booth,' he replied. 'Buddhist monks take a vow of hospitality. That means, they are obliged to give succour – food and shelter – for free, to anyone who demands it. But when people like us come to stay here we make an offering to the monastery and pay the cost of our food and lodging.'

'Why?'

'Because we are rich *gweilos* and they are poor Chinese monks,' Mr Borrie replied. 'A dollar to us is a pack of cigarettes, but to them . . .' He paused then went on, 'Tonight, you'll live like a Buddhist monk, just as they have for a thousand years.'

'I've not got any pyjamas,' I admitted. My mother's omission was worrying me.

'Don't fret,' Mr Borrie reassured me. 'Neither have any of us. Except perhaps your father.' He winked at me and went on, 'We'll be having supper soon. Don't be late.'

I left him and went into the temple. It was like all the other temples I had visited, with an ornate altar, smouldering incense, embroidered tapestries, offerings, lanterns and censers. The one difference was the statue of Buddha. In the curio shops and gold dealers of Hong Kong, Buddha was represented by a fat, grinning man with a paunch of obese proportions. This Buddha, by contrast, was a benign seated figure with a peaceful expression, its right hand raised in blessing. There were no demon warriors or guardians of heaven. I lit a joss-stick, genuflected – after checking my father was not about to enter – and placed it in the sand-filled urn. Had my father, who professed Christianity but never went to church, caught me worshipping false gods and idols, I dared not think of the consequences. He would probably have personally condemned me to eternal damnation.

Returning through the moon gate, I followed the sound of the bell and came upon a hall in which lines of monks sat at a square of low tables finishing a meal. At one end of the room, a monk stood at a simple lectern reading a collect as his brothers ate. The only sounds were his chant-like reading and the tolling of a bronze bell which was shaped like an inverted tulip. It was rung by a log of wood suspended horizontally by two ropes from a ceiling beam.

I lingered in the doorway. The monks paid me not the slightest attention and, after a few moments, I slipped away.

'You forgot my pyjamas,' I said to my mother as I came upon her by a small pond in which a number of red-eared terrapins floated in the water or lay on a rock in the centre.

'Do you know why they keep terrapins?' she rejoined.

'To eat?' I ventured.

'No,' she replied. 'It's because terrapins and turtles – especially marine turtles – are considered very lucky and stand for longevity. That means long life. The turtle supports the elephant upon whose back rests the world. A long time ago, the Chinese believed the world was a giant turtle's shell. Besides,' she finished, 'what do you want pyjamas for? It's going to be far too cold for py-jams. When you go to bed, just take your shoes off, keep all your clothes on and wrap yourself up in the quilt.'

'But Daddy's got his,' I argued, ignoring the homily on the universal and divine turtle which I already knew from my visits to numerous back-street temples.

'Well, he would, wouldn't he?' was my mother's response.

We ate by lamplight in a large room at the other end of the monastery from the monks' hall. The food was delicious, the flavours subtle and the textures exquisite. Yet, although I was an experienced *dai pai dong* diner, I was unable to recognize many of the dishes and asked my mother what meat was in them.

'None,' she answered.

With my chopsticks, I picked up a piece of what looked like and tasted like braised duck's breast.

'I know what you're thinking,' my mother said, 'but it's not duck. It's against the Buddhist religion to take life. All the food is made out of *dofu*, fungi and herbs. The vegetables are grown in the plots we saw as we arrived. The monastery is virtually self-sufficient in everything except paraffin, candles and joss-sticks.'

At nine o'clock, we turned in. There were eight of us in the dormitory. My *kang* was in a cubicle on its own, my father's the far side of the screen separating my space from the others'. I removed my shoes and snuggled under the quilt fully clothed. Outside, a cold wind had sprung up, rattling the shutters of the window by my head. My father came round the end of the screen to say goodnight. He was wearing his dressing gown over the flannel pyjamas. His slippers clicked on the wooden floor.

The boards of the *kang* were hard, as was the pillow block, but I soon fell asleep, a cold draught blowing over my face.

During the night, I was woken by a strange noise. It sounded like castanets being played in slow motion or a convention of geckoes. On consideration, I knew it could not be the latter. One rarely saw geckoes in the winter: it was too cold for them. It then occurred to me that it might be the skeleton of a lonely spirit wandering the earth. If there were spirits anywhere, they would surely be in a monastery high in the mountains.

Then a muted voice said, 'For heaven's sake, Ken, put your clothes back on. Your shivering's keeping us awake.'

Around dawn, I was woken again but this time by muffled chanting. Slipping my shoes on, I tiptoed down the stairs and went outside. The sound was coming from the temple. I went to the main door and stepped inside. The monks were kneeling in front of the altar, chanting prayers. Their shaven heads shone in the lamplight. Buddha seemed to hover in mid-air in the semi-darkness, the lamps glinting off the brass cups. The joss-stick smoke hung marbled in the air, moving only when a finger of breeze blew in. It was an unearthly experience. I felt I was wrapped in the pure essence of divinity. Somehow, I had transcended the ordinary in my life and was now in what an adult might have termed a state of grace.

By the time the prayer session ended, it was fully day-light. I left the temple to find the men from my dormitory sluicing their faces at a water trough fed by a small stone-lined gully. A few had loosened their shirts and were rubbing their armpits. I followed their example. The water was only a few degrees above freezing and tightened my skin the moment it touched it, stealing my breath. The cold breeze chilled my wet skin until it hurt.

I was pondering on whether or not to fetch my towel when my father appeared, fully dressed but dishevelled, his towel around his neck. Not greeting me, he balanced his wash bag on the edge of the trough and removed from it a razor, shaving brush and a bowl of shaving soap. He wet his face with a flannel, soaped himself without being able to build up much of a lather, and started shaving. Several of the other men gave each other knowing glances.

It must have been hell. Over the sound of the wind, I could hear the blade of his safety razor rasping at his stubble. More than once, he winced but kept his jaw set and his razor hand firm. He had just finished his chin when the towel slipped from his neck, caught his wash bag and the two of them fell into the water. His shaving brush followed, the weight of its ivory handle sinking it to the bottom of the trough. My father had no alternative but to strip to the waist and immerse himself to the shoulder to retrieve it.

An hour later, warmed by a bowl of tea and a serving of *congee*, we bade the guest master farewell by bowing to him and left the monastery. We headed for Mui Wo, otherwise known as Silvermine Bay, seven and a half miles away over the mountains. It was quite heavy going in places but, by mid-morning, the sky was cloudless and blue, the sunlight sharp and warm on the skin.

As on the day before, I forged ahead of the party and thought over my brief stay in the monastery. I could never, I decided, adapt to the life of a monk, yet it certainly held a distinct attraction. The monastery had been so peaceful, my father's chattering teeth apart, and the chanting had somehow lifted my soul. I knew, there and then, that I would return to the monastery one day.

On Hong Kong-side, in addition to rickshaws, taxis and buses, there was a double-decker tram system that ran from Kennedy Town in the west to Shau Kei Wan at the eastern extremity of the city. A branch line veered off to Happy Valley where it went in a circuit round the race-course and was diverted to the tram depot. The newer trams were made of metal panelling on a steel chassis, the seats were wooden slats and the windows went up and down on a sash. Power was supplied by overhead poles connecting to wires, the trams driven by electric motors. On those that were older, the front and rear upper decks were open whilst one or two very old models had upper decks that were completely open to the sky.

The trams were slow and noisy as they rattled and ground their way along tracks set in the metalled surface of the streets, yet they were also almost romantic, a means of locomotion from another age. Furthermore, they were cheap. The fare was ten cents, no matter how far one travelled. This was ideal for me. I would walk towards Kennedy Town and mount a tram heading east. If I got on near the start of the journey I was assured a top-deck front seat.

The vehicle seemed to clatter and clank its way through a history of urban Hong Kong. From Western District with its narrow nineteenth-century streets lined with traditional Chinese buildings as old as the colony itself, the tram tracks entered Central District, swaying by the plush prestige stores such as the Dragon Seed Company. Running down the centre of Des Voeux Road, it went along the edge of Statue Square, by the façades of the Hongkong and Shanghai Bank and the Bank of China – under the impassive bronze gaze of Stephen and Stitt – before skirting the Hong Kong Cricket Club pitch.

From my vantage point on the top deck I could look down on the pedestrians, coolies and rickshaws, old crones pushing wheeled trolleys piled with bags of laundry, Chinese school children in pristine uniforms, amahs immaculate in black and white, policemen in their khaki uniforms, with their black Sam Browne belts and revolvers in holsters, directing the traffic from their pagoda-like platforms. Conservative-looking British and brash American cars drove by. Cyclists wove in and out of the traffic.

Next, the tram would enter Wanchai, sliding past bars, tea houses, mahjong schools and restaurants. Passengers boarded or alighted at tram stops on small traffic islands, getting on the tram at the front and off at the rear. Onwards then along the edge of the Causeway Bay typhoon shelter, North Point, Quarry Bay and Sai Wan Ho. Eventually, after more than an hour, the tram would reach Shau Kei Wan where, turning in a circle by a junk-building yard, it would set off on the return journey. I would break my journey here, sit on the sea wall over which I knew the invading Japanese Imperial Army had swarmed in 1941, drink a Green Spot and watch the carpenters shaping planks to make a junk before me, the keel laid and the air scented with the perfume of teakwood shavings.

One summer's afternoon, I was sitting on the upper deck of an eastbound tram when an elderly European woman carrying a silver-topped walking cane and a bunch of yellow roses wrapped in cellophane sat next to me.

'Excuse me, young man,' she said, 'but can you tell me if this tram is for Happy Valley?'

'No,' I replied, 'this tram goes to North Point.'

'Oh, dear!' she exclaimed, suddenly clearly distressed. 'I need to get to Happy Valley. It's all most confusing.'

I realized then that she was not a *gweipor* and offered to take her there. She readily accepted and, after changing trams at the Percival Street switch-over, we proceeded around the race course perimeter.

'Where exactly are you going?' I enquired.

'To the cemetery,' was her answer.

The Happy Valley cemetery was the second oldest in Hong Kong, the earliest graves dating to the foundation of the colony.

As we approached the tram stop by the cemetery entrance, she asked, 'You wouldn't help me, would you, young man? I'm afraid my legs aren't what they used to be.'

I helped her down the stairs and across the road into the cemetery. The graves were arranged on a series of stepped terraces running up the side of the valley.

'I need to find a grave,' she said as we entered the cemetery.

I looked in dismay at the serried ranks of perhaps a thousand tombstones. Those higher up the cemetery were overgrown with creepers. Ideal snake terrain, I thought. And I was wearing shorts, short socks and sandals.

'Could you help me find it?'

I was beginning to think I had been suckered by this sweet old lady but decided to assist her nevertheless.

'What is the . . . ?' I was not sure how to refer to a corpse.

She gave me the surname, adding, 'He died in 1879.'

While the elderly lady perched on a grave, leaning on her cane and wiping her brow, I started to trot methodically along the lines of graves. In three-quarters of an hour I had viewed all the graves except those in the corner which I was most loathe to approach.

All the graves were of Europeans, predominantly men under the age of thirty. Some were military graves, others civilian. Yet what astonished me was their causes of death. Diseases I had expected, but not 'fell from the rigging', 'lost overboard', 'murdered in the pursuance of his duty', and 'killed by pirates off Cheefoo'. Many of the memorials had been erected 'by his shipmates' or public subscription.

The elderly lady was disappointed I had not found her grave but she gave me a ten-dollar note.

I thanked her and asked why she was seeking the grave.

'It's my great-grandfather,' she replied. 'He was one of the first British people to live here.'

I thought for a minute then said, 'The oldest graveyard is in Stanley. I go swimming near there.'

'And how might I get to Stanley?'

'There's a bus,' I told her, 'but I don't know where to catch it.'

She bent down and kissed me on my cheek. 'You are a little angel,' she praised me.

At that, she picked up her roses and hailed a taxi.

'Can you tell the driver where I want to go?'

I leant through the window and said, '*Chek Chue.*'

With that, she was gone. The last I saw of her were her yellow roses on the back parcel shelf of the taxi.

When I arrived home, I told my mother what I had been up to.

'Well, you did your best for the poor soul,' she remarked.

'But the graves . . .' I said. 'No-one died of old age.'

'No, I'm sure they didn't,' my mother replied. 'That was their sacrifice. Those people founded Hong Kong. They set the ball rolling for all of us.' She was pensive for a moment before adding, 'I wonder what they'd think of it now.'

That evening, I sat on the balcony with all of Hong Kong spread out at my feet and tried to imagine it without streets and buildings and ferry boats. Instead of grey British and American warships I attempted to visualize men-o'-war and opium clippers and war junks. And it came to me that I was a descendant of those men, keeping the ball rolling merely by my being there.

My father had a fierce hatred of the trams based upon the facts that they had no brake lights, they caused traffic jams at tram stops where vehicular traffic had to give way to alighting or embarking passengers, and they had a right of way over the traffic lights. Worse, however, was their inability to stop as quickly as a car.

The first incident happened on Yee Wo Street. My father wished to turn right into Kai Chiu Road. Disregarding a tram coming up behind, he pulled smartly into the centre of the road – where the tram tracks lay – and waited for a break in the traffic. There was the sound of tearing metal. Sparks flew from the tram wheel. A North Point bound tram slid into the back of the Ford at an impact speed of about three miles an hour. I was mildly jolted in the back seat. My father got out to survey the damage. The rear offside lights of the Ford were smashed, the bumper and rear wing dented and deformed. The tram driver alighted, surveyed the situation then gesticulated for my father to get his car out of the way. On the tram, all the passengers were leaning out of the windows.

My father refused to move. My mother and I joined him. A crowd began to gather on the pavement expectantly awaiting what was an inescapable confrontation.

'Move the car towards the kerb, Ken,' my mother suggested.

'No, Joyce! Not until the police have seen it.'

'You've got me and Martin as witnesses.'

'No!' my father repeated bluntly. 'I want independent third-party verification. The law clearly states that the driver of any vehicle that goes up the back of another vehicle is liable. I'm not at fault here . . .'

My mother sought to placate my father. 'No-one says you are, Ken.'

'He's culpable,' my father said, pointing an accusatory finger at the tram driver, who took umbrage at being pointed at and let off a stream of invective in Cantonese that even I could not translate.

'Don't you speak to me like that!' my father retorted. 'You should have kept your bloody distance . . .'

At this, the driver decided not to keep any distance at all and closed on my father.

'Don't you come on to me like that!' my father muttered loudly and he removed his blazer, putting it in the car.

'Ken, I don't think this is helping matters,' my mother observed. 'Just let it go.'

'I'm damned if I will!' my father exclaimed over his shoulder. 'I'm not in the wrong here.'

The passengers in the tram, like schoolboys in a play-ground seeing a fight in the offing, started to egg the tram driver on. He commenced bouncing about on his heels like a boxer warming up.

This, I knew as a spectator at any number of coolie arguments, did not bode well, yet there was nothing I could do to defuse the situation.

Suddenly, the tram driver lunged at my father who blocked the blow. My mother tried to step between the combatants, safe in the knowledge that no-one would dare hit a *gweipor*. The tram driver dodged round her and took another swing. My father blocked it once more and managed to land a clout around his opponent's ear. The passengers on the tram and the audience on the pavement gave vent to a loud *Whoa!* intermingled with an undertone of *Ayarhs!*

Needless to say, this enraged the driver further. He had lost face in front of at least two hundred onlookers.

Feeling I should do something, I stepped forwards and yelled at him, '*Wei! Lei! Heui la! Diu nei lo mo!*' (literally, Hey, you! Get lost! Go fuck your mother!).

At the time, I was ignorant of the exact meaning of the phrase but knew it was pretty expressive. My knowledge of the language of the streets exercised, I then stepped forward and shook my finger at him in a school-ma'amish fashion.

The crowd on the pavement broke out into hoots of hilarity. So did the passengers. The driver just stared at me, taken aback by this little *gweilo* who spoke at least a smattering of colloquial Cantonese.

A police traffic patrol arrived.

As the Ford was now askew across both the east- and westbound tram lines, it was quickly causing a backlog to build up in both directions. A traffic patrol had come to see what was creating gridlock half a mile down the road.

'This bloody fool—' my father began.

'I can see what's happened, sir,' a European police inspector interrupted him. 'Now, with your permission . . .'

A Chinese constable drove the Ford to the kerb whilst four others directed the traffic. The westbound trams started moving again. After a few words from a Chinese police corporal, the tram driver returned to his place and the tram went on its way.

The inspector took out a notebook and pencil then came over to my father.

'Not very lucky, are we, sir?' He opened the notebook. 'First the tricycle . . .'

He took down the details. The tram company paid for the damage. They also accepted liability for the next two, identical accidents. On the fourth, they sued for remuneration of income lost due to delayed services. They did not win the case. As a result, however, my father – like my mother before him – was the cause of a change in the law. It was henceforth illegal to stop a vehicle on the tram lines.

For as long as we lived in Hong Kong, my mother had attempted to get me to swim. She was a fairly competent swimmer herself and wanted me to be likewise, ostensibly as a life skill such as playing tennis or bridge or being able to ballroom dance, but actually so as to have someone to swim with.

At least once a week throughout my school holidays and often at a weekend during term, my mother and I would go to the beach together, sometimes in the company of friends, sometimes just the two of us. Her favourite spot when we lived at the Fourseas and on Boundary Street in Kowloon was 11½ Mile Beach. It lacked any amenities whatsoever and the only shelter was three or four ruined beach houses destroyed in the war and a row of trees. However, a Dairy Farm popsicle seller was usually to be found in the vicinity.

The beach was of sand with a freshwater stream cutting through it at one end. Transport was provided by the Navy, which ran a daily families' bus service to Kadoorie Beach, seven miles further on with beach toilets, deck-chairs, ice-cream sellers and a *dai pai dong* or two. Whereas the latter was frequently crowded, *sap yat bun* (Cantonese for 11½), as my mother called the beach, rarely had two dozen people on it.

As soon as her foot touched sand, my mother undressed. Wearing only a pair of shorts and a blouse over her swimming costume, she was stripped for action in seconds. I took longer out of a reluctance to join her. I would rather have spent my afternoon catching fish in the stream or hunting for tree frogs in the ravine down which it ran. Finally, unable to dismiss my mother's entreaties any longer, I would take off my clothes and, grudgingly be-trunked, wade out to join her.

The sea was always warm and lapped at my stomach. The sandy bottom was firm with only a few rocks here and there to which clung barnacles, minuscule sea anemones that packed a vicious sting and urchins with long black spines as sharp as hypodermic needles. A crevice in a large submarine rock was the residency of a small octopus which could be lured out with a dead fish or a piece of meat. It never completely quit its shelter but I often managed to encourage its tentacles and head into the open.

Yet we were not there to enjoy the wonders of marine nature. My mother would take my hands and, towing me as she walked backwards, attempt to get me to kick my legs. I watched as the water rose up her body and knew that once her bosom was submerged I was out of my depth. At this point, she would let go of one hand and tell me to move it breast-stroke fashion. I would obey but grip her other hand so tightly she could not cast me adrift. All the while, I would be breathing hard in panic and begging her not to let me go. She promised she would not and she never did. As a consequence she didn't betray a trust nor did I learn to swim. I possessed plenty of theory but precious little courage.

After a while, she would give up and swim out to the swimming platform where she would sit absorbing the sub-tropical sun, her head tilted back, her short blond hair golden in the light and her eyes closed, day-dreaming.

I would sit on the beach and look out at her, often wondering how life would be if it were just her and me. I think it was at those moments I came to love her rather than just rely upon her as children do their mothers. I was becoming independent and my feelings for her were altering – maturing – as a consequence.

At five o'clock, the grunting horn of the Bedford bus would summon us from the beach and we would climb the concrete steps to the road and board it. Because the seats were wooden and slatted we did not even need to change out of our wet costumes.

After our move to the Peak we frequented Tweed Bay, a secluded sandy beach set aside for the exclusive use of the members of the Prison Officers' Club at Stanley, of which my parents were curiously members. It lay in a tiny bay under the very walls of Hong Kong's top security jail and was reached by passing through several guarded gates. No-one had ever escaped from the place: only one prisoner had ever scaled the walls and he had broken his legs in the process. Every bather was a turnkey, his superior or their families.

I liked Tweed Bay the least of all the beaches we visited. There were no food or popsicle sellers, no streams or woods to explore – and if there had been, they would have been out of bounds as I found out when I tried to climb the hill behind the beach to get a look into the prison. I had not gone fifty yards before I was apprehended by two warders. In short, Tweed Bay was boring.

It was here I finally learnt to swim.

One Saturday afternoon, my mother and I drove to Tweed Bay with Philip and Ray as our club guests, riding in their Jaguar. Both the Bryants were good fun and, as they had no children of their own, I became a surrogate son whenever we were together. In retrospect, I think Philip appreciated how my father regarded me with indifference and decided to fill in a few of the cracks in his non-existent paternity.

We parked by the prison walls and walked to the beach. There were no changing facilities but, as usual, we wore our swimming costumes in lieu of underwear. In next to no time, the adults were in the sea and I was paddling in the shallows.

Eventually, tiring of this, I sat on the beach, absent-mindedly and unsuccessfully digging for the small opaque crabs that lived in holes in the sand. After a while, Philip left the sea and walked up to me.

'I think it's time,' he said.

'Time for what?' I rejoined.

'To swim. Before we go home, I'll have you frolicking like a porpoise.'

This I very much doubted but I trusted Philip and agreed he could have a go where my mother had failed. I was not to know that she and Ray were in on it too.

Philip and I walked out until the water was up to my chest. He then held his arms out and I lay across his hands, face down. The wavelets broke in my face, stinging my eyes.

'Now,' Philip said, 'kick your legs like frogs do.'

I did as he suggested.

'Now, don't stop kicking and move your arms, fingers closed, as if you were pushing the water behind you.' Again, I complied.

Suddenly, I sensed his hands were no longer touching my stomach. Indeed, he was at least ten feet away and treading water. I panicked, stopped kicking, tried to stand up and sank vertically. I was going to drown. I knew it. I opened my mouth to scream. At that moment, my head broke the surface, strong hands under my armpits.

'I want to get out!' I spluttered, clinging to his neck.

'If you want to get out,' he answered calmly, 'you'll have to swim to the beach. I'll come with you.'

'I can't swim,' I pleaded.

'Yes, you can,' he declared, smiling at me. 'The human body is less dense than seawater. It floats. Look at your mother and Ray.' Sure enough, they were holding hands and floating on their backs. 'Now, let's try again.'

I wanted to trust Philip. I liked him and I knew he would never let me come to harm, but . . . He put his hands on my stomach again, held me horizontal in the water and off we went. He removed his hands and, with much splashing and gasping, I made it to the beach.

My mother and Ray kissed me; Philip shook my hand, man to man.

'You see,' he said when the clamour of female congratulation had died down, 'in life we can do anything within our physical power if only we have the courage. You could climb Mount Everest if you genuinely wanted to.'

That hot Saturday in the South China Sea, I learnt more than how to swim. Philip had shown me that much more was possible if one pushed the limits a bit and, from then on, I did.

As my mother and Ray got changed behind a towel, Philip and I did the gentlemanly thing and looked out beyond Tweed Bay into the greater Ty Tam Bay beyond.

'A good place to learn to swim,' he remarked off-handedly. 'Not much current, and if you knew about the place you'd never let your feet touch the bottom.'

'Why not?' I asked, picturing giant clams or beds of sea urchins.

'Do you know who Colonel Noma was?'

I shook my head.

'Well,' Philip told me, 'after the war, the Japanese in Hong Kong who had murdered a lot of our chaps – and local Chinese, too – were rounded up and tried in a court of law for what were called war crimes. That was not just killing people in the fighting, which is what happens in war, but afterwards. Killing wounded soldiers instead of treating them, unarmed prisoners, women and children. That sort of thing. Those that were found guilty were hanged in the prison behind us. There were nine of them in all. The most senior were Colonels Noma and Tamura. When they were dead their bodies were weighted with chains and dumped in the sea.'

'What did they do?' I asked.

'Noma was head of the gendarmerie. He killed and tortured many people.'

'How many?'

'Certainly hundreds, probably thousands.'

'Why didn't they dig graves for them?'

'Because the British and Chinese wanted to punish them for ever. The Japanese believe a man's soul cannot go to heaven if he is drowned or buried at sea.'

'Where did they dump them?' I asked.

'Here,' Philip answered, taking his pipe out of his mouth and pointing with it. 'In Ty Tam Bay.'

Immediately, my toes curled into the damp sand.

'Touch bottom here and you might be standing on the bones of Colonels Noma and Tamura themselves.'

I am sure Philip told me this to make certain I continued to swim and, over the coming months, I came to do so quite well, but never again at Tweed Bay.

Not long after my grandmother's departure back to England, my mother's health had begun to deteriorate. She had previously contracted jaundice whilst my father was away in Japan. At the time, I was bundled off to stay with a Mr and Mrs Everett who lived at Magazine Gap and my mother was admitted to the Royal Naval Hospital at Mount Kellett. Now, a year or so later, her illness was less immediate but more insidious. She started to suffer pains in her joints, periods of weakness and migraine headaches. There seemed to be no apparent cause for this but the diagnosis was the onset of rheumatoid arthritis, the prognosis (which fortunately turned out to be erroneous) being that she would be crippled by the age of fifty and probably dead by fifty-five. As she was then thirty-four, this promised a bleak and brief future with considerable pain. It was noticed that she felt worse when our apartment was in the mist which, being the better part of fifteen hundred feet above sea level, it was quite frequently. Particularly during the hot season, the top of the Peak could become shrouded in warm mist. It was not polluted but simply water vapour that had condensed around the summits, cooled by the rising breezes and rock faces.

I found walking to school in this mist an exhilarating experience. When the mountain was in the mist, the pace of life slowed. Birds ceased to sing so much, people moved with a measured speed. In the servants' quarters, fingers of mist inveigled themselves through the lattice stone work and laundered clothes had to be brought in to the kitchen to dry. By the Peak Tram terminus, all would be quiet, no tourists thronging the observation point, no American sailors patronizing the Peak Café. Cars crept along in low gear, their headlights dipped, the drivers peering through the windscreen to follow the line of the road. Often I would not meet another living soul. It was as if I had the Peak to myself. Sounds were suppressed, my footsteps barely audible to me. Shadows loomed up in the mist, boulders and trees with which I was more than familiar taking on alien shapes. My over-active imagination tinkered with them. It was a scary time. On rare occasions, I woke in the morning to find the apartment above the mist. The view from the windows was much as I expected it might be from a high-flying aircraft, the solid-looking billows of cloud beneath bathed in pristine sunlight.

Due to my mother's adverse reaction to the mist, her doctors suggested we leave the Peak and move back down to the city or at least to Mid-Levels, the band of housing halfway up the mountain and usually below the cloud line. The problem was that there were no available quarters.

Throughout the summer term, I hurried home from school every day to be with my mother. Those few friends I had were obliged to come to my home to play. She liked meeting them but there were times when our boisterousness tired her quickly and we had to leave. She and I would also go for walks, my mother strolling rather than striding out as she was wont. I shared my places with her – the rifle range where she dug for bullets with me, Governor's Walk where she marvelled as had I at the fact that tiny fish lived at the top of a mountain and the ruins of Mountain Lodge and Pinewood Battery.

It was when we were sitting on the wall of one of the gun emplacements at Pinewood late one afternoon that she first broached the subject with me that had clearly been in her mind for a while.

'Martin,' she began, 'do you like living in Hong Kong?'

'Yes,' I answered, wondering where the conversation was going.

'More than England?'

'I think so,' I said. 'I can't really remember it except Nanny's house, and Granny and Grampy's house . . .'

'You know that in less than six months we have to go back to England, don't you?'

I had not really given this much thought.

'Your father's tour of overseas duty ends and he's being posted to a naval stores depot at Corsham, near Bath. You'll be going to a prep school to cram for the eleven-plus examination. If you pass, you'll go to the Royal City of Bath Boys' Grammar School.'

'And if I don't,' I said glumly, 'I suppose I'll be a dustman.'

'Like hell you will!' she retorted. 'Whatever you choose to do, you'll succeed. Isn't that what the fortune-teller predicted? Don't listen to your father. He's a plodder. Twenty years before the typewriter and he hasn't even made Commander . . .'

She fell silent for a while. I watched the kites soaring over Sai Ying Pun. On the slopes of Mount Davis, the most westerly high point of the island, the squatters' cooking fires were visible as sparks in the shadow of the hill.

'I don't want to go back,' my mother said emphatically, breaking our silence. 'England is dreary, colourless, down-in-the-mouth. Lifeless. Just look at this.' She turned and faced distant Lan Tau, the rays of the setting sun fingering between the mountains. 'How can I live in Romford or Woking or Basingstoke after this?'

'Or Bath,' I suggested.

She laughed ironically and stood up, suggesting, 'Let's go back via Lugard Road.'

As we walked slowly round the mountain, the city unfolding beneath us, my mother said, 'I want to stay here. In Hong Kong. And I've been thinking. Your father will have to resign from the Admiralty and get a job here. In the government, perhaps. Tax is much lower here than in Britain and the salaries are a good deal higher.'

I noticed she did not say 'Back home' as so many of her friends did.

'Will he change jobs?' I wondered aloud.

'Oh, yes!' my mother replied quietly and with a cast-iron confidence. 'Maybe not this week, maybe not next month, but he will. You mark my words!'

My mother adored the apartment at Mount Austin. It was spacious and had views from every window for which any Hollywood star would have inserted bamboo splinters under their fingernails, she had Wong and Ah Shun to attend to the chores, Su Yin to cosset and Tuppence to spoil. Her Chinese circle of friends, larger than her crowd of *gweipor* acquaintances, regularly visited for tea, often staying on into the evening, much to my father's chagrin: as long as my mother had guests he had to ease up on the pink gins and whisky sodas.

At other times, she continued to go for picnics with them, swimming parties or *chow*, which meant a meal in a Chinese restaurant. To her friends' children, she was universally known as Auntie Joy. When festivals came round, she was invited along to the celebrations as an ersatz relative.

The *gweipor* in her only came out in the mornings when she went to play canasta and drink coffee with other European women. She went swimming as much as she could, the exercise keeping her joints flexible. When that was not feasible, she wrote letters and poetry and knitted baby clothes either for Su Yin, the various new-born of friends or a squatter charity. Yet both she and I knew the time was coming when we would be presented with the opportunity to leave the Peak. And we would have to take it.

Finally, after six weeks of intermittent mist and continuous painkillers, with no quarters becoming available, my parents decided there was only one thing they could do. Just in time for the beginning of the new academic year in September, we packed up the apartment, put our

GWEILO

furniture in store, reluctantly dismissed Wong and Ah
Shun with much shedding of tears (but with references so
glowing Wong could have landed a job in the Savoy or the
Ritz had he so chosen), signed me off the roll at the Peak
School and moved across to take up residency once more
in the Fourseas Hotel.

10

MONG KOK REVISITED

LITTLE HAD CHANGED IN THE STREETS AROUND THE FOURSEAS Hotel during my Peak-side sojourn. Mr Tsang, the shop-keeper, remembered me and greeted me with a stroke of my hair. The Communist Chinese school still held its patriotic morning assembly but with the stirring music now blaring from loudspeakers rather than the scratchy phonograph. The late-morning quayside at Yau Ma Tei was still slick with fish scales and entrails and the rickshaw coolies still slept with their machines in Soares Avenue at night. Ah Sam was not amongst them. I was told he had died of a weak heart, weakened no doubt by his rickshaw and the *nga pin*. His number 3 hat was being worn by another now.

When I went up there, I found the Ho Man Tin squatter area had been rebuilt but now it had a rudimentary sewage system and was provided with standpipes and a concrete laundry area. The thoroughfares between the houses were wider in order to serve as fire breaks.

The Queen of Kowloon still lived in her cockloft and was still tormented by the local children. Yet, now, I did not join in their mockery or railway gravel throwing. I had learnt much about the world since I had last seen her, learnt to differentiate between fun and cruelty, humour and contemptuous laughter, love and hate. On one occasion, I approached her with the intention of buying her a meal at a *dai pai dong*. I wanted to see if I could extract some of her life story. I knew enough of adults now to be aware that they all possessed incredible tales – if only one could get at them. I was taller now than when she had first seen me but, otherwise, I was little altered in appearance.

It was early one evening in Mong Kok that I saw her for the last time. She was being chased by a woman who owned a fruit stall, with a stiff bamboo broom. The Queen was shuffling along as fast as she could go, dropping apples and oranges in her wake. At the sight of me, the stallholder immediately gave up the chase and started to retrieve her stolen merchandise. I went up to the Queen and addressed her in Cantonese.

'Good evening, madam,' I began politely. 'You should not have to steal. I would like to buy you food.'

She squinted at me, her eyes beady slits under a fringe of dishevelled, badly trimmed and matted hair. For a moment, I thought I was going to get a lucid answer. I was wrong.

She recoiled from me. Her hands rose over her head to the complementary stench of her armpits and general rank body odour.

'*Kwai! Kwai!*' she screamed in a falsetto voice that could have cracked a wine glass.

With that, she fled with far greater speed than she had to avoid the broom. A month later, I risked approaching her cockloft. It was occupied by a Chinese family. I felt guilty then. Had I, I thought, unwittingly driven her away? It was only later I realized she must have thought I was the ghost of the young heir to the Russian throne, returned from the dead to haunt her in her opium- and alcohol-befuddled dreams.

Things had changed, however, inside the Fourseas. Mr Peng was still the manager, but Ching had left, along with at least half the other room boys I had known. Ah Kwan was still the third-floor captain, but the whores had been moved out, the clientele now predominantly tourists or expatriates waiting for housing. The latter were exclusively British, the former almost exclusively American. The skull-faced gardener was no longer employed, his place taken by a kindly, elderly man who wore a battered trilby hat at all times and spoke to the plants in undertones of affection. Rumour had it that Skull-face had been 'chopped' – attacked with a meat cleaver – and done a runner for China. It was also discovered that he was more than just a card-carrying member of the Communist party. As such, he must have fallen foul of the fiercely patriotic and anti-Communist local Triad society and narrowly escaped a traditional execution of death by a thousand cuts.

Politics did not really enter into the lives of the Hong Kong Chinese. They were presided over by gods not governments. They had no vote, for elections were never held: members of the Legislative Council, Hong Kong's parliament, were appointed by the Governor. However, once a year, the spiritual world stepped aside momentarily and the population could display their political allegiances.

10 October was known as the Double Tenth, a public holiday celebrating the anniversary of the Wuhan uprising which sparked the 1911 Chinese Revolution and was the foundation of modern China. Strings of firecrackers were exploded. Buildings were decked out with huge and often badly executed portraits of Generalissimo Chiang

Kai-shek. They were surrounded by red and gold bunting and the Chinese Nationalist Kuomintang flag, which was then the national flag of Taiwan, whence Chiang had fled on losing mainland China to the Communists. The flag also fluttered in squatter areas and from tenement roof tops, washing poles, trees and even bicycle handlebars.

Not every building was so decked out, however. Some carried defiant Communist Chinese flags and a picture of Chairman Mao. This sometimes resulted in scuffles and street fights, observed by a large crowd of detached onlookers until broken up by the riot squad which arrived on grey-painted, open-sided police vehicles. Armed with long truncheons and rattan shields, they formed a phalanx and moved into the fray in complete silence save for the thump of their boots and a *gweilo* officer barking orders in fluent Cantonese through a loudhailer. After a few skulls were cracked and arrests made, the remaining assailants melted away. The onlookers followed them in suppressed mood, like football fans leaving a stadium after their side had been trounced. The fun was over until another Chiang supporter tore down a red flag or a Mao supporter desecrated a picture of the Generalissimo.

Street fights in general were often spectacles to behold, little short of urban, outdoor theatre. Normally docile, when the Chinese lost their temper they did it in style, shouting abuse with astonishing intensity and originality before eventually resorting to blows. Sometimes, the fighting consisted of little more than face slaps and the occasional artless punch, but if the protagonists possessed even a modicum of martial arts knowledge, the fights would involve back kicks and short leaps, stabs with fingers, and rabbit punches with hands shaped into hard blades. The injuries in the *kung-fu* type fights were always the worst unless a knife appeared from a sleeve: then the pavement would be spattered with blood before the police arrived. After a bloody fight, the street dogs would lick the pavement clean.

I came to realize that the Chinese were a nation of spectators. From a full-scale riot to two rickshaw coolies squabbling over a parking space, they would gather to watch. On one occasion, I even saw bets being made on the outcome, with side bets being placed on spin-off likelihoods.

Gambling and being Chinese were synonymous. Apart from mahjong, they indulged in *tin gau*, a strategy game played with tiles vaguely similar to dominoes. It was the first Chinese game I learnt to play and, in time, I became sufficiently proficient as to risk a part of my pocket money on it with the rickshaw coolies and mechanics in the Fourseas garage. I seldom left a session down.

Other gaming pastimes included heads 'n' tails and coin tossing. Played with ten-cent coins, the players stood in a line facing a wall. The first player threw a coin at the wall. It bounced off and settled on the ground. The idea was to throw one's coin so that it would land as near to the bottom of the wall as possible, but not touching it. He who succeeded took all the money but there were strategies. One could hit another's coin away from the wall or one could partly cover it, in which case, your coin took its place.

Although by law gambling was illegal unless conducted in a licensed mahjong club or through official Royal Hong Kong Jockey Club horse betting offices, it went on everywhere. To eradicate gambling was akin to prohibiting the eating of rice. I not infrequently saw policemen on the beat call into a tea house for a bowl of gunpowder tea and a few

GWEILO

hands of *tin gau* and, for all his gentility, the new Fourseas gardener kept a stable of fighting crickets in minute, ornate bamboo cages. He fed them grass and chrysanthemum sprouts but, despite my attempts to bribe him, he never took me to a match.

The fact that anyone in Hong Kong could support the Communist cause seemed beyond me. They had butchered, dispossessed and robbed millions. Not a single squatter had avoided Communist brutality and yet even some of the squatter shacks flew the scarlet flag of mainland China with its five gold stars.

One of the hotel staff, although not a Communist sympathizer, had fought as a partisan with them during the Japanese occupation. His name was Ah Lam. When I discovered his past, I sought him out and asked him why.

'Japanese more bad Communist,' was his pragmatic response.

'But why do people support the Communists now?'

'They wan' China one country. No like Taiwan, China, Hong Kong, Macau. Wan' China be one place for all Chinese.'

This seemed reasonable to me but I could not equate it in my mind with the atrocities of the recent civil war.

'But the Communists were very bad to the people.'

'All pe'pul bad to all pe'pul in war,' Ah Lam stated bluntly.

'Were you bad in the war?' I enquired.

'Me ve'y bad in war. One day, I show you.'

A few days later, as I was in my room doing my homework, there came a knock at my parents' door. It was Ah Lam asking to see them. I put down my pen and went through the adjoining door into my parents' suite.

'Master and Missee Bo Fu,' Ah Lam began, 'I wan' ask

352

you for me take Martin New Te"ito'ies-side, show him some t'ing from the wartime. In wartime, I fighting Japanese for English. I East 'iffer B'igade man. Not Communist. Fight for England.'

He fumbled in his pocket and took out a small, brown cardboard box. On the lid were printed the letters *OHMS* and a crown with the words *Official Paid* round it. He handed it to my father who opened it and took out a medal. Cast in silver and attached to a red, white and blue ribbon, one side showed a lion standing on a dragon whilst on the other was the head of King George VI.

'Governor give me,' he continued, 'for fight Japanese. If Martin can come, I look-see him ve'y good. No p'oblem.'

My father had a we'll-let-you-know look on his face but my mother immediately acceded to the request, saying, 'Yes, I'm sure that's fine, Ah Lam.'

That Saturday afternoon, Ah Lam and I set off in the hotel Studebaker bound for Sai Kung, a fishing village at the far eastern end of the New Territories famous for its seafood and the distinctly Communist leanings of its populace. Ah Lam told me that the narrow road to Sai Kung, known as Hiram's Highway, had been built by the British military but had been much improved by the Japanese, using allied and Chinese slave labour. It was the only road that penetrated the Sai Kung peninsula, an area of mountains, forests and isolated villages approached only by remote footpaths and known to the Japanese as a hotbed of sedition.

As we drove over the airport runway, he said, 'We go Sai Kung-side, you no talk-talk about Communist. You just no talk, boy.'

Sai Kung was quiet. Fishing junks lay three deep at the quayside. On a few, children or women were washing down the decks. The nets hung from the masts, drying in the sun like giant furled spiders' webs. Scattered here and there on the dock were dead fish or their remnants, the leftovers from the catch landed that morning. Outside the quayside buildings stood buckets of sea water containing live fish or lobsters, their massive claws secured by wedges rammed into the claw joints, jamming them closed. Crabs clicked in other buckets, ten deep, their claws manacled by pliable bamboo twine. Seated on a low stool, a fisherman was tying them in bunches of three with a loop to act as a carrying handle.

Ah Lam parked the Studebaker in the shade of a wide-spreading tree and we walked through the village to a tea house, sitting at an outside table under an awning. He entered into a long conversation with the proprietor whom he obviously knew well. I sipped my tea and kept quiet. At length, Ah Lam introduced me to the tea house owner.

'How do you do?' he said, shaking my hand.

'*Ho! Ho! Nei ho ma?*' I replied.

He laughed at this, but I sensed the threat of malice hiding behind his laughter.

'You don't need to speak Cantonese with me. I speak English. So,' he went on, 'you are going with Lam here to see something in the hills. Do you know what you will see?' I said I did not. 'You will see what Lam and I did in the war. Lam is my good friend and old comrade.' He put his hand on my shoulder. 'Are you a strong boy?'

I considered the question and said, 'I think so. I can walk a long way. I walked from Tung Chung to Ngong Ping without—'

'I do not mean strong in your legs but . . .' his hand shifted to my head '. . . in your mind.'

I did not quite understand what he meant but answered that I thought I was. He grinned.

'It is a long walk. Maybe two miles. And it is a hot day.'

He put four bottles of Coke in a small string bag and handed me a tiny bottle opener in the shape of a Coke bottle. Thus provisioned, Lam and I set off along a wide path across paddyfields of waving green rice, the pale white grain hanging down like cascades of tiny opals, ready to ripen. As we walked, frogs leapt from the path into the paddy. Where there were stone bridges over watercourses, lizards ran helter-skelter ahead of us making for the security of a crevice.

'Who was that man?' I enquired.

'He my boss in war,' Ah Lam replied.

'Your boss?' I repeated.

'He East 'iffer B'gade off'sser.'

'What is the East River Brigade?'

'In war,' Ah Lam explained, 'many Chinese pe'pul wan' fight Japanese but he no can do. Got no gun. But some pe'pul got gun. Communist got gun. They make small-small army, liff in mountungs . . .' He pointed to the east where the land was mountainous with narrow wooded valleys between grass- or bush-covered ridges. 'Dis mountungs. He call East 'iffer B'igade. He fighter, not sol-jer. Sometime Communist, sometime Kuomintang, sometime just man no like Japanese.'

'But what did you do?'

'Make trubbul for Japanese.'

After about half a mile the path, now narrower and cut into earth steps, left the paddyfields and started up a hillside carved into terraces upon which was growing a variety of vegetables. Here and there between the terraces were small platforms bearing rows of golden pagodas and one or two graves.

'What sort of trouble did you make?' I asked.

'Big trubbul. You know Watah-loo Road, near hotel, is a b'idge for t'ain. Kowloon-Canton . . .' he struggled with the word '. . . Wailway? One time, we blow up. Put plenty PE under b'idge. *Phoom!* No t'ain can go China-side long time.'

'What is PE?' I enquired.

'In English he call plas-tic ex-plo-sif,' he enunciated slowly. 'B'itish sol-jer come China-side, giff us.'

We carried on up the hill to a point where the path ran horizontally along the hillside, following the lie of the land. It was easier going now and, in twenty minutes, we reached a steep-sided wooded valley. Just as we were about to enter the trees, Ah Lam froze. I did likewise. Crouching down, he signalled me to move to his side and pointed ahead. Not twenty yards away was a wild boar, his tusks like old ivory, his back bristled. He did not look in our direction and, after a moment, moved off into the undergrowth. I began to stand up, but Ah Lam held me down. In less than a minute, the boar's sow crossed the path followed by seven piglets with light brown coats and thick, dark horizontal stripes.

No sooner were they gone than Ah Lam stood up and, in a loud voice, said, *'Ho sik!'*

At the sound of his voice there was a crashing in the undergrowth as the boars fled.

'In war,' Lam went on, 'we eat dis pig. Taste ve'y good! Much more better farm pig.' We crossed a dry water-course in the centre of the valley then began to follow the ever diminishing path through the remainder of the trees. Halfway to the edge of the woodland, however, Ah Lam stopped by a huge boulder, so big it had created a clearing for itself. He sat down on it and gave me two of the bottles of Coca Cola which I opened, handing him one. The Coke was warm but quenched a thirst I did not realize I had until then.

When he had drained his bottle Ah Lam, with characteristic Chinese disregard, tossed it into the trees. I heard it smash on a rock. This done, he slithered down the boulder, crossed the path, squatted down and started to clear away the leaf litter with his hands.

'You come see,' he said.

I joined him. A few steps from the path, he had uncovered six dull white stones. Each was about the size of a small watermelon and decorated by a similar series of thin, jagged cracks. They were in a line about three feet apart.

'You know dis one?' he asked.

'No,' I answered. The stones were a puzzle to me, all the more so for their being in a line.

Ah Lam patted the top of his pate. His hair was cut short, not much longer than a well-used toothbrush.

'Japanese sol-jer head,' he declared matter-of-factly. 'Six piece. We kill him here. Hide behind rock, jump on him. Very quick! No noise.'

My toes curled involuntarily as I looked down on the tops of the soldiers' skulls. It seemed incredible to me that there were dead people at my feet, buried in the earth with no coffin, no headstone, no epitaph. Then it occurred to me. Why could I see the tops of their heads? Dead people lay down in their graves.

'Did you bury them?' I asked.

Ah Lam nodded, grinning. 'Mus' do or Japanese come fin', take away, maybe kill pe'pul in Sai Kung for punish.'

'But why are they . . . ?' I mimed upright as opposed to supine.

Ah Lam's grin extended further as he replied, 'Japanese man no like die up.' He stood to attention to emphasize the point. 'If no lie down no can go to heaven.'

My father did not like having to return to the hotel. In part, I sympathized with him. He could no longer live as he had done in an apartment, with servants, entertaining in style, enjoying as prestigious an address as one could get in Hong Kong without living in a house on the mountain.

There was another reason for his dislike of the hotel. My mother was back in close contact with her Chinese friends amongst the staff. In my father's eyes, it was beneath her to befriend what were in effect her servants.

'In my opinion, Joyce,' he said frostily one evening as he waited for her to dress to go out to dinner, 'you're going native.'

I could hear the conversation through the adjoining door which was ajar.

'Letting the side down,' my mother replied.

'Precisely!'

'Don't be such a bloody fool, Ken!'

'I don't like it.'

'In that case,' my mother said, 'you can lump it.'

At this juncture, I knocked and went into their room.

'I've gone native,' I announced proudly.

My father stared at me for a moment then addressed my mother again. 'And that!' He pointed at me. 'Your son's more Chinese than a coolie. He'll have a bloody pole and a rattan hat next. Is this what you want?'

'Yes!' my mother replied emphatically. 'It is just what I want. I want a child who knows the world, knows the value of people whatever their race or rank and can appreciate what he sees.' She picked up her evening bag: it was black with silver beads sewn on to it. 'What I don't want is a boring, narrow-minded bigot with a drink problem.' She smiled amiably. 'Shall we go?'

Bit by bit, my parents grew even further apart. My mother maintained her gradually increasing coterie of Chinese friends, seldom inviting my father into this circle but, whenever she could, including me in her excursions. I particularly loved going with her to festival celebrations.

Some, such as the Moon Festival, involved little more than a slap-up meal taken *al fresco* with the moon high in the sky and the children carrying multi-coloured lanterns shaped like rabbits, birds, butterflies, dragons and fish. If clouds threatened to obscure the moon, everyone made a loud noise by banging saucepans together or letting off a short string of firecrackers to drive the clouds away. The only aspect of the festival I just could not abide was the moon cakes, one of the very few Chinese foods I found it impossible to swallow. They came in a variety of sizes and looked vaguely like English pork pies. The dough was made of flour, syrup or honey, rice wine and eggs. After some hours, it was rolled out and a filling made of lotus seed paste and whole duck egg yolks, care being taken not to break them. Once filled and shaped in a ball, they were pressed in wooden moulds, glazed and baked. The Chinese adored them but most *gweilos* found them inedible. The glutinous contents had the unpleasant habit of sticking to the roof of the mouth.

Other festivals, like Ch'ing Ming (or the Hungry Ghosts' Festival) in the spring, were a more exclusive matter and it was a sign of the regard in which my mother was held by her Chinese friends that, after only three years in Hong Kong, we were invited to attend this most personal of ceremonies.

On the morning of the appointed day in early April, we rendezvoused with a noisily joyful gaggle of thirty Chinese in a hundred-yard-long queue at the railway station in Tsim Sha Tsui. Everyone was weighed down by a parcel, wicker basket or string bag. After twenty minutes, we were herded aboard a train which set off immediately.

The train trundled through Kowloon and entered a tunnel in the hills. When it emerged in the Sha Tin valley, it was as if I were riding a time machine. At one end of the tunnel was a mid-twentieth-century city, on the other a timeless landscape of tiny villages, paddyfields, salt pans and fishing junks. If a British man-o'-war had sailed into the cove, cannons blazing, it could have still been the Opium War.

Following the coast to Tai Po, the train then headed north to Fanling, where we disembarked. Once we were all gathered together, the party headed into the low hills to the south. It was a long walk, first up a disintegrating concrete road then along a path through brush and scattered trees. Finally, we arrived at our destination: three graves and a row of a dozen or so golden pagodas. The women – including my mother – swept the semi-circular platforms before the graves. A man with a tin of red paint touched up the characters on the grave doors. This done, joss-sticks were produced and burnt with everyone, including my mother and me, kow-towing to the ancestors.

After this, food was produced, including, incredibly, a

whole suckling pig. Bowls of hot rice ladled from a thermos were placed before the entrance to each grave with a piece of the pig, some steamed vegetables and a little bowl of rice wine. The label on the bottle read *Sam Sheh Jau* – Three Snake Wine. Pickled in the bottle was a small nondescript snake. On the top of the graves, thick wads of Hell's Banknotes were weighted down with a stone. Next to them was placed a car made out of tissue paper stretched over a split bamboo frame. This was set alight, the ashes blowing away on the breeze and adhering to the crackling on the pig.

'The money is to pay the ancestors' bills in heaven,' my mother whispered in explanation.

'And the car?'

'They haven't got one in heaven, so . . .'

Two of the men approached with armfuls of human bones. Behind them, one of the golden pagodas was open. The bones were placed on the ground where several women dusted them down and set about buffing them up with light tan Cherry Blossom shoe polish. I watched utterly mesmerized, wondering what it would be like to dig up my grandfather and give him a shine.

While the contents of all the nearby ossuaries were cleaned, a picnic was laid out. The human bones were then arranged around the picnic cloth. Every skeleton was set a place. I found myself sitting between my mother and a skull carefully balanced on a heap of its associated bones, the lower jaw dropped as if the ancestor who owned the bones was having a damned good laugh at the rest of us.

'What happens to their food?' I asked my mother, not letting my eye off my neighbour's rice bowl. I think I half expected to see it gradually disappear, consumed by the ghost of the skeleton.

'The ancestors in heaven soak up the essence of the food, then it's thrown away,' my mother informed me.

'Including the pig?' I enquired, my mouth watering at the thought of it.

'No,' my mother answered. 'Only the food in the bowls. We eat the rest.'

No-one spoke to the bones and, when the picnic was eaten, we indeed threw the ancestors' food into the bushes for the ants and birds. With the bones returned to their golden pagodas, we set off for the railway station. As we descended the hills, I saw other families scattered across the slopes of the hills doing as we had done.

Arriving home, we found my father sitting on the balcony of my parents' room reading a month-old copy of an English newspaper and puffing on his pipe. He had temporarily grown a full beard, partly, I suspected, because naval officers were permitted to do so. Indeed, he had unnecessarily asked Mr Borrie's permission.

'So, feel you've done your bit for someone else's fore-bears?' he asked acerbically.

There was, however, one festival my father was actually prepared to attend, despite the fact that it contained much that he abhorred – joss-stick smoke, firecrackers, dense jostling crowds and (to him) inedible delicacies. This was the birthday of Tin Hau and my father tolerated it because it entailed a boat trip.

The primary festival of the sea-going folk of Hong Kong, it was held not only at all the Tin Hau temples around Hong Kong but also at the ancient temple in Tai Miu Wan, named – literally – Joss House Bay by early European settlers who referred to temples as joss houses.

The journey to Tai Miu Wan was explained to me by my father, who insisted I sat at a table in the hotel lounge with him as he pored over our impending nautical experience with military precision, plotting it with dividers and a navigational ruler on a naval chart. He might have been preparing an invasion.

'It'll take us about ninety minutes to get there from HMS *Tamar*,' he began. 'Our party will be taking one of the larger, faster launches. At first, we head towards the eastern harbour, then – pay attention – go on to a bearing east-south-east through Lei Yue Mun and into . . .' he jabbed the point of the dividers into the map '. . . the Tat Hong Channel. We change to a north-easterly bearing here . . .' he moved the dividers '. . . once clear of the island of Tit Cham Chau.'

I looked at the map and said, 'It's not very far.'

'Dangerous waters,' my father replied. 'Rocky shores, rip tides.'

'How far is it?'

He spun the dividers round in his fingers and said, 'Seven-and-a-half nautical miles, give or take.'

'Don't you have to be very accurate?'

My father did not reply and rolled up the map.

The naval launch had been decked out in signal flags and pennants including a huge scarlet triangular Chinese one at the bow with a black serrated edge and black characters in the centre.

We cast off and joined a veritable flotilla of vast fishing junks, motorized sampans, walla-wallas and pleasure craft, all extravagantly decked out in the same fashion. By the time the launch reached its destination, it was reduced to barely moving, jostling with the other craft. A hundred yards off shore, the bos'n dropped anchor and prepared to lower a dinghy. It had not been readied on its derricks before two sampans arrived alongside, a vociferous argument ensuing between the Chinese naval launch crew and the women in the sampans. It seemed no-one was allowed to organize their own landing arrangements, the sampans being the only permitted 'ship-to-shore' craft. They had fixed a monopoly so, in the name of colonial expediency and not wanting to arouse the anger of the Triads on the beach, we all clambered into the sampans and were oared ashore.

I had never been in a sampan before and was fascinated at how it was propelled by its single stern oar, twisted on the out-stroke to give forward momentum then twisted back on the in-stroke to avoid drag. The woman driving the boat stood barefoot on what my father called the stern flat, wearing a loose jacket and baggy trousers cut of a shiny black material that seemed to be steeped in tar. Her face was wrinkled and tanned by a life at sea.

We reached the pebble beach, went ashore down a plank extended from the bow of the sampan and joined the dense throng of celebrants. Entering the temple itself was impossible.

'Can't see why you wanted to come, Joyce,' my father grumbled. 'We can't get in the damn temple. Why couldn't we come on a day . . . ?'

'For the atmosphere,' my mother replied in a weary tone.

'Atmosphere!' my father retorted. 'Smoke more like.'

As he spoke, an elderly lady pushed past him carrying a bundle of lit joss-sticks, three feet long and as thick as Churchillian cigars. My father got the full benefit of the drift of their smoke right in his nostrils. He let out a gargantuan sneeze which had the lady turn round and briefly give him a piece of her mind.

In front of the temple, to appease those who could not

get in to pay their homage, a secondary shrine had been set up on the beach. The image of Tin Hau was made of tissue stretched over a bamboo frame and surrounded by red and gold paper and small brightly coloured plastic propellers that spun like miniature windmills in the sea breeze. Before the image was arrayed a number of fully grown roast pigs, cooked chickens and ducks, bowls of pink bread buns, cakes, a large pile of pink-coloured boiled eggs and joss-sticks of all sizes. In the temple, gongs clanged and a deep bell continuously rang. Several bands played against each other from opposite ends of the temple.

Many of the junks riding at anchor were of the huge, deep-sea variety, vessels from another century. Every so often, the crews let off strings of firecrackers hanging from the masts, the blue smoke and fragments of paper drifting over the sea towards land. I half closed my eyes and imagined they were war junks fighting off pirates or East Indiamen running opium up the Pearl River to Canton.

After an hour at the festival, we returned to the launch and sailed three miles across open sea to the Ninepins, a group of four uninhabited islands with a natural rock archway on one. The water was as clear as – as my father put it – chilled vodka and we could see the rocks of the sea bottom six fathoms down. Every so often a dark shadow drifted over them and was the reason no-one swam. Due to a confluence of currents, this place was notorious for its sharks.

As the adults drank, ate and talked, I lay on the deck at the bow and looked down, watching the sharks glide by and thinking all the while that an instant and terrible death moved by only twenty feet below me. I only had to roll off the deck . . .

'What're you up to?' my mother asked, kneeling on the deck beside me.

'Watching the sharks,' I replied.

At that moment, a vast shape like that of a delta-wing bomber passed beneath me.

'What's that?' I almost shouted.

Everyone looked up and some came over to stand by me. Something broke the surface a short distance off. It floated just beneath the light waves as a sodden face flannel might.

'It's a manta ray!' someone exclaimed.

The launch crew quickly raised the anchor and started the engines. The ray began to move away. We set off in slow pursuit. The creature had a wingspan of at least fifteen feet and was, someone reckoned, over twenty feet from its bizarre, horseshoe-shaped snout to the tip of its long, quite rigid tail. It was dark grey in colour with a few cream patches and did not so much swim as gracefully fly under the water, its vast wings beating like a great bird's but in slow motion. It looked the epitome of marine beauty and yet simultaneously exceptionally sinister and dangerous.

'I wouldn't like to meet him when I was swimming,' I said to no-one in particular.

A man clutching an expensive German camera and kneeling on the deck next to me replied, 'You'd have nothing to fear. All they eat is plankton.'

I considered this information. That such a huge creature could live only by consuming the microscopic creatures that made phosphorescence was, at that moment, one of the wonders of my world.

'That ray was astonishing,' my mother remarked as my father drove our car on to the vehicular ferry that evening.

'Not really,' he commented dismissively. 'I saw bigger in west Africa during the war.'

'Well, you would have had to, wouldn't you, Ken?' my mother answered. 'If I had a boil on my bum, you'd have had a bigger one during the war.'

She leant back in the passenger seat and winked at me. My father glanced in the driving mirror to see my reaction. I kept my face deadpan. Had I been caught grinning, I would have been belted for some mis-demeanour, trumped up or otherwise, by bedtime.

11

'HOMEWARD' BOUND

AS 1955 ADVANCED, THE WEATHER HEATING UP AND THE DAILY humidity rising, my parents' life became increasingly frenetic and fraught. At his office, my father was preparing to hand over to his successor. This caused him frequently to return to the Fourseas in a flaming temper.

'I don't know how they do it!' he would mutter. 'The oldest bloody civilization on earth and they can't file. I've put a chart up. What goes where. Anchor butter is not the same as anchor chains. Dear God! My life is blessed with blithering idiots.'

This tirade made, he would pour himself a pink gin and sit on the balcony, watching the traffic go by and the setting sun illuminate the hill opposite.

My mother spent much of her time packing for the voyage 'home', which she no longer considered her home – or mine. Our larger possessions – furniture and the Ford – had already been sent ahead by cargo ship. When she was not packing or visiting friends, my mother quietly wept to herself. She did this in private, but I heard her through the door between our rooms. On just one occasion, my father found her wiping her eyes.

'What's the matter, Joyce?' he enquired as he poured

himself a gin and tonic, the hotel being temporarily out of Angostura bitters, much to his vexation.

'Nothing.'

He sat down in one of the armchairs, rolling the ice round in his glass.

'Must be something.'

'I got some dust in my eye.'

'Right,' he said and sipped his drink.

My mother gave him the sort of look she might have afforded a street cat that had just regurgitated the half-digested intestines of a rotten garoupa on her bed.

'What?' he asked, catching the look.

'You're an unfeeling bastard, Ken.'

My father, having no direct response to this, replied, 'I've had a hell of a day in *Tamar*, Joyce, and I didn't come home to have to take this display of petulance.'

He put his half-finished drink down and walked to the door.

'Off to the wardroom?' my mother called out to his receding back.

He slammed the door and returned at midnight.

My preparations for leaving Hong Kong consisted of stocking up on *wah mui*, packets of joss-sticks and dried melon seeds, and buying presents for my grandparents. For my father's mother, I bought a table linen set embroidered with Chinese scenes, whilst for Nanny, who had stocked up on table linen during her visit, I bought a folding octagonal waste-paper basket with little Chinese figures of playing children appliquéd to its sides. For Grampy, a seafaring man, I bought a rosewood model of a sampan which cost me three weeks' pocket money.

My mother was invited by her Chinese friends to a number of farewell banquets as the date of our departure drew nearer. My father was not always invited and, when he was, he more often than not declined.

'Silly old sod!' my mother said to me one day after he had rejected yet another invitation. 'He's not happy unless he's bloody miserable.'

I accompanied my mother to a few of these banquets, the best of which was given by the hotel room boys. We met at a restaurant in Tsim Sha Tsui just as night fell. The neon shop signs were coming on, the air was warm and moths were beginning to flicker around the lights. In the trees that lined Nathan Road, birds squabbled noisily over roosting perches.

The banquet was superb and went on well past midnight, the dishes appearing with a mouth-watering regularity: sharks' fin soup, abalone, quails' eggs and hundred-year-old duck eggs (which my mother tasted for the first time and was amazed to discover I not only knew of but also liked), chickens' feet, braised duck, soft-shelled hairy crabs cooked in salt and sugar, chicken wrapped in pickled cabbage and baked in clay, various fish, pork and beef with chillies and garlic . . . We were showered with farewell gifts. They were simple things, like sets of chopsticks, chopstick rests, decorated porcelain bowls and soapstone figurines, but to my mother they were as precious as gems and she prized them for the rest of her life.

After the banquet my father, who had attended on this occasion, returned to the Fourseas in a taxi, but my mother elected to walk. It was at least two miles but this did not deter her. I walked at her side, holding her hand despite the fact that I considered myself too mature now to do such a thing. In the circumstances, it just seemed right.

The air was warm. From the windows of the tenements

came the sounds of everyday Chinese life – the song of caged birds, the clack of mahjong tiles, the raucous chorus of a Cantonese opera playing on the radio. The shops were shuttered. Under the arcades sat old men in their pyjamas with the legs rolled up to the knee, reading Chinese comic books or the past day's papers, talking to each other, smoking cigarettes of Chinese tobacco, some mixed with opium.

My mother and I did not speak. In our own ways, we were letting Hong Kong impinge itself upon us.

'Will you be sad to leave?' she asked, finally breaking our silence as we turned into Waterloo Road.

'Yes,' I admitted. 'Very.'

'Would you like to come back?'

'For a holiday? Yes!'

'No. For good.'

I thought about it. I had been happy in Hong Kong. It had been an exciting place in which to live and I was sure it had much to offer that I had yet to uncover. However, there was more to it than that. I felt I had grown up in Hong Kong. I could recall little of my life prior to the *Corfu*. It was as if my memory – my actual existence – had begun the minute my foot had touched the dock in Algiers. England was as strange a place to me now as Hong Kong had been on that June morning in 1952. In short, I felt I belonged there.

'Yes,' I said at last. 'Definitely.'

'In that case,' my mother replied, 'we'd best see what we can do about it.'

On my last night in Hong Kong, I went down Soares Avenue bidding farewell to the shopkeepers. Mr Deng, the seller of cherry bombs, gave me a ten-cent biro and ruffled my hair. Mr Tsang cut open a pomelo.

'You can buy in Ing-lan'-side?' he enquired, handing me a piece and taking one for himself.

'Lo can buy Inglan'-side,' I confirmed, biting into it and spitting the flat pips on to the pavement. This, I thought at the same moment, was a habit I would have to lose. And quick!

'*Ayarh!*' he exclaimed. 'You mus' come back Hong Kong-side!' He too stroked my head for a last fix of luck. 'You come back. I low. One day, no long time, you come see me one more time.'

Halfway down Nathan Road, my mother said suddenly, 'Ken . . . ! Stop the car!'

My father, sitting in the front passenger seat next to a young naval rating with a flat Birmingham accent and a badly sunburnt neck, ordered the driver to pull into the kerb.

'Give me the boarding passes, will you, Ken? Mine and Martin's.'

For the briefest of moments, I saw a sense of intense fear pass over my father's face. My mother had always been an expert at timing. If she really were going to leave him, and I assumed it was possible, this would be the supremely appropriate moment. And he knew it. Yet he reached into his jacket pocket, removed his wallet and handed her two pieces of folded green-tinted paper.

'How long will you be?' he asked.

'How long is a piece of string?' she replied evasively.

It was one of her stock answers and she knew it

infuriated my father, whose life was filled with certainties to which there was never any string attached.

'Depends on the size of the parcel,' I said, aping my mother's usual response to further interrogation.

My father gave me a scathing look and went on, 'Well don't be long, that's all.'

We stepped out of the car and it drove away. I briefly saw my father's face through the front passenger door window. He looked crestfallen, defeated and scared. I felt strangely, guiltily jubilant.

Directly across Nathan Road was Whitfield Barracks, two sentries with cockades in their berets and Lee Enfield .303 rifles in their hands standing either side of a gateway. Through it I could see an armoured scout car of which I had an exact Dinky replica.

Without any haste, my mother and I walked down Nathan Road. Ahead of us, between the buildings, rose the Peak, hazy in the mid-afternoon sun. It was hot, the humidity high. Rickshaws passed us, carrying people, boxes and bales of cloth. Red and cream Kowloon buses sped by, washing hot air over us. My mother looked at them and I wondered if she was watching out for Her Russian Majesty.

At the southern end of the barracks, we crossed Nathan Road, entered Haiphong Road and took the second left into Hankow Road. Hing Loon Curio and Jewellery Company was open but we did not go in for a chat or a free drink. We had already said our goodbyes.

My mother, who had not spoken twenty words since we got out of the car, said, 'Well, what do you say?'

I made no answer. We both had the same thought in mind and entered the Pen. We were shown to a table and my mother ordered tea for two. She specifically requested

Chinese tea. It soon arrived at our table in a bone china teapot accompanied by wafer thin sandwiches and a silver stand of dainty cakes. On a balcony above, a string quartet started up, playing tunes from recent hit musicals.

'This is living,' my mother said after a long silence. 'Really living . . .' She looked about her. 'Haven't we been the lucky ones!'

'Yes,' I said, 'we certainly have. And', I added, 'we will be again.'

My mother reached across the table and took my hand in both of hers.

'Too bloody right!' she said with characteristic defiance. 'You can bet your bottom dollar on it.'

She looked at her watch and summoned a waiter Chinese style, her palm downwards and all her fingers beckoning together.

'*Mai dan, m'goi*,' she said as he drew near. Her accent was almost perfect.

The bill was presented. My mother paid it, smiling at me with the memory of our first tea here. We left through the grand front entrance as if we were minor royalty, a Chinese boy in the hotel livery holding the door open for us, another asking if we required a rickshaw or taxi. That tart – I understood the meaning of the word now – the Duchess of Windsor could not have been better treated.

Beside the Tsim Sha Tsui fire station was a short concrete slope to the hillside on the top of which stood the marine police headquarters. A tree hung over it. In its shade, as usual, was the old grasshopper man seated on a folding stool, a rattan basket of bamboo splints and leaves by his side. With them, he skilfully wove grasshoppers, arranging them around his feet or along the top of a culvert. As we approached, he held one out.

'You wan' g'asshoppah, missee? B'ing you plenty good luck. Only one dollar.'

I bought two and gave my mother one.

'You good boy for you muvver,' the old man said and, getting up, stroked my hair.

We walked on, past Sammy Shields' dental surgery and into the Kowloon Docks. Alongside the first pier was the P&O liner *Carthage*, the sister ship of the *Corfu*. Her white hull towered over us, gleaming in the sunlight. Smoke drifted from her funnel. Signal flags flew from her mast. The Blue Peter announced she was soon to sail.

The dock was crowded with baggage coolies, rickshaw pullers, cars, trucks and well-wishers. Along the hull, sampans bobbed on the waves. Junks sailed by out in the harbour and walla-wallas puttered about, tossing in the wake of a Star Ferry leaving its jetty. I glanced at the Peak across the shimmering water. Block A, Mount Austin stood out, silhouetted against the sub-tropical sky and I thought that, no matter what, I could always claim I once lived there.

Plank by plank, hand in hand, clutching our lucky grasshoppers, we slowly climbed the gangway. My mother was crying.

It was the afternoon of Monday, 2 May 1955, and I was ten.

Four years later, exactly as my mother had predicted, my father was a colonial civil servant and we were back. For good.

GLOSSARY

THE SPELLING OF CANTONESE WORDS DOES NOT NECESSARILY follow the accepted Pin Yin or other linguistic systems (such as Wade-Giles) but is the roughly phonetic spelling of how Cantonese was spoken by the average European (*gweilo*) at the time. It may well be inaccurate, for which I apologize. The spelling of pidgin English is also phonetic.

atap a woven bamboo and/or rice straw matting used to cover bamboo windbreaks, peasant buildings and temporary structures

ayarh! a common expletive: it has no literal meaning

baksheesh alms (of Middle Eastern origin) cf. *kumshaw*

cash ancient Chinese copper coins with round or square holes in the centre

chau island

cheen money

chop noun: an ivory carved seal; verb: to attack with a meat chopper or knife

chop! chop! pidgin English for *get a move on/hurry up*

chow food: a generic word (*small chow* means canapés)

congee a form of rice gruel-cum-porridge eaten for breakfast

dai big – e.g. *dai fung* (typhoon) means big wind

dai pai dong a street-side cooked-food stall (not a fast-food purveyor)

dim sum small steamed dumplings containing bite-sized lumps of shrimp, pork, beef and other ingredients

diu nei lo mo Literally *go fuck your mother* but often used coarsely as an epithet the equivalent of *You don't say!* or *Well, I'll be damned*; also used vindictively or pejoratively

dofu known in the West as tofu or soya bean curd

dor jei *thank you* (for an item or gift)

Fide! Fide! literally *Quick! Quick!* but implying the more impolite *Get a move on!*

fung shui pronounced *fong soy*, it is the art (or science) of achieving harmony in one's surroundings by balancing the influences of wind (*fung*) and water (*soy*)

gai doh cheen *how much?* Literally, *how much money?*

Gai duk toh a Christian

garoupa a large sea fish, a delicacy frequently served in Chinese cuisine

godown a warehouse

golden pagoda an ossuary urn

heui la! *go!/let's go!*

ho *good* or *yes*

Ho! Ho! Nei ho ma? *Good! Good! How are you?* (a common polite greeting)

ho pang yau good friend

Ho sik! Good to eat/eating/food

hutong alley or passageway

kai fong associations Chinese social charities

kam taap golden pagoda: see above

kang a traditional Chinese sleeping bed or platform made of wood or stone, the latter often having a fire beneath it for warmth

kukri an exceedingly sharp, curved fighting knife used by Nepalese Gurkha troops

kumshaw alms (of Cantonese origin)

kwai a ghost; more accurately a disembodied spirit

Kwan Ti the god of war and literature, and the patron god of secret brotherhoods, the police and many others

lai see packet a red paper envelope printed with gold lettering and containing money: usually given as a gift at Chinese New Year

loh siu a rat (or mouse)

mai dan the bill

Mat yeh? *What?* (rudely implying *What do you want?*)

m'ho bad or no

m'ho cheen Literally, *no money*

m'koi *thank you* (for a service or act); also, on occasion by implication, *please*

muntjak a small, indigenous deer, also known as a barking deer on account of its dog-like call

Nei wui mui gong ying mun? *Do you speak English?*

Nei giu mut ye meng? *What is your name?*

Nei ho ma? *How do you do?* – a common greeting

nga pin opium

ng mun five dollars

Ngo giu jo *My name is . . .*

nullah an open drain, varying in size from two feet wide and three deep up to sixty feet wide and fifteen deep; usually built to cope with heavy rain or effluent

pi lau a ceremonial archway

praya a stone-fronted dock or esplanade

pu-erh a variety of Chinese tea

roorkee chair a folding camp chair used in India and rather like a film director's chair

sarong a Malay (usually Tamil) ankle-length cotton skirt worn by men

saw hei combed or combed back (of hair)

Sei Hoi Jau Dim Fourseas Hotel

shadouf an ancient Egyptian crane-like irrigation mechanism for raising water

shéh snake

skink a common lizard

suq an Arab market or bazaar

taipan a wealthy businessman, traditionally the expatriate head of a major trading company or 'noble house'

ushabti a small ancient Egyptian funerary sculpture

wan bay or inlet

wei! *hey!* or, if used on the telephone, *hello*: the American equivalent would be *Yoh!*

wok a type of cooking pot, used especially for shallow frying or searing

won ton a deep fried dumpling of minced beef and pork, water chestnuts and onions

yamen a building housing the home and office of a mandarin, magistrate or other regional administrator in dynastic times

yat, yee, sam, sei, ng, lok . . . one, two, three, four, five, six . . .

yum cha literally *drink tea*

CANNABIS: A HISTORY
by Martin Booth

'So good no one will need to do another for at least fifty years . . .
mesmerizing detail, fantastical digressions, lots of jokes and wry asides'
James Delingpole, *Literary Review*

'*After two puffs on a marijuana cigarette, I was turned into a bat*'
Dr James Munch, pharmacologist and special adviser to the
Federal Bureau of Narcotics, 1938

To some it's antisocial anathema, to others it is a harmless way to relax, or
provides relief from crippling pain. Some fear it is a dangerous drug that
leads to 'reefer madness' and addiction; to others still it is a legal anomaly
and should be decriminalized. Whatever the viewpoint, and by whatever
name it is known, cannabis – or marijuana, hashish, pot, dope, *kif*, weed,
dagga, grass, *ganja* – incites debate at every level.

In this definitive study, Martin Booth – author of the acclaimed *Opium: A
History* – charts the history of cannabis from the Neolithic period to the
present day. It is a fascinating, colourful tale of medical advance, religious
enlightenment, political subterfuge and human rights; of law enforcement
and customs officers, smugglers, street pushers, gang warfare, writers,
artists, musicians, hippies and pot-heads.

Booth chronicles the remarkable and often mystifying process through which
cannabis, a relatively harmless substance, became outlawed throughout the
Western world, and the devastating effect such legislation has had on the
global economy. Above all, he demonstrates how the case for
decriminalization remains one of the twenty-first century's hottest topics.

'Booth tells this story with admirable restraint . . . this book should be on the
shelf of anyone interested in human freedoms and bad laws'
Independent

'Enlightening . . . a very engaging history'
Daily Telegraph

'Amazingly informative . . . fascinating stuff'
Financial Times

0 553 81418 4

BANTAM BOOKS

GERMS
A MEMOIR OF CHILDHOOD
Richard Wollheim

' A GREAT BOOK, STRANGE AND BEAUTIFULLY WRITTEN . . .
TO BE COUNTED AMONG THOSE MASTERPIECES OF WHICH
THE FADING MEMORY CONTINUALLY DEMANDS RETURN
AND REFRESHMENT'
Frank Kermode, *Times Literary Supplement*

The son of affluent parents – a distant, dandified impresario father he
revered; a beautiful, mindless 'Gaiety Girl' mother he came to regret
loathing – Richard Wollheim grew up in the English suburbia of the 1920s
and 1930s. *Germs* is his account of those years. It is a book like no other; a
remarkable exploration of childhood by one of the English-speaking
world's most distinguished postwar thinkers.

'A HUMAN DOCUMENT OF CONSIDERABLE POWER AND
IMPORTANCE'
John Armstrong, *Independent*

'WOLLHEIM'S POWERS OF DESCRIPTION ASTOUND . . .
BECAUSE OF THE INTENSITY WITH WHICH A REMARKABLE
MAN HAS OFFERED US A VIEW OF HIS INNER SELF, I DOUBT
WHETHER ANYONE WHO HAS READ IT WILL FORGET IT'
Diana Athill, *Literary Review*

'PUNGENTLY TRUTHFUL, COMPLEX AND ORIGINAL'
Alan Hollinghurst, *Guardian*

'THE VOICE IS INIMITABLE: SUBTLE, SEDUCTIVE, MOVING
FROM DEADPAN HILARITY TO ACHING SADNESS'
Roy Foster, *Times Literary Supplement*

'A MASTERPIECE – AN UNCLASSIFIABLE WORK OF
STARTLING ORIGINALITY IN WHICH THE ACUTELY SENSUAL
AND CONFUSEDLY CEREBRAL EXPERIENCE OF INFANCY,
BOYHOOD AND ADOLESCENCE IS BRILLIANTLY RECREATED'
Francis Wyndham, *Spectator*

0 552 77314 X

BLACK SWAN

A POUND OF PAPER
Confessions of a Book Addict
by John Baxter

'After 400 pages of enjoyable, diverting material, the discerning reader will surely grasp one point above all others: that this is an excellent book'
Sunday Telegraph

In the rural Australia of the fifties where John Baxter grew up, reading books was regarded with suspicion; owning and collecting them with utter incomprehension.

Despite this, by the age of eleven Baxter had 'collected' his first book – *The Poems of Rupert Brooke*. He'd read it often, but now he had to own it. This modest purchase marked the beginning of an obsession that would take him all over the world . . .

In the comic tradition of Clive James' *Unreliable Memoirs, A Pound of Paper* is a brilliantly readable, honest and funny account of a life spent in pursuit of a passion – of how a boy from the bush came to be living in a Paris penthouse with a library worth millions.

'His extraordinary enthusiasm for his subject is infectious . . . a wonderful memoir'
Literary Review

'Extremely entertaining and unusual . . . an account of a lifetime's passionate pursuit of signed copies and biblio-rarities'
Sunday Times

'Packed with characters . . . and rich with anecdotes. Fascinating, funny and informative, *A Pound of Paper* should surely be the cornerstone of any respectable collection'
Time Out

'A valuable record of a passing, ephemeral era; before the price of everything became known'
Guardian

0 553 81442 7

BANTAM BOOKS

A SELECTION OF NON-FICTION TITLES
AVAILABLE FROM BANTAM AND BLACK SWAN

THE PRICES SHOWN BELOW WERE CORRECT AT THE TIME OF GOING TO PRESS. HOWEVER TRANSWORLD PUBLISHERS RESERVE THE RIGHT TO SHOW NEW RETAIL PRICES ON COVERS WHICH MAY DIFFER FROM THOSE PREVIOUSLY ADVERTISED IN THE TEXT OR ELSEWHERE.

40664 7	CHE GUEVARA	Jon Lee Anderson	£14.99
81523 7	THE MAN WHO MARRIED A MOUNTAIN	Rosemary Bailey	£7.99
81442 7	A POUND OF PAPER	John Baxter	£7.99
81418 4	CANNABIS: A HISTORY	Martin Booth	£7.99
81506 7	GALLIPOLI	L.A. Carlyon	£9.99
81710 8	MEENA: HEROINE OF AFGHANISTAN	Melody Ermachild Chavis	£6.99
81447 8	INTO AFRICA	Martin Dugard	£8.99
50692 7	THE ARCANUM	Janet Gleeson	£6.99
81521 0	ARBELLA: ENGLAND'S LOST QUEEN	Sarah Gristwood	£9.99
81445 1	HIMMLER'S CRUSADE	Christopher Hale	£7.99
81485 0	THE AIR LOOM GANG	Mike Jay	£7.99
81264 5	TEN THOUSAND SORROWS	Elizabeth Kim	£7.99
81353 6	THE DEVIL IN THE WHITE CITY	Erik Larson	£7.99
81642 X	ANCIENT MARINER	Ken McGoogan	£7.99
81498 2	GENGHIS KHAN	John Man	£7.99
81522 9	1421: THE YEAR CHINA DISCOVERED THE WORLD	Gavin Menzies	£9.99
81655 1	THE FUNNY FARM	Jackie Moffat	£7.99
81460 5	THE WAR AND UNCLE WALTER	Walter Musto	£7.99
81551 2	THE BIG YEAR	Mark Obmascik	£6.99
81554 7	DAD'S WAR	Howard Reid	£6.99
81528 8	NOBODY IN PARTICULAR	Cherry Simmonds	£6.99
81610 1	THE LAST MISSION	Jim Smith and Malcolm McConnell	£7.99
8'1360 9	IN HARM'S WAY	Doug Stanton	£6.99
81656 X	EDUCATING ALICE	Alice Steinbach	£7.99
81425 7	A COUNTRY LIFE	Roy Strong	£6.99
81444 3	WHERE THEY LAY	Earl Swift	£7.99
81476 1	HALFWAY HOME	Ronan Tynan	£6.99
81555 5	AN EMBARRASSMENT OF MANGOES	Ann Vanderhoof	£7.99
77314 X	GERMS	Richard Wollheim	£7.99
81439 7	LEARNING TO FLOAT	Lili Wright	£6.99

All Transworld titles are available by post from:
Bookpost, PO Box 29, Douglas, Isle of Man IM99 1BQ
Credit cards accepted. Please telephone +44(0)1624 677237, fax +44(0)1624 670923, Internet
http://www.bookpost.co.uk or
e-mail: bookshop@enterprise.net for details.
Free postage and packing in the UK.
Overseas customers allow £2 per book (paperbacks) and £3 per book (hardback).